ADVANCE PRAISE FOR *ANIMAL JOY*

"To read *Animal Joy* is to become alive to the condition of wakefulness in the world. This spectacular achievement by the psychoanalyst
and writer Nuar Alsadir provokes and destabilizes our understanding of a life's competing narratives. I can think of no other contemporary work of nonfiction that brings together autobiography, a learned
history of psychoanalysis, lyrical poetics, ontological investigations
of our attempt to manage our own feelings with such astute engagement. This is a work that will change conversations about who we are,
what we think motivates us, what makes us *us*. The meeting place of
the intentional and the unintentional erupts in *Animal Joy* in order
that we might reinvestigate our incoming thoughts and feelings with a
sense of vigor and curiosity. If you are open to introducing 'tiny revolutions' of thought into your life by resisting received and uninterro-
gated scripts, read this book." **—CLAUDIA RANKINE**

"Few things feel as important right now as what Nuar Alsadir is thinking about in her brilliant new book. She considers the ways in which,
despite our most determined curation of our public faces, and despite
our approval-seeking and plain old quotidian bullshittery, laughter reveals to us (and sometimes others) what we might really feel. What
happens when we wonder beneath or into that unexpected chortle or
snort, that losing it, that dying, when we spend a little curious time with
what, in fact, beyond sanction or affirmation, moves us? Re-makes us
animal to ourselves? I'm not exactly sure, but I have a hunch that *for
lack of what is found there we die miserably every day*. Nuar Alsadir has
written such a beautiful and important book." **—ROSS GAY**

"With *Animal Joy* Nuar Alsadir is in a relentless pursuit of authentic life, slaying the endless ways we accept falsehoods and store-packaged simulacrums, in search for what is beyond the obvious. Alsadir radically foregrounds inner over external reality as an act of subverting convention. Moving seamlessly between the most intimate to the political reality of our time, she leans hard into the absurd, harnessing the engines of psychoanalytic theory, philosophy, and her poet's love-hate relationship with language to bring back from exile what has been rendered unthinkable by social contract. Reading this book you are on a joyride with the mind of a free thinker who will surprise you, make you laugh uncontrollably, and trouble you until you come out changed. You will gain a different relationship to what is before you, less tolerant of the lies and defenses that keep us apart from the impulse of our true self, joys, excitements, and devastations."

—ORNA GURALNIK, PSYCHOLOGIST, PSYCHOANALYST,
COUPLES THERAPY (SHOWTIME)

"Nuar Alsadir's lyrical, hilarious, and beautifully undefended meditation has the capacity to widen our consciousness to allow notice of what occurs in the interstices of attention and mortification. In that way, *Animal Joy* is a book that seems compassionately able to read us as we turn its pages." —JONATHAN LETHEM

"Where do laughter, psychoanalysis, poetry, motherhood, creativity, thought, language, and so much more intersect? In *Animal Joy* Nuar Alsadir shows us in dazzling fashion, demonstrating what only the essay form, in the hands of a true artist, critic, and thinker, can achieve." —JOHN KEENE

ANIMAL JOY

ANIMAL JOY

A Book of Laughter and Resuscitation

Nuar Alsadir

Graywolf Press

Originally published by Fitzcarraldo Editions in Great Britain in 2022

Excerpt from the Shirley Jackson papers used by permission of the Shirley Jackson Estate. Copyright © 2016 Laurence Jackson Hyman, JS Holly, Sarah Hyman DeWitt, and Barry Hyman.

Excerpt from *Thus Spoke Zarathustra* by Friedrich Nietzsche, translated by Walter Kaufmann, translation copyright © 1954, 1966 by Penguin Random House LLC. Used by permission of Viking Books, an imprint of Penguin Publishing Group, a division of Penguin Random House LLC. All rights reserved.

This publication is made possible, in part, by the voters of Minnesota through a Minnesota State Arts Board Operating Support grant, thanks to a legislative appropriation from the arts and cultural heritage fund. Significant support has also been provided by the National Endowment for the Arts, the McKnight Foundation, the Lannan Foundation, the Amazon Literary Partnership, and other generous contributions from foundations, corporations, and individuals. To these organizations and individuals we offer our heartfelt thanks.

Published by Graywolf Press
212 Third Avenue North, Suite 485
Minneapolis, Minnesota 55401

www.graywolfpress.org

Published in the United States of America

ISBN 978-1-64445-093-2 (paperback)
ISBN 978-1-64445-181-6 (ebook)

2 4 6 8 9 7 5 3 1
First Graywolf Printing, 2022

Library of Congress Control Number: 2021945914

Cover design: Frances Baca

Cover image courtesy of the author

The author has used labanotation, a notation system developed in the 1920s by choreographer Rudolf Laban to represent bodily movement, as section breaks in this book.

ANIMAL JOY

The so-called pure childlike joy of life is animal joy.

—ANTON CHEKHOV

Ӿ

My daughter sits down to dinner, looks at the food on the table, and says, I'm not hungry.

That's rude, her sister tells her.

I don't care what you think.

That's rude as well, I say. You should apologize.

She looks directly into my eyes and blurts, I'm sorry for you. The moment the slip registers, her lips bunch quickly inward as though someone had tugged a drawstring. She successfully suppresses a laugh until her sister lets out a muffled snicker and they both break into a fit of hysterical laughter.

"A thing is funny," writer George Orwell explains, "when—in some way that is not actually offensive or frightening—it upsets the established order. Every joke is a tiny revolution."

∧

After my first day of clown school, I tried to drop out. The instructor was provoking us in a way that made me uncomfortable: to the nervous, smiley woman, "Don't lead with your teeth"; to the young

1

hipster, "Go back to the meth clinic"; and to me, "I don't want to hear your witty repartee about Oscar Wilde."

I was the only nonactor in the program and had made the mistake, as we went around the circle on the first day, of telling everyone I was a psychoanalyst writing a book about laughter. As part of my research, I explained, I had frequented comedy clubs and noticed how each performance, had it been delivered in a different tone of voice and context, could have been the text of a therapy session. Audience members, I told them, laughed less because a performer was funny than because they were honest. Of course that's not how all laughter operates, but the kind of laughter I'm interested in— spontaneous outbursts—seems to function that way, and clown performances push that dynamic to its extreme, which is why I decided to enroll in clown school, and how I earned the grating nickname "smarty-pants."

But if I dropped out, I would lose my tuition money. So I decided to stay and, by staying, was provoked, unsettled, changed.

There's a knee-jerk tendency to perceive provocation as negative— like how in writing workshops participants often call for the most striking part of a work to be cut. When we are struck, there's a brief pause during which the internal dust is kicked up—we lose our habitual bearings and an opening is created for something unexpected to slip in. Habit protects us from anything we don't have a set way of handling. Because we are least automatous when caught off guard, it's in those moments that we are most likely to come up with spontaneous responses.

It turned out that the perpetually smiling woman was sad, the hipster (who didn't even do drugs) acted high as a way of muting the parts of his personality he was afraid we would judge, and I found it easier to hide behind my intellect than to expose myself as a flawed and flailing human being. Each role, in other words, offered a form of protection: by giving off recognizable signals to indicate a character type, we accessed a kind of invisibility. We cued people to look through us to the prototypes we were referencing. When the instructor satirized those roles, he defamiliarized them so the habitual suddenly became visible. His provocations knocked the lids off the prototypes we were hiding inside of, in a similar way to how many psychoanalysts, in the attempt to understand a person's conflicts, begin by analyzing their defenses—what is being used as a cover—before moving on to what is being covered up and why.

Both psychoanalysis and the art of clowning—though in radically different ways—create a path toward the unconscious, making it easier to access the unsocialized self, or, in philosopher Friedrich Nietzsche's terms, to "become the one you are." Psychoanalyst D. W. Winnicott considers play to be "the gateway to the unconscious," which he divides into two parts: the repressed unconscious, which is to remain hidden, and the rest of the unconscious, which "each individual wants to get to know" by way of "play," which, "like dreams, serves the function of self-revelation." In clown school, the part of the mind that psychoanalysis tries to reveal—by analyzing material brought into a session, including dreams and play—is referred to as a person's "clown."

Each of us has a clown inside us, according to Christopher Bayes, head of physical acting at the Yale School of Drama and founder of the Funny School of Good Acting, where I was taking my two-week, six-hours-per-day workshop. The theatrical art of clowning—commonly referred to as "clown"—is radically different from the familiar images associated with birthday parties, circuses, and horror stories. Bayes's program helps actors find their inner clown. The self-revelation that results provides access to a wellspring of playful impulses that they can then tap into during creative processes. His method stems from the French tradition developed by his former teachers Jacques Lecoq and Philippe Gaulier—the kind of training the fictional main character of actors Louis C.K. and Zach Galifianakis's TV series *Baskets* seeks, and that Sacha Baron Cohen, Emma Thompson, and Roberto Benigni underwent early in their careers.

Lecoq, who began his career as a physiotherapist, believes that "the body knows things about which the mind is ignorant"—a phrase that can be applied to the unconscious. The process of trying to find your clown involves going through a series of exercises that strip away layers of socialization to reveal the clown that has been there all along—or, in Winnicott's terms, your "True Self."

Various experiences affect our ability to make contact with our true self. Winnicott sees the first signs of the True Self in the spontaneous gestures of an infant, which would develop if a "good enough mother" was able to affirm and accept them, or be hidden if she disapproved of or corrected them ("It's not *moooooah*, it's *Mama!*"). When an infant modifies its behavior to please—a survival mechanism at base, given the infant's dependency on the mother for its basic needs—the socialized self begins to develop.

The more our concerns surround survival, in fact, the more we suppress our primal instincts and try to blend in—or, in the extreme, play dead (like hiding among a pile of bodies during a mass shooting). The social equivalent of playing dead is to put forward a facade—what Winnicott terms the "False Self," built around manners and protocols as opposed to spontaneous expression—that flies under the radar in order to ensure the survival of the True Self. It's a kind of psychological slouching based on the belief that whatever stands out is dangerous: the tallest sunflower gets snipped.

The clown is different. The clown gets up before an audience and risks letting whatever is inside them seep out, just as analysands in psychoanalysis free-associate, let their thoughts go wherever the mind takes them. While the analyst searches for the analysand's True Self by way of material that reveals the unconscious, the actor in clown school seeks to discover it by way of their spontaneous expressions. These processes are similar to what philosopher Martin Heidegger terms *aletheia*, or truth as unconcealment. The clearest expression I've heard of *aletheia* came years ago, when I overheard my then three-year-old daughter call someone beautiful. I asked, What does beautiful mean? Still close to her clown, she replied, Beautiful means most self.

Like a clown's red nose, beauty reveals: "You know the clown is present," according to Bayes, "when you no longer see the nose." Gaulier runs a clown school in Paris that actors flock to from around the globe for its famous yearlong training program. His purported definition of beauty as "anyone in the grip of freedom or spontaneity" functions as a guiding principle in the clown community. The clown is the embodiment of this beauty in the unmediated expression of raw emotion—the mask, according to Lecoq, "draw[s] something from [the actor], divesting him of artifice." The mask, in other words, unmasks.

Ten years later I asked my daughter, Is it better to be beautiful or photogenic? She paused for a while, thought about it, then said, I'd rather be beautiful, but I think you get more out of being photogenic.

Our preoccupation with perfecting our exteriors, our profiles—which often determine what we have access to in the social world—has caused us to lose touch with our interiors. The dominant issue bringing people into my office for psychoanalysis is the sense that, after sacrificing so much to achieve the lives they had dreamed of, they're unable to experience the pleasure they had expected to accompany those ideal lives they labored to construct. The False Self may be attractive to onlookers, but it is not connected to the emotional panelboard, into which the clown sticks every finger without fear of getting shocked. Whereas most people are encouraged to work to line up their external chips and let the internal chips fall where they may, the clown does the inverse: lines up the internal chips and lets the external chips fall where they may. The beautiful mess that results reveals the clown's interior and the interior of the audience members, who recognize themselves in what the clown is expressing. They mark that recognition with laughter, sometimes the only socially acceptable form of catharsis, as philosopher René Girard puts it.

The desire for acceptance prompts people to hide whatever they imagine may be judged, their True Selves and their clowns, the motley colors within. "It's easier for other people," Bayes told us repeatedly, "if you're less":

That's why we have the social contract on the subway: no eye contact, don't take up space. I want you to be more. You can be less if you're going to sell real estate, but not if you're going to be an artist. It demands that you live hotter. I'm trying to undo socialization: *stop wiggling, sit still, please behave.* When someone says *please behave,* it means please behave less.

Behaving less supports the status quo and increases your chances of having access to the benefits that accompany belonging, which is often achieved by putting others first. Giving the mother what we know she will affirm trains us to develop a radar for what is wanted by other people, as opposed to tuning in to what is inside us. The result is a sense of alienation from ourselves that gets transmitted to others and is often rewarded, as it keeps the wheels turning without catches or snags.

Yet things are different in the consulting room and the theater for the person trying to access the deepest recesses of the self within a framed environment. Psychoanalysis tries to understand the forces that bend our psychic development and to understand how those forces shape us and the choices we make. Clown, like analysis, raises our awareness of our impulses to accommodate others in the pursuit of affirmation, and, by removing the social filter, pushes us to explore what might have been possible had we continued to believe that what is most beautiful is the moment when we are most ourselves, even if that means being messy, vulnerable, or despairing. "Imagine what you would be like," prompted Bayes, "if you'd never been told *no.*" If we resist aligning our interiors with the social order, we create openings into which we can spontaneously grow.

The road to growth, however, often passes through the towns of awkwardness and shame. As we performed the given exercises, Bayes would look for what he called our "catch places": "Where are your catch places? Where are the places you're reluctant to go—when you feel you're going there, you instinctively avoid it? How does something catch? Move it around to see if it engages, catches. It's okay if it's fake; it's part of the growth."

In one of the exercises, we were told to take turns coming onto the stage and telling the audience about something we had just seen—something so funny that the laughter that would erupt in recalling it would prevent us from being able to speak. When the laughter didn't come naturally, Bayes would coach us on how to try to evoke it synthetically by moving the laugh sounds around—going low (*ho*), high (*hee*), shaking our bodies—because "body and sound travel together without filter." The hope was that if we worked on opening ourselves up, regaining contact with our mental and physical drives, we could more easily access authentic laughter—an eruption from the unconscious—even if by way of the synthetic.

Our daily morning warm-up was choreographed to help us "get out of 'the body of the commuter'" and find "the body of curiosity, appetite. If you're curious, ready, and available, have an appetite for fun, it will show up. When you're trying to work from a good idea or solution, you're no longer listening to the world and what it has to offer you. You're imposing something onto what could be magic."

Of course, the magic didn't always come. "We feel the work," he told one student. "It's okay to feel that the work is hard. It's part of the process, to be in the middle of your growing, your changing." The job of the performer is to let go, resist having an agenda, and allow an impulse to emerge spontaneously from the body.

My catch place—what made me fall to the ground in hysterics—was when I shot a zinger at someone that crossed the boundary of the appropriate. As a child, the first "big word" I learned was *facetious*, which I heard repeatedly from my parents, who would snap, "Stop being facetious!" Because *facetious* had come to mean *bad*, each time I made a puckish comment in clown class, I felt the imp of my irreverent childhood self slip out. And accompanying its release was a massive discharge, in the form of ecstatic laughter, of the energy that had been mobilized toward holding it down.

"This work can change you," Bayes warned, using logic very similar to what an analyst presents to a person beginning analysis. "The only thing is that you don't get to choose how you're going to be changed. You just have to be ready for change."

At Jack, a small theater in Brooklyn, New York, a day of clown began in a circle, shaking out our bodies, stretching, softening our faces, mooing like cows. We would walk around the room, accessing emotions called out by an apprentice of Bayes's, who'd prompt us to explore our anger, nervousness, despair. Having stirred up a range of feelings, we were instructed not to "tuck it away." We were to resist exerting control over our emotions and "let the little one drive, the one who doesn't know how to drive but loves to drive," by allowing our impulses to extend into outward expression. We lined up the internal chips and let the external chips fall where they might. "Once you give the body freedom," Bayes cautioned, "it's reluctant to be put back in the drawer."

We performed in front of one another, and understood the vulnerability involved in trying to break into a spontaneous outburst of laughter or sing a solo about a naughty little secret. One day, particularly anxious about taking my turn, I confided in the woman beside me. Just get up there, she said matter-of-factly. We're not going to judge you.

It is difficult, even with reassurance, to trust others, to take off your armor and set the little one free—which is why in daily life it is rare that the little one gets to peek out except in the form of parapraxes (slips of the tongue, forgetfulness, or unintended actions that reveal unconscious motivations).

Often, in the midst of an attempt to laugh, a performer burst into tears. "The *wah-wah* is attached to the *ha-ha*," Bayes told one person this happened to. "Crying is just laughing larger." He then instructed him to walk upstage, stand "in the zone of the pathetic," raise his arms, look above the heads of the audience members, and wail, "Pick me up!" As the actor sobbed, we in the audience burst into laughter, tears, or a combination of both. We invariably laughed when a performer cried, yet in a profoundly empathic way. "The clown gets all up in your humanity," Bayes told us, encouraging the expression of all emotions without prioritizing the more comfortable ones. When the actor tried to compose himself, Bayes admonished, "Don't wipe it till it's done!" He flipped what would have been shameful in an ordinary social interaction into inspiration: "Get all up in your humanity and celebrate your courage and audacity, your elastic connection to emotion, and we'll envy your ability to do that. We'll want to be you." It's not the content of what you bring onto the stage that has an effect, but "your reaction, your relationship to what you bring that the audience connects to—we crave an authentic conversation."

Communication that originates in the True Self, according to Winnicott, feels "real," whereas communication from the False Self does not. A similar distinction exists in the way a performer connects with the audience, and the audience, in turn, with the performer. If a performer's expressions feel honest, of the moment, rather than rehearsed, the audience senses "an authentic conversation," connects, and marks that connection with laughter. If not, there's silence. The way others receive you is communicated simply and quickly in clown. As the performer, you want the laughter and fear the silence but are made to explore both—if you value one over the other, go after the laughter and avoid the silence (or pretend it isn't happening); in Bayes's terms, you "lead with your desperation":

> If you're honest in the moment when something isn't working, we love you more. Acknowledge it. When it's going well, you can celebrate that. If it's going badly and you admit that, you're alive. If you pretend it's okay when we know it isn't, we hate you a little bit. If you're bad and you admit it, we love you again. Like a shark, you have to keep moving.

In order to keep moving, you need to be fully present and take in what is before you, as opposed to trying to force the world to conform to your hopes, expectations, or desires. This advice applies regardless of the position you occupy, whether you're an artist, instructor, analysand, or analyst.

The psychoanalyst W. H. Bion, writer Samuel Beckett's analyst, advises that a psychoanalyst approach each session without "memory, desire, [or] understanding." As the analysand free-associates and puts into words the leaps their mind takes, the analyst takes in the analysand's train of thought through an equally unguided thought process. By not always linking back to previous comments as though there were a fixed self, and by not desiring a certain outcome or matching individual experiences to meta-psychological theories, the analyst gives the analysand room to grow and change in whatever direction they're headed.

Similarly, when you take the stage, you're not supposed to use something that worked in the past, to want to make the audience laugh, or to have an idea of what you're going to do. You have to "soften your brain," Bayes told us, perform without an agenda at "the speed of fun, faster than your worry, louder than your critic," and trust whatever gets dislodged. "By not planning, you train yourself to listen." Bayes explained:

> When you wonder, How do I make them do something, affect the audience, you disconnect from the source. Your good ideas will kill you because they're attached to your ego. Don't present ego material; it's not funny. Let it not be so precious, whether you succeed or fail.

"Ego material" doesn't always prove fruitful in psychoanalysis either. Pursuing something that erupts from the unconscious—such as spontaneous laughter, a slip of the tongue, or transference (expectations and emotions that get transferred onto the analyst)—is far more likely to lead to insight. Connection occurs between two people not simply when they communicate from ego to ego, but from unconscious to unconscious—and the form that connection takes varies depending on the context.

Unconscious communication is marked by laughter in clown and by emotion in psychoanalysis. Sometimes an analysand will cry but have no idea why they are crying—just as we are sometimes overcome by a fit of laughter that has no clear trigger. These moments are meaningful even if they cannot be logically explained. The True Self is not something reason can circumscribe but an emotional wellspring you tap into. You know you are close to it when you *feel*, when you are brought, in Lecoq's terms, "into contact with the *essence* of life, which I call the *universal poetic sense.*"

It is difficult to resist the urge to play it safe, to play the part you imagine the other person will find interesting or entertaining, despite the fact that in doing so you hem yourself into a ready-made position. Even my daughter, who once divided her peers into the categories of "store-bought" and "homemade," intuitively recognized at a young age the sad fate of the store-bought. "The middle is boring," Bayes asserted. "There's nothing to be found there, the socialized mask that is desperate to convince the world you're fine. That's what everybody does. We don't want to reflect that back to the world unless we are shining a light on it."

One of the actors in clown school had the nervous tendency to say, "It's cool," when he was floundering, and we would boo because we knew he was being disingenuous. It's devastating to flop, and when someone pretends everything is fine when we know it isn't, we disconnect. Another actor, by contrast, began to sob and berate herself in the face of the audience's silence, sparking us to laugh uproariously. "We love her when she despairs, because we understand her," explained Bayes. "We have our own version of that."

Failure brings with it the possibility of growth and change, which is its own kind of hazard when you don't get to decide how you're going to be changed. At the same time, Bayes told us, "if you have a clear idea of the path you want to follow, you're just going to live in the part of your talent that you like and that you have confidence in. There is no surprise there." You will slowly morph into a prototype, even if it's self-fashioned—like poets who receive recognition and then imitate their own work to maintain their standing.

In clown school, Bayes kept describing the moment when the audience felt moved by the clown onstage as "poetry," which, because I'm a poet, caught my attention. I thought of the poet J. H. Prynne, who once, after listening to a poetry reading, described the poems read as "written by a poet," from a prototypical position, which he "could do without." Prynne explained that he wanted "a poet to break out of his or her poetic identity, to establish a whole new set of possibilities for the reader and for him- or herself."

A new set of possibilities can unsettle the poetic order, as it can the social order—as when a poem doesn't look like a poem, which most often results in it not being published. Most poets struggle with this split between the True Self urge, as poet Sylvia Plath describes in a notebook, to "grow ingrown, queer, simply from indwelling and playing true to my own gnomes and demons" and the False Self desire for approval, to catch what she termed "New Yorker fever, as if I could by main force and study weld my sensibility into some kind of articulateness which would be publishable." Yet in lining up the external poetic chips into publishable "articulateness" rather than "indwelling," you face the danger of writing what poet Derek Walcott terms "a fake poem." Still, many yearn for the status that public recognition brings, even as they recognize the possible falsity involved. As the poet Theodore Roethke quips in a notebook, "We all long to create a great dreary masterpiece that everyone will have to pretend to read."

The fake poem, like the performance or session you enter into with the goal of manipulating the response, will not lead to an authentic conversation with your audience or with yourself. The cost of not playing true to your gnomes and demons—your clown or True Self—is, for some, too high. To live by formula, according to Emily Dickinson, leads to feeling closeted:

> They shut me up in Prose—
> As when a little Girl
> They put me in the Closet—
> Because they liked me "still"—

Here, the equivalent of staying still is writing in prose, which restricts one to the sentence, described by philosopher Roland Barthes as "hierarchical: it implies subjections, subordinations, internal reactions." To write in poetry is to write *outside the sentence*, to take pleasure in the text, which, Barthes says, "is (should be) that uninhibited person who shows his behind to the *Political Father*." Political resistance, poetry, and self-revelation spring from that provocative, impish drive to burst free from external constraints—like my facetious zingers or my daughters' outbursts of laughter. It's fitting that at the end of Dickinson's poem, the mark of the speaker's resistance, her psychological break from "Captivity," is to "laugh."

The defining element of poetry—whether on the page, in the theater, or in life—may very well be the transformative feeling it creates in its recipient, that "*universal poetic sense*," in Lecoq's terms, of having been brought "into contact with the *essence* of life." "So far, about morals," writes Ernest Hemingway, "I know only that what is moral is what you feel good after and what is immoral is what you feel bad after." Perhaps Hemingway's thinking can be extrapolated to poetry. Regardless of expectations surrounding form, poetry, at base, is what you feel moved after, when another unconscious has made contact with your unconscious, when your True Self has been stirred.

Often what moves us is beauty, that feeling that crops up when we are at play, in the grip of freedom or pleasure, most self—but that can just as easily be expressed through messier emotions, such as rage, repulsion, or despair. For an authentic conversation to take place, you have to be willing to follow whatever comes up in whatever form—the free-associative path your mind takes—so long as it is accurate and honest.

We can be as moved by one another as we can by art. After all, everyone is a poem, as psychoanalyst Jacques Lacan has it: "A poem that is being written, even if it looks like a subject." But I suppose that means each of us faces the danger of becoming a fake poem—a static prototype—as well.

We were allowed to put on our red noses in the wings only before taking the stage. The nose is a mask that allows the actor, in Lecoq's terms, "not to play *themselves* but to play *using* themselves"—much as a poet does in writing out of the voice of a speaker, an analyst in using themselves as an instrument, and an analysand in reflecting on their experiences within the frame of the session, which, like any performance, has set parameters that signal a transition out of lived life and into the symbolic.

As the course progressed, I began to see the necessity of these parameters everywhere, nowhere more starkly than in the field of politics. Donald Trump, for instance, has been referred to repeatedly as a clown, but he is a clown who does not clearly step out of reality and into the show. He is a fake clown—what actor and writer Mary-Louise Parker describes as "the opposite of all things clown." Rather than revealing his humanity, Trump "is always trying to pass off one emotion as another. He plays indifference when obviously enraged, which is like playground sarcasm. He sells you steadfast when at his most unsteady, and that makes him transparently insecure. Most of all why I could not connect to him if he were even the greatest leader on earth is because at his core, he's just a terrible actor":

> Terrible actors always telegraph, always have to indicate because they can never fully inhabit. They never own it to the point to where you can't separate them from the moment, it's always hanging off of them a little, like an ornament. The really tragic thing about mediocre acting, for me, is that shitty actors are routinely convincing to most. They have a big audience on their side be-

cause they play to what that majority asks for and those people are so happy to see it. Too happy.

Trump reveals the reality he would like to construct—which coincides with the way many would like the external chips to be lined up—but not the honest expression that gets at a *universal poetic sense* and moves the audience. When self-interest is passed off as self-revelation, we sense the presence of something store-bought—we can see the role hanging off him, can smell the packaging.

This terrible acting, however, is nothing new in the methodology of American politics. Journalist Ron Suskind recorded an exchange he had with an aide to President George W. Bush in 2002 that depicts this same grafting of a false reality onto the world:

> The aide said that guys like me were "in what we call the reality-based community," which he defined as people who "believe that solutions emerge from your judicious study of discernible reality." I nodded and murmured something about enlightenment principles and empiricism. He cut me off. "That's not the way the world really works anymore," he continued. "We're an empire now, and when we act, we create our own reality. And while you're studying that reality—judiciously, as you will—we'll act again, creating other new realities, which you can study too, and that's how things will sort out. We're history's actors . . . and you, all of you, will be left to just study what we do."

History's actors, like bad actors, create realities from the outside in. Clown is closer to the project of late-night comedians, who, rather than impose a fake reality on the one before them, pursue truth as unconcealment. Humor, as John Lennon explains, has the power to disarm:

> When it gets down to having to use violence, then you are playing the system's game. The establishment will irritate you—pull

your beard, and flick your face—to make you fight. Because once they've got you violent, then they know how to handle you. The only thing they don't know how to handle is nonviolence and humor.

We know how to handle prototypes, but not the provocations that jolt us out of them. For Winnicott, creativity, aliveness, and feeling real—the hallmarks of a healthy individual—are accessed through play. By behaving spontaneously, in line with our instincts, we have the potential to provoke ourselves—and others—into possibility, whether it's personal, poetic, or political.

It's subversive not to hide behind a prototype, to take up space, to resist behaving for the comfort of others. To act according to instinct. After clown school was over, I found it difficult to engage in a number of social interactions—I had, it turned out, a range of prototypes for different situations, and straying from those given roles proved disruptive. When I expressed myself spontaneously, stepped outside of established social scripts, other people became thrown off, uneasy. Destabilizing someone, as I discovered from my own reaction on the first day of clown school, can be perceived as a provocation, aggressive.

To utilize all I learned during those two weeks at Jack and to tolerate the fallout would require great inner strength. It is difficult to give up the social tokens you receive for staying in line, but it is perhaps more difficult, once your freedom and pleasure have been unleashed, to put them back in the drawer. To engage in anything unrelated to survival that mitigates your sense of aliveness will feel like too great a sacrifice, even after factoring in the cost of not taking up an assigned position. Learning to prioritize the arrangement of my internal chips changed my relationships, my poetry, the way I work as an analyst, and, perhaps most crucially, how I approach the world. Now I try to listen to what it has to offer, rather than immediately wanting it to conform to my expectations, ideas, or desires. And letting-be, it turns out, is a form of rigorous self-gathering.

λ

During college, I spent a summer at the University of Oxford studying James Joyce. I had just decided to drop my neuroscience major and was there to immerse myself in modernist texts after having experienced, through *Ulysses*, the excitement (*I will Yes*) of being close to a mind that had not been calibrated to ready-made forms. I was in awe of the graduate students who would gather at the pub, sometimes on the lawn of my college, in animated conversation.

One evening on the lawn, the friendliest member of the group signaled me over. Excited to finally have the opportunity to get to know them, I blurted a series of questions: How long have you been here? What are you working on? They offered detached, clipped answers until one advised, "Here in Europe, when we try to get to know someone, we don't ask questions. We enter into conversation and get to know a person by the way they think."

Whether or not that is, in fact, the European way, I was captivated by the idea that you could know someone by knowing how their mind moves.

But what does it mean to know someone? My daughters know me very well. They watch me with vigilance. One of my daughters went through a phase of asking me if I was angry with her. Out of the blue, as I was chopping vegetables at the kitchen counter or performing whatever mundane task needed to get done, she would ask, Are you mad at me? Each time I said no, it didn't register, until one morning, in the wee hours, she walked into the room where I was writing and asked again. I looked up, surprised to see her, and answered, No; I was thinking.

I get it! she said, lighting up. Your thinking face and your angry face are the same.

What she had been picking up on wasn't the contents of my mind, but a closed door between us. Whether from anger or thought, she had been momentarily shut out.

For years, I believed my dog had an uncanny—almost prophetic— ability to read people. When someone entered the house, he was able to instantly assess their character. One day, however, as we both backed away from a guest simultaneously, I realized it wasn't the other person he was reading, as I had always imagined. He was reading me. After watching me closely for years (his well-being, after all, depended on it), he had become skilled at picking up on my micro-expressions, perceiving feelings that, though they belonged to me, had not yet registered, made their way into my consciousness.

Being known can also feel inhibiting. I have a memory from high school of sitting in the back seat of the car. My mother was driving. My father must have been there as well, or I would have been sitting in the passenger seat. I was crying—sobbing, actually—because my mother and I were having an argument. I don't remember what the conflict was over, only that she was turning onto an exit ramp when I wailed, You don't know me! You don't know me like my friends know me!

I may not know you the way you want to be known, she said calmly, but, believe me, I know you.

Philosopher Jean-Paul Sartre, in *Being and Nothingness*, sketches a scene in which a man who is peeping through a keyhole, completely absorbed in looking at what he sees on the other side of the door, suddenly hears a creaking of the floorboards behind him and realizes he has been seen. Sartre uses this scenario to explain the loss of subjectivity that occurs when a person shifts from being a subject looking out at the world to an object in another's field of vision, from the one who looks to the one who is being seen.

The man then imagines that the person who has seen him peeping through the keyhole knows him as he cannot know himself—knows him, in fact, better than he knows himself. He can now know himself only by reading the other's knowledge, can see himself only through the gaze of the other. This transformation from being a subject with agency (the one doing the looking) to an object in another's world to be evaluated (*What do they see?*) results in what Sartre calls existential shame—the shame of having been caught in the act of being who you are.

If, like the man at the keyhole, you are preoccupied with how others see you—and particularly with how they see you through something external to you (your children, possessions, or work)—you run the risk of believing you can know yourself only through their perspective, determine your value only by reading their knowledge. You're then less likely to create or behave according to what you feel compelled to express than what you imagine will win approval, what you imagine others will like or want to hear.

The figure we imagine as we speak or write reshapes our communication, a process that philosopher Mikhail Bakhtin calls "addressivity." In the split second before speaking, we project ourselves into the position of our addressee, imagine how they will take what we are about to say, then adjust our communication to fit those expectations. This mechanism, performed in milliseconds, leads us to utter not what we had intended but an edited version that accounts for—protects against—the ways that the psychic representation of our addressee thinks and feels.

Addressivity explains why you can feel connected speaking with one person but talk about the same thing in the same way with someone else and feel like a fumbling bore. The other person may or may not match up to the imagined persona you project onto them, but you will adjust in relation to that psychic representation, regardless.

In considering your audience, therefore, it may be helpful to think about who you become in relation to them, and about how, through the process of addressivity, your perception of yourself as seen through their imagined eyes will reshape you and what you express. When I like one of my daughters' friends, my feelings have only partly to do with who they are. My feelings are influenced more by what the specific person brings out in my daughter, the person she becomes when she enters their force field.

A friend of mine used to like to challenge people to try and smile without making their eyes smile. This is particularly challenging in a playful context, as I have observed between my daughters, who invented a similar game they named Expressionless Face, in which two people stare at each other blankly until one of them—the loser—breaks into laughter.

Expressionless Face is similar to the "Still Face Experiment," conducted by psychologist Edward Tronick, who studied the effect on an infant's psychological state when a mother is emotionally unavailable. The study filmed interactions between mother-and-infant pairs. In one, the pair relate in an attuned way—the mother responds to the baby's sounds, looks where it points, smiles when it smiles—until, after a few minutes of playful interaction, the mother is cued by a researcher through an earpiece to shift into a still face for a solid two minutes.

What happens next is difficult to watch. The baby tries to engage her mother with smiles, pointing, babble, whatever would usually lead to connection. When nothing seems to work, she begins to panic, scream, break down. Finally, the mother responds and the two reconnect, repairing the momentary disruption of their bond.

Long before acquiring language, an infant develops complex skills of communication that are necessary for survival. As a person's basic needs are extrapolated to include emotional survival, feeling shut out by another person, even when literal survival is not at stake, can be threatening. Shattering an intolerable sense of disconnection is, for most people, worth losing a round of Expressionless Face (the grown-up version would be attempting to reestablish connection by picking a fight).

Maybe the game was my daughters' way of trying to master moments when they felt emotionally abandoned (*Your thinking face and your angry face are the same*). Small doses of still-face disconnection are experienced throughout our daily lives—someone looks at their phone while you're speaking, half listens, smiles at you with their mouth only.

The eyes tend to smile along with the mouth if the smile is sincere, as was invariably the case during a night out when my friend presented the challenge. The muscles around the mouth obey the will, but the muscle to the side of the eyes—the orbicularis oculi—which contracts to make your eyes smile, does not. Guillaume-Benjamin Duchenne, the nineteenth-century French neurophysiologist who first discovered this connection by stimulating muscles in the face using electricity, found that the orbicularis oculi contracts only when a person feels genuine positive emotion: "Its inertia in smiling," he wrote, "unmasks a false friend."

Feeling is body driven, whereas thinking, according to Bion, is "called into existence to cope with thoughts." He explains this counter-intuitive precept through a scenario involving a hungry infant who yearns for the breast to suddenly materialize and satisfy its need. When the infant feels hunger and expects the breast, but no breast turns up—or expects a smile and only the lips turn up—instead of the yearned-for satisfaction, it feels frustration, which then leads to a thought (*The breast is not there*). The "development of an ability to think," in Bion's words, occurs as a way of coping with the thoughts that crystallize from frustrated feelings: in philosopher Emil Cioran's terms, "Every thought derives from a thwarted sensation." With the breast—or its metonym—in the mouth, however, there's no need for thinking. You are free to feel.

Or, as poet E. E. Cummings has it, "since feeling is first / who pays any attention / to the syntax of things / will never wholly kiss you."

But our tendency in daily life is to value thinking, the rule-driven syntax and facts about a person's existence, over feeling. Those who foreground emotion, the way the mind moves, generally forgo the rewards—chief among them belonging—that accompany thinking that is easily calibrated with the thoughts of others.

Neurologist Oliver Sacks writes about a set of autistic twins, who, though they could not perform basic mathematical calculations, had an extraordinary ability to "see" prime numbers—breasts of sorts—"in an entirely sensual and non-intellectual way," and to "savour" them through play with "holy intensity":

They seemed to be locked in a singular, purely numerical, converse. John would say a number—a six-figure number. Michael would catch the number, nod, smile and seem to savour it. Then he, in turn, would say another six-figure number, and now it was John who received, and appreciated it richly. They looked, at first, like two connoisseurs wine-tasting, sharing rare tastes, rare appreciations.

Others quoted by Sacks with similar sensory relationships to numbers experienced them as living things, like the "unanalysable essence of all musical sense" based on tones that are like "'faces' for the ear, and are recognised, felt, immediately as 'persons.'" This recognition, "involving warmth, emotion, personal relation," is akin to the recognition of a friend. "Numbers are friends for me, more or less," Sacks quotes mathematician Wim Klein as saying. "3,844? For you it's just a three and an eight and a four and a four. But I say, 'Hi! 62 squared.'"

Poetry needs to wholly kiss, have holy intensity.

That is because, for me, poetry is not defined by form but by effect. A piece of writing can look like a poem, use words that are considered poetic, but without the ability to move readers, it becomes an example of Walcott's fake poem, which can be unmasked the same way that Duchenne's false friend can—there is no physical contraction, no movement in the body. "Poetry is not the poem," writer Jorge Luis Borges explains, "for the poem may be nothing more than a series of symbols." Regardless of whether we are looking at a sonnet, a sculpture, or a newborn infant, we know we are in the presence of poetry, its "magical, mysterious, unexplainable—although not incomprehensible—event," when we feel moved.

But what does it mean to feel moved? Right now, I'm communicating with you ego to ego. An ego communication is one in which you communicate information that can be processed by logic and reason. In psychoanalytic sessions, ego communications aren't always easy to work with. Someone comes in, tells you about their week, a recent job interview. You can, of course, listen through the material for feelings around the thoughts, the trail of associations, what is being communicated by way of the material being conveyed (*What are they telling me by telling me this?*), but the profound work is most readily accessed through a communication from the unconscious.

Communications from the unconscious are often received as bodily sensations. For example, when I'm working as a psychoanalyst, I occasionally begin to feel sleepy during a session, sense a pull toward slumber so strong it's as though I had just taken cold medicine. I have experienced this dynamic often enough to know I'm not literally sleepy but am colluding with the analysand to close my eyes to something, usually some feeling they don't want me to see. Communicating outside words makes it possible to get at felt realities without distorting them to match linguistic forms, providing us with a more direct way of giving others access to our interiors. Abstract art can operate in a similar way: like representational work, it's mimetic, but instead of representing an identifiable object, like a tree, it may represent feelings, images, or perceptions from the interior.

Unconscious communication involves an interpersonal process described by Bion through a model involving a mother communicating with her preverbal infant. Even though an infant doesn't have language, its mother (or any caregiver, of course, gender aside) can still receive its communications. Let's say the baby is crying. The baby's cry isn't heard the way words are generally heard: cognitively. It enters the body. Rather than coming to know what the infant is feeling by understanding it—as you understand directions to the closest grocery store—the mother accesses the emotion by feeling it. The infant projects raw emotion into the mother, which the mother then feels inside her body as though it were her own. She processes that raw emotion with the tools she's developed through experience, then puts that processed emotion back into the world in symbolized form, in words— for example, "You're tired."

In Bion's theory, the raw emotional data that the infant gives off are termed "beta elements," which must then be ruminated on, metabolized by an "alpha function," the mechanism of experiencing

23

emotion from within, digesting it, and putting it back out in symbolized form. Alpha functions process beta elements so that they become available for thinking.

Beta elements pass between people who are close—a parent and an infant, lovers, friends, siblings—but also strangers on the street, on the subway, at the checkout counter of a store. We project and contain beta elements, and perform alpha functions on those elements, without being conscious of doing so.

Bion's definition of beta elements focuses on split-off negative parts of the self that get projected into others, but it can just as easily be applied to all energies that are projected into us and that we emit when interacting with others. Sigmund Freud thought about the drives—the impulses that power our life force—in terms of energy. Beta elements, like energy, pass between bodies, continuously changing form.

Empathy, which is articulated in German as feeling into the shape of another, also gets at this shape-shifting of emotion as it passes between people. We now understand, through neuroscience, what happens when a person feels into the shape of another—say, if they see someone trip. Mirror neurons fire within the brain of the observer, causing the tripping sensation to be mirrored within, as though it had originated there, the way the mother feels the infant's emotion within her body as her own. Because the same mirror neurons fire when a person witnesses an emotion or action as when they feel or act that way themselves, we are able to experience what happens outside of ourselves as part of our own subjective experience—to feel moved by experiences that are not our own.

It can be helpful, therefore, to think about the extent to which you are performing alpha functions and processing your beta elements, your raw emotions and impulses, for others. If you are performing alpha functions, digesting your beta-element communications for your addressee or audience to the extent that they become like a piece of American cheese in plastic wrapping, they can take them in as we take in processed foods, but it's unlikely that much will remain for their bodies to contain and metabolize. That is the danger of overediting, shining the surfaces, airbrushing, combing out the knots ("The lines I love now," writes Walcott, "have all their knots left in"). A clean, processed communication with no bumps or snags may not trigger existential shame, but it is also unlikely to emit beta elements from your body to your addressee's body, your unconscious to their unconscious—to move them.

Like the infant does in early-stage addressivity, trying to give the mother what she will affirm, putting forward ego material in an attempt to control the audience's response, will strengthen the development of a False Self, which, detached from Winnicott's True Self and what Bayes termed "the source," won't have the capacity to move anybody.

"The essence of pleasure," writes philosopher Søren Kierkegaard, "does not lie in the thing enjoyed, but in the accompanying consciousness." Think of a madeleine, which, without Marcel Proust's writing, would be nothing more than a bland bit of cake. We love it because he loves it.

That is not to say that ideas and thinking do not have equal significance in poetic communications, interpersonal relationships, or our experience of the world. Yet just as the first step in ethical thought is to feel into the shape of another, bodily communication has the potential to widen our horizons of understanding by way of the direct access it gives us to another's experience. A communication from the unconscious that provokes feeling in the body will have been encoded by the specific body that created it—with all its genetic, racial, and desirous markings—and will therefore, in being incorporated into the experience of others, have the potential to expand our modes of relating.

It's difficult to resist the urge to play the part you imagine other people will find interesting or entertaining, the part you think will receive approval. We all want to be loved. The problem is that you're less likely to connect with others on an emotional level if you're leading with a prototype or idea, an ego communication, rather than with a spontaneous impulse. When your goal is to get a certain response—which involves projecting yourself into the position of another to anticipate and meet their imagined expectations, as opposed to staying connected to the source—you're bound to flop.

The most direct way of connecting with others is to experience genuine feeling within yourself, so that your emotion, transmitted to others as beta elements, triggers their mirror neurons to fire. It is then that they will experience and process your emotion as though it had originated within their own bodies, that they will feel moved. "Indeed, a work of art," writes composer Arnold Schoenberg, "can produce no greater effect than when it transmits the emotions which raged in the creator to the listener, in such a way that they also rage and storm in him."

At the end of clown school, Bayes named our clowns through a process that lasted days. We each took the stage and underwent a kind of interview process that culminated in his deciding on a name that flagged something in us he believed we needed to explore. Most people cried—I mean sobbed, snot into red nose—as their clown was being named: Everyday Spencer, Take It or Leave It Karen, Maybe Someday Donna. One actor was given a name he hated—Little Tiny Regret—but accepted it in the expressionless way most artists are trained to listen to a critique. Bayes pushed him:

You come all this way, and what are you waiting for? Yourself. Don't regret the things you've done; regret the things you haven't done. Don't regret the mistakes; regret the mistakes you didn't make—because you tried. Did you try? Did you really try? You have to really try. Why do you want to be invisible? Get out of your own shadow. Say, "I'm alive!" Roar.

The actor, sobbing, said, "I'm alive." Then repeated it a second time, with a roar: "I'm alive!"

"Now we see you," said Bayes.

On the day I was to be named, I was terrified. I knew I had been seen but didn't feel ready to own it. As Winnicott says, *"It is joy to be hidden but disaster not to be found."* Unable to access a state between being hidden and found, joy and disaster, I scrambled my signals. My clown name reflected the ambivalence I often experience being onstage—lost in a holy intensity until the floorboards creak behind me and I become gripped by existential shame, imagining how others will perceive me if they see my enjoyment.

In the end, he named my ambivalence, marking it as the thing I needed to explore. My clown name was Next! The name incorporates the inflection of a director calling the next actor onto the stage for their audition, being dismissed, sent away, an irrelevant number. If you're not going to bring it, really give it your all, let yourself be mostself beautiful, seen, then get off the stage. You had your chance. *Next!*

One of the first steps in change, from the perspective of many psychoanalysts, is to recognize your patterns of thought and behavior, make the unconscious conscious. That way you can pause in the moment rather than act on autopilot, take in the information before you, and decide how you want to behave. The ability to make conscious choices is the crucial freedom that psychoanalysis can offer.

We are our choices, Sartre says; "an individual chooses and makes himself." Our choices determine our identity. If we choose to act courageously, we become courageous. But the moment we make a different choice—say, to act cowardly—we become that next thing. We are always becoming the self our most recent choice calls into being, painting our portrait anew.

Psychoanalysis, too, posits a continually evolving self: we are each "[a] poem that is being written," as Lacan has it, even if the living text of our unconscious is inscribed in an indecipherable code. To take responsibility for who we become, for the poem that gets written, we must understand our unconscious. Deciphering the unconscious is what makes it possible for us to become the one we are and, from that position, direct our choices. "The analyst," writes Bion, "is trying to help the patient to dare to be himself, to dare to have enough respect for his personality to be that person."

Sartre's "existential psychoanalysis," on the other hand, "rejects the hypothesis of the unconscious." But if there is no unconscious, how do we account for the choices that seem to be made not by us but through us? My phone operates as though it has an unconscious that, like the raw impulses of the id, seeks to be expressed. If I behave appropriately, in a well-mannered way—if I try, for example, to apologize—my phone reverses my intent, changes *sorry* to *dirty*, a genuine apology into innuendo, as in, *I'm writing to let you know how dirty I am*—

Recently, I overheard someone use the word *feckless*. Having never uttered the word before, I typed it into the Notes app on my phone. A few days later, I was texting with the mother of one of my daughter's friends about plans. *Hoping she can sleep over with us tonight*, the mother wrote. *Only bummer is we have to leave early tomorrow to LI. Can you pick her up at 8:00 a.m.?? Is that too horrible?*

Perhaps having internalized the sense that I was feeling feckless, my phone changed the word *actually* in my response to *act risky*, so that it read, *I may act risky have to come even earlier.* I had unintentionally given the impression that I was going to stay out all night and pick up my daughter on my way home.

We all need slips from the unconscious to nudge us to take risks, align our outward selves with the interiors we desire. But what mind does a phone's unconscious belong to, and is it always, even in invisible ways, cutting into our line?

As we become better able to clear our histories, act through avatars, and tweak our profiles, we live in the fantasy that we are expunging the unconscious, deleting it, seizing the blank moment with a cleared past, tabula rasa. Bookmarked tabs are the personal myth we prepare for an imagined Other—not necessarily the sites most visited, but the ones we identify with ourselves, the outwardly directed persona we would tolerate another person apprehending if they were to catch a glimpse of our screen.

A similar statement of identity can be made through clothing and numerous other concrete possessions one chooses to make visible to others. Some even enlist designers to manage the signals emitted by their surrounding objects. Actor Gwyneth Paltrow, it was reported, hired a personal book curator to select hundreds of books for her shelves. An article in the *Modern House* featuring the home of author Rachel Cusk included a photograph of a wall of books, prompting people on Twitter to attempt to collaboratively decipher the spines and determine what she reads (or chose to exhibit for the shoot) as a way of gaining access to her.

Some people refer to the emotions and perceptions they signal about themselves to others as their "brand." A personal brand is maintained through a set of consistent choices that signify corresponding character traits—an approach that shows how an essentialist idea of identity (*We are our choices*) can be manipulated for strategic purposes.

Focusing on the surface, lining up your external chips, often results in immediate social reward, yet it can also cause you to lose sight of your interior. In extreme cases, the surface may even become the interior, like the map that comes to stand in for the territory, as philosopher Jean Baudrillard describes it: a simulation that takes the place of the real. The virtual can even feel more real than the real, as happened to a couple in Korea who left their infant daughter at home while they camped out in an internet café playing a video game in which they successfully raised a virtual child. Their daughter starved to death.

When a person becomes a simulation—when it is difficult to distinguish between their self and their role in the game—they may be said, in psychoanalytic terms, to have an "As-If" personality. An As-If person, according to psychoanalyst Helen Deutsch, who coined the term, appears "intellectually intact," able to create a "repetition of a prototype [but] without the slightest trace of originality" because "expressions of emotion are formal . . . all inner experience is completely excluded." She likens the behavior of someone with an As-If personality to "the performance of an actor who is technically well trained but who lacks the necessary spark to make his impersonations true to life." Bion gets at this As-If quality in relation to psychoanalysts who, regardless of training and their familiarity with "psycho-analytic theories" and "labels [they] can collect and wear," may still lack the necessary spark to fully inhabit the moment, make themselves available for conscious and unconscious communications: "Why is it that one person is capable of tolerance, compassion, concern or respect for his fellows, and another isn't?" The answer is inside us. "We ought to know something about ourselves," he says of psychoanalysts who "are [not] in any way exempted from the characteristics of the rest of the human race." Anyone who has lost contact with their True Self, their inner world, and merely repeats a prototype that has been internalized from the external world will inevitably lack that true-to-life spark of authenticity and an ability to seem or feel, as Winnicott has it, real.

Increasing access to a person's interior—trying to reach the source, the wellspring of energy and impulses that make up the True Self—can be achieved by attending to unintentional manifestations from the unconscious that slip through in the form of linguistic displacements, bungled actions, spontaneous outbursts of laughter, or other forms of parapraxes. When the unconscious slips out of repression, it most often does so in an altered form, through a process seen most clearly in dreams.

Freud observed that dream images work through condensation and displacement. For example, you can condense the characteristics of two people who remind you of each other (say, your mother and your lover), or displace one person with another who is somehow associated with the first (Sam, the neighbor who stole your package, with your best friend, who shares his name). Both scenarios allow you to circumvent a direct thought that has the potential to be disturbing (*I'm sleeping with my mother; My best friend is stealing from me*), offering a way of dreaming about emotionally charged figures or scenarios in low-stake form.

Lacan noticed that such condensations and displacements, which are central to Freud's dream theory, function very similarly to the linguistic devices of metaphor and metonymy, which led him to conclude that the unconscious is structured like a language. A metaphor condenses two things in such a way that a similarity is brought into relief—for example, the world and a stage, as in William Shakespeare's line "All the world's a stage"—while a metonym displaces one term with another that is different but associated.

I learned the definition of *metonym* in graduate school. The professor wrote on the blackboard: *All night long.* He then asked, What is associated with the night? Someone called out, The moon! The professor then added a second sentence: *All the moon long.* The moon, he explained, was an association with night that then displaced it. You can build a chain of metonymic associations, he continued, with each new word linking to and displacing the last: *All night long. All the moon long. All the stars long.*

The definition of a particular literary device is easiest to remember through example. Whenever I think of a synecdoche—a part that stands in for a whole—I recall an example from the anthology we had been assigned in that class: "All hands on deck!" People often confuse metonyms and synecdoches. The clearest way for me to distinguish between them is through example—curses, in particular. A synecdochical curse, for instance, substitutes a part of a person for their whole (*asshole, dick, heel*), whereas a metonymic curse displaces the entire person with something outside of them that is somehow associated (*douchebag, bitch, pill*).

My ex-husband sometimes called me a pill. You're such a pill, he would say, and I would assume he meant *pill bug,* because that is how I often felt: rolled up inside myself, retracted, disappeared. You're such a pill bug! I would hear and feel guilty for my emotional withdrawal.

One of the challenges of growing up with parents who aren't native English speakers is grasping figures of speech. Why, for example, can't you have your cake and eat it too? Can't you have a slice, pack up the rest, and save it for later? ("Because I'm human," writes poet Adélia Prado, "I zealously cover the pan of leftover sauce.") Is the presentation of cake—placing the perfectly iced, untouched object on a stand for all to see—more important than the pleasure in eating it? Why have a cake, if not to eat it?

"By the same token," in my mother's mouth, became "by the same talkin'," which condensed in my mind with the expression "talking out of both sides of your mouth." This composite phrase made sense to me because I always imagined the token as a coin with two sides that could not be viewed at once, like the optical illusion that lets you see only a beautiful woman or a hag but never both at the same time. "By the same talkin'," then, comes to mean talking out of both sides of your mouth in two streams of speech that can never be perceived simultaneously, much like the psychoanalytic term *vertical splitting*, conveying a kind of compartmentalization that allows you to hold two contrary thoughts in your mind in an unconflicted way because they don't enter your consciousness at the same time (a way of having your cake and eating it too?).

My first piano teacher, Mrs. Muselmann, had her couch and sat on it too. I would step out of the elevator into the overheated hallway on the nineteenth floor of her building and enter her apartment through a foyer that led directly into the living room, where the piano was, along with a white couch and an armchair, both covered in thick plastic. During the summer, when I sat on the couch waiting for someone else to finish their lesson, I remained perfectly still, having learned that when I moved, the skin on my legs would stick to the plastic and make a suction sound that I worried would be mistaken for a fart.

On one side of the living room was a kitchenette and dining room, with a table where Mrs. Muselmann occasionally invited me to sit and eat cookies. On the other side was a small hallway that led to a bathroom and a bedroom, the door of which was always shut. Her husband, who my mother told me had had a stroke, was always in the bedroom—or so I assumed, sensing his presence through the closed door regardless of whether or not there was evidence of his being there. Never in my six years of lessons in Mrs. Muselmann's apartment did I set eyes on Mr. Muselmann, but sometimes, as I was playing my arpeggios, I would hear a moan from the bedroom. Mrs. Muselmann, an upbeat older woman with a high-pitched voice, would continue singing the rhythm she would use for triplets—*tan-ti-vy, tan-ti-vy, tan-ti-vy*—as though she hadn't heard a thing. My entire being would halt, even as my fingers went on without me.

Our minds enlist various maneuvers that allow us to keep our hands moving across the keyboard, to remain composed, regardless of our emotional state. After Trump took office, in 2017, I noticed an increase in people's use of the phrase *make do* in psychoanalytic sessions. The phrase is short for *make something do well enough* and has within it a kind of resignation, a powerlessness—what more can you do than play the hand you've been dealt?

"We did not want to work with Mr. [Rudy] Giuliani," European ambassador Gordon Sondland testified during the 2019 Trump impeachment hearings, in an attempt to explain his having engaged with the government of Ukraine outside of official channels. "Simply put, we played the hand we were dealt." The dealer, in this case, was Trump, and Sondland's defense was that he was not making choices but following orders passed down the chain of command. If the choice was not his, he seemed to be arguing, then it did not attach to his person. Of course, he could have chosen to object or to question—not choosing is also a choice, as historian Howard Zinn says: "You can't be neutral on a moving train."

Perhaps there is always a power dynamic behind the impulse to *make do*. Some use the homophone *due*, creating a condensation that brings an additional meaning into the phrase. *To make due* gets at making something do well enough with what is accepted or proper, in accordance with dominant values, the cards the dealer has dealt, and the rules of the game. When we *make due*, we are not only accepting our circumstances but aligning ourselves with systems of power, playing the game from an As-If prototypical position, at the expense of making choices directed by our feelings and beliefs, and ultimately compromising our ability to feel alive and real.

A couple of years out of college, I was in a bar on Seventh Street in the East Village in New York with my boyfriend at the time, a novelist who carried a small notebook with him that he would suddenly take out of his pocket and write in during conversations. We were breaking up, although that didn't become clear until an extremely drunk woman stumbled over to our table and asked, What does *arbitrary* mean?

Random, I said. Like if you decided to move to Montana but had no real reason for doing so, the choice would be arbitrary.

I see. She nodded, then turned to my soon-to-be-ex-boyfriend who was half listening, because he only ever half listened to anyone. You keep using that word, she said to him, then paused longer than was comfortable. What's wrong with you? Have you stopped feeling?

Thinking metonymically offers us a roundabout way of getting at what is too difficult—or impossible—to approach head-on. This project, for instance, began as a book about laughter, because that is what I saw when I turned away from what felt too disturbing to approach directly. A fetish is another example of a mental process that is based on looking away from what is too overwhelming, as Freud illustrates through a scenario involving a little boy who notices that his mother doesn't have a penis and assumes it has been cut off. The thought is too upsetting for him to hold in mind, because with it comes the fear of castration, so he looks away.

In turning away, the little boy focuses on something else in his field of vision that becomes a substitute, "a token of triumph over the threat of castration and a safeguard against it." By the same token of triumph, then, one expresses both a threat and a safeguard against it, creating a vertical split in the mind, what Freud calls a "splitting of the ego," which allows a state of knowing and not-knowing, seeing and unseeing, to exist—but not register—simultaneously. The token's triumph is splitting off the threat and metonymically displacing it with another object (a shoe, if feet were seen when looking away, or under-

34

wear, if that is what the eyes focused on, et cetera) that soothes the sense of threat by keeping the cake, or idea of self, whole.

"The meaning and purpose of the fetish," writes Freud, ". . . is [to] substitute for the woman's (the mother's) penis that the little boy once believed in and . . . does not want to give up." Creating a fetish, in other words, is a way of twisting your perception of external reality to maintain an idea or belief that would have to be altered if the evidence before you were taken into account. Rather than change your thinking, then, you change reality, so that your beliefs about yourself, others, and the world do not have to be adjusted.

Contemporary notions of castration anxiety have evolved beyond the (limiting) gendered fear of losing a literal body part to losing a part of the self—or idea of the self—that a person does not want to give up. The worry that you might not be able to fulfill your desires or be rewarded for fulfilling the desires of others—failing to please the mother, for example, or whatever figure has come to displace her (*What will they think?*)—is a kind of castration anxiety, particularly if not getting what you had expected or hoped for shakes your sense of self or triggers shame.

Imposter syndrome—the feeling that you may not live up to the fixed-portrait sense of self you've invested in and that you may, at any moment, be exposed as a fraud—has its basis in external chips being lined up beautifully, but in a way that does not necessarily connect to inner experience. ("So you are the one," Beckett said to his biographer Deirdre Bair upon first meeting her, "who is going to reveal me for the charlatan that I am.")

Being seen as you are as opposed to as you seem or would like to be—having your story of self disrupted—can provoke shame, which creates a gap between your experience and the perspective an observer takes, or is imagined to take (*What do they see?*), about that experience. The phrase *Okay, Boomer*, for example, attempts to shame a person twice over: once for having a dated perspective and again for being so checked-out they don't even realize it. You become a "comic character," who, philosopher Henri Bergson explains, "is generally comic in proportion to his ignorance of himself." He is "unconscious . . . invisible to himself while remaining visible to all the world."

In psychoanalytic sessions, people sometimes protect against this particular kind of shame, inadvertently revealing parts of themselves they cannot see, with defenses that limit how much gets disclosed (not saying what comes to mind, forgetting, falling silent, planning sessions in advance, trying to be entertaining, showing up late, going to the bathroom beforehand to be sure not to bring any shit into the room). One analysand had a constant worry, while lying on the couch, that his fly was undone. The fear expressed his anxiety around exposure, a fantasy about what might slip through an unintentional opening to reveal the gap between who he was and his representation of who he would like to be, as well as what I might do with that knowledge—his privates—if they were laid bare.

We elude being known even by ourselves. The way we remember our own experiences is also subject to psychic displacement, placing things in what Freud calls "substitutive relation," through "screen memories" that screen out upsetting thoughts and feelings that might get in the way of our daily functioning if they were allowed into consciousness. Screen memories operate by a process similar to that of dreams—retaining neutral information and repressing anything we might find disturbing—with a similar aim: keeping us asleep.

We need sleep so we can get the necessary rest to function and survive. In order for a dream not to become disturbing and wake us, images get split. The latent content, the powerful thought or emotion that stirs us, detaches from the manifest content, the neutral container for the emotion, which makes its way into the dream as seemingly meaningless content that rouses neither the dream censor nor the dreamer. When successful, what Freud calls "dream-work" represses disturbing feelings or thoughts that may wake us, while permitting the dispassionate containers housing them to make their way into dreams as tokens that show only one side, the beautiful woman, and obscure the hag.

The image of leaves turning to brown mulch where the gutter rises to meet the sidewalk's edge at the corner of Dorchester and Fifty-Second in Chicago has, for years, appeared in my mind in place of a thought or emotion I cannot access. Instead of a memory, my mind produces this image, which functions as a kind of recall, though I have no idea what is being called back.

The image of the leaves, I suspect, is an example of a screen memory, which censors powerful emotion by displacing what has the potential to be distressing with a trivial image or clip from experience. Like a fetish, the screen is often what the eyes see when looking away from what overwhelms. The trivial image—which serves as a neutral container for all that is important from the past in encrypted form—then becomes over-endowed with a vivid brightness, as with my mulching leaves. The work of psychoanalysis is to extract the meaning within the screen memory, which, like all other content within the unconscious, can be accessed only indirectly, through the analysis of its derivatives, which slip out in the form of dreams, parapraxes, superstitions, random thoughts, or associations.

My own associations led me to the realization that the street corner at which I have placed the memory of those leaves was on my walk home from school, at the end of a block where a girl in my grade lived. A sudden storm hit while she and her father were out sailing: he drowned; she survived. As I think about the image of the leaves, my mind associates it with fathers and daughters, storms, protection, vulnerability, drowning, loss, being engulfed. The image often comes to mind in place of forlornness, a sense that something horrible is about to happen that I will have to handle on my own ("When we speak of forlornness," writes Sartre, "a term Heidegger is fond of, we mean only that God does not exist and that we have to face all the consequences of this").

Unconscious processes that operate metonymically are all structural variations, for Freud, of how dreams function. Because one can get at the contents of the unconscious only through its derivatives, Freud's theory of dreams offers a way of understanding deeper meaning by way of the surface. In *Jokes and Their Relation to the Unconscious*, Freud proposes that jokes operate by the same process as dreams, in that they hide a powerful unconscious "kernel of thought" in what he calls a "joking envelope," a neutral container that seems innocent, unalarming. A joke—like a dream or a screen memory, or even a fetish object—allows a suppressed thought to enter the mind without anxiety or disruption, because it appears in a disguised form that elicits laughter, which allows an escape from the unconscious that is socially sanctioned due to the positive associations most people have with humor.

When someone laughs spontaneously at a joke, it is a sign that the latent part of the joke—the kernel of thought—has resonated with something in their unconscious, even if the content of the reverberation does not register consciously. The *aha!* becomes a *ha!*, and, because laughter flies beneath the radar, it offers us a way to express emotionally complex—even troubling—communications without detection.

Sometimes, however, a disquieting element can slip through a laugh and cause a rupture in the social fabric, much as a disturbing dream image can disrupt sleep. In 2006, comedian Dave Chappelle described to Oprah Winfrey how he had felt deeply disturbed upon hearing a particular kind of laughter during the taping of a skit in the third season of *Chappelle's Show*. The skit—and the show in general—used stereotypes ironically as a way of highlighting and subverting them. If irony does not register in the mind of an audience member, however, the method runs the risk of strengthening stereotypes rather than destabilizing them.

The problematic laugh broke out during the filming of the skit "Racial Pixies," in which Chappelle plays a tiny minstrel performer in blackface wearing a bellhop's uniform, holding a cane, and dancing to banjo music—"the visual personification," as he described it, "of the N-word." The laugh that disturbed him, which he described elsewhere as being particularly loud and long, came from a White person working on the show:

So then when I'm on the set, and we're finally taping the sketch, somebody on the set [who] was white laughed in such a way—I know the difference of people laughing with me and people laughing at me—and it was the first time I had ever gotten a laugh that I was uncomfortable with. Not just uncomfortable, but like, should I fire this person?

He found himself in a "complete moral dilemma." If he couldn't control whether the audience took his use of stereotypes ironically or literally, he also couldn't control whether he was subverting stereotypes or reinforcing them.

The so-called pixie incident provoked Chappelle to flee to South Africa without explanation, abandoning a $50 million dollar contract with Comedy Central. "That was the last thing I shot before I told myself I gotta take [f-word] time out after this," he explained. "Because my head almost exploded."

In order to keep our heads intact, most of us, rather than flee, exile our unthinkable thoughts. One method of doing so is to develop bodily symptoms, which disguise what is too difficult to face directly by displacing it into the body in encrypted form. Like a dream, a symptom has encoded within it the meaning of what has been repressed so that, successfully ciphered, it becomes inaccessible to the conscious mind. I went through a period of experiencing a twitching in my left eye. This symptom would occur most often when a thought or feeling I didn't want to see began to enter my psychological field of vision. The twitching, I came to understand, literalized my desire to hinder my perception so that I would have to take in only as much as I could tolerate.

We sometimes strive to unsee what we see, unknow what we know, because anything that destabilizes our psychic equilibrium can get in the way of our ability to perform the daily tasks that are expected of us. Taking in information that runs counter to our beliefs presses us to adapt our perspective, whereas perverse thinking allows us to maintain our beliefs by disavowing what is before us if it feels too unsettling. It can be destabilizing to change long-standing ideas about ourselves, others, and the world, which is why, even as evidence contradicting a belief should lead us to adjust the belief to accommodate reality, many people will bend the evidence before them to keep their thinking intact—the fundamental maneuver marking perverse thinking.

Freud describes neurosis as the negative of perversion. Whereas neurosis pushes an unthinkable thought into repression, perversion recognizes the disturbing piece of reality, then contorts it—as an optical illusion might—so that the tolerable part is kept in mind, while whatever may feel destabilizing is twisted out of view. Like a fetish object, a belief that reverses, recasts, or covers up what feels too upsetting to accept can soothe any perturbance by returning the thinker to a comfortable and familiar perspective on the world, however detached from reality.

A professor of mine in graduate school, perhaps seeing the ghost of *Alasdair* in my last name, kept insisting that I was Scottish even though I told him repeatedly that I was an Arab. Once, I ran into him on the street, and he introduced me to a companion. Noire, she said, clearly associating the sound of my name with *noir*, the French word for "black." That's beautiful. Is it French?

No, I said. It's Arabic. My parents are from Iraq—

But, the professor cut in, she's part-Scottish.

I relay these stories the way others tell jokes. I've got another. After a night at the pub during my summer at Oxford, a group of us decided to buy food from the local kabob cart parked outside the college gates. I asked the woman who lived in the room next to mine if she wanted to come along. I wouldn't eat food from those dirty Arabs, she said, disgusted.

I'm an Arab, I told her.

But you're different—

I began recounting this anecdote to my daughter and she cut me off. You've already told me this, she said impatiently. I had been helping her with a paper she was writing about *The Adventures of Huckleberry*

Finn, about how Huck needs to see Jim, in Mark Twain's words, as "white inside" in order to feel okay about loving him. My daughter, the one writing the paper, was very blond as a child, leading people to assume—because of my dark features, perhaps—that I was her nanny. When they realized I was her mother, that she had come through me, I would sense a subtle but palpable shift in their perspective on me, like when you pour boiling water over a duck before cooking it, and, as the heat tightens the skin, it appears to be moving (Is it coming back to life? my daughter would ask, half in fear, half in exhilaration). Perhaps I became to others what Jim is to Huck, "white inside" (less dirty? alive? okay to love?).

It is always easier to change a person who doesn't fit our expectations than to change a stereotype. This is what the woman who lived next door to me did when faced with me, evidence in the world that didn't fit her thinking: she changed me (*You're different*) instead of changing her idea about Arabs. In late 2017, Ahed Tamimi, a light-haired, light-skinned, blue-eyed Palestinian sixteen-year-old referred to by Amnesty International as "the Rosa Parks of Gaza," was arrested and imprisoned for eight months after slapping an Israeli soldier who had entered the yard of her house hours after her cousin had been shot at close range by a different soldier with a rubber bullet. There was an uproar of international objection. Tamimi is from Nabi Saleh, a Palestinian village in the occupied West Bank that held weekly non-violent protests from 2009–2017, when some of its land, including its water source, was confiscated by nearby Israeli settlers. Her sentence, according to Amnesty International, was "clearly disproportionate to her actions and a blatant attempt to intimidate anyone who dares challenge the human rights abuses that Palestinians experience under Israel's brutal occupation."

She is not the only Palestinian child to have been subjected to a disproportionate sentence, but the story spread across the globe, along with her photo, likely because of her appearance, which does not match up to the stereotypical image of a Palestinian. Her contradictory image might have changed people's assumptions about Palestinians, but instead, accusations surfaced that she was not a real Palestinian. Israeli security services even investigated her and her family members, who also have fair features, suspecting they were actors hired as a propaganda tool. If the evidence had been accepted—that the sixteen-year-old and her family were not actors, As-If characters, but real people (*white inside?*)—those in the region and beyond might have felt compelled to change their expectations about Palestinians and the ethics surrounding how they are treated.

Trump likewise perverted evidence while in office to keep his story intact. After he was exposed in 2020 for using the military to disperse people engaged in peaceful protest against the murder of George Floyd so he could walk to a nearby church in Washington, DC, for a photo-op, Trump tweeted a letter from his former lawyer saying the "phony protesters" were "not peaceful" or even "real"—contradicting video footage—but "terrorists." Days later, he tweeted a similar conspiracy theory alleging that a seventy-five-year-old White man in Buffalo who had fallen to the ground and lay bleeding from the head after being shoved by police was "an ANTIFA provocateur" who was part of a "set up." Because Trump had deemed Antifa a terrorist organization days earlier, he was effectively calling the man a terrorist, attempting to frame the public's interpretation of the facts so they saw the police officers' behavior as justified. Changing evidence is more effective than changing our long-standing ideas about others and ourselves, if the objective is to maintain the status quo.

More and more often, comedians have begun to stand up and point out when evidence and fact have been perverted in the political sphere. In a *Washington Post* op-ed in late 2019, Sacha Baron Cohen warned against the danger of conspiracy theories and fake news supplanting evidence-based conclusions and factual truth. He knows these strategies intimately because he uses them in his comedy. Take, for example, Borat, whom Baron Cohen refers to as "the first fake-news journalist." By pretending to film a documentary, Borat, a fictional character from Kazakhstan, draws real people into fictional scenarios they believe to be nonfictional in order to reveal their genuine—perverse—feelings and beliefs.

During the summer of 2020, Baron Cohen pranked a group of conservatives in Washington State who organized a rally, "March for Our Rights 3," protesting safety regulations instituted to stop the spread of COVID-19. "Video that was streamed live from the event," writes CNN reporter Harmeet Kaur, "appeared to show a singer in a red shirt and blue overalls engaging the crowd in a racist singalong." The songs exposed the extent to which the "rights" the protesters were defending were entangled with the infringement on the rights of others. The lyrics referenced Barack Obama, Hillary Clinton, Dr. Anthony Fauci (director of the National Institute of Allergy and Infectious Diseases), and called the coronavirus by one of the racist names it had been given, "the Wuhan flu." The call-and-response lyrics became more and more offensive as the sing-along continued ("Chinese people, what we gonna do? Nuke 'em up like in World War II"). People sang along ("Journalists, what we gonna do? Chop 'em up like the Saudis do"), until one of the organizers realized they had been had and unplugged the microphones. The prankster-activists hopped into the back of an ambulance and sped away.

Baron Cohen's method creates "a new style of comedy" that uses the real world as its stage. As with clown, which he learned from Gaulier, we laugh not simply because something is humorous but because it is honest. In a 2018 interview, Baron Cohen described the genesis of his comedic style at a pro-hunting rally in England that "every member of the upper class" attended "save the royal family." He put on "a hat from Astrakhan in Southern Russia" that happened to be in the back seat of his car and went "undercover as a foreign character"—"basically an early form of Borat"—and approached the participants at the rally.

> Hello, my name is . . . [he assumes the Borat accent]. I would start asking people, "excuse me. When we went hunting in Moldova, we like to hunt the Jew. Would you hunt the Jew here?" And they'd start answering . . . [assumes upper crust British accent] "Well, actually . . . yes, so long as he was given a fair start. Yes, I would." And

I suddenly realized here was a method that allowed people to really reveal their true feelings on camera. I came back home and I said to my flatmate, I think there's a new style of comedy here that I've accidentally chanced upon, an undercover character comedy.

This undercover character comedy is humorous because it is honesty framed by the absurd, which makes it, like Chappelle's comedy, ironic.

Without the fictional frame, which creates a disjunction between what is being spoken and what is being said, the same communication would be threatening. In 2020, for example, Congressman Matt Gaetz, a Republican from Florida, posted on Twitter just after Trump designated Antifa a terrorist organization—during the same month as Baron Cohen's sing-along—"Now that we clearly see Antifa as terrorists, can we hunt them down like we do those in the Middle East?" Unlike Baron Cohen, Gaetz means what he says literally, and there's a history to his threat. A self-proclaimed "Antifa Hunter" was sentenced to three years in prison during the same time period for making racially motivated threats and cyberstalking people he perceived to be "enemies." The term *Antifa*, short for *anti-fascist*, is vague, and it loosely includes leftists who are willing to use physical force when they deem it necessary to oppose fascism, neo-Nazis, and White supremacists. The murkiness of Antifa's identity—like that of a terrorist or an enemy combatant—makes it easy to apply the label to people irresponsibly and then use it as a justification to do whatever you want with their bodies and lives.

The definition of *Antifa* is relational: it means "enemy," but only from a particular standpoint (Trump's), much like the term *Middle East*, used by Gaetz in his tweet, expresses, in literary scholar Edward Said's terms, an Orientalist attitude that is more cultural than geographic, in that the countries referred to are Eastern only if you assume the central position—the standpoint from which you are looking—to be North America or Europe. (Australia is considered part of the West even though it is geographically located in the Southern and Eastern Hemispheres.) Exposing the ways in which we unthinkingly fall into these strategically constructed positions that do not match up to what is factual underlies a key strategy in Baron Cohen's comedy.

"Democracy," Baron Cohen writes in the *Washington Post* op-ed, "which depends on shared truths, is in retreat, and autocracy, which thrives on shared lies, is on the march." His method of combating this trend is to spotlight the false beliefs people adopt unknowingly in hopes of reversing the process of unseeing.

Our collective sleep is dangerous. "Habitualization," the literary theorist Viktor Shklovsky explains, "devours work, clothes, furniture, one's wife, and the fear of war." America is suffering profoundly from such habitualization at the moment: there's an apathy, a deadness, even when the stakes should feel high, where human life, basic rights, and our environment are concerned.

When children were first separated from their parents at the border between the United States and Mexico under Trump's 2018 order, for example, the anecdotes, images of children in cages, and sound clips of desperate sobbing were so disturbing that it was difficult to think of anything else. News outlets attempted to track the children, figure out where they were. Yet eventually, other stories dominated, and, as with the wars we are engaged in abroad, it became necessary to proactively search news sources for updates. Horror, too, can be habitualized. Horror at the habitualization of horror can also be habitualized, as can our ability to empathize, which is increasingly excused as "compassion fatigue," as writer Susan Sontag explains:

> In fact, there are many uses of the innumerable opportunities a modern life supplies for regarding—at a distance, through the medium of photography—other people's pain. Photographs of an atrocity may give rise to opposing responses. A call for peace. A cry for revenge. Or simply the bemused awareness, continually restocked by photographic information, that terrible things happen.

The bemused awareness that terrible things happen is itself a kind of sleep. The purpose of art, according to Shklovsky, who came up with the literary device of defamiliarization, is to resist emotional fatigue, "recover the sensation of life; it exists to make one feel things, to make the stone stony . . . to impart the sensation of things as they are perceived and not as they are known." In order to recover a sense of aliveness, we must shift from what we know—or assume we know—to what we perceive at the bodily level. It's like driving along the same road you've traveled for years and suddenly noticing a house your perception had taken for granted until it was stripped of its ivy. Perhaps you had never noticed the ivy before, but the absence of ivy makes you notice retroactively the ivy that had been there all along, on the bricks and in your mind.

"Habit is the ballast," writes Beckett, "that chains the dog to his vomit." Because the world is "a projection of the individual's consciousness," he continues, "(an objectivication of the individual's will, [philosopher Arthur] Schopenhauer would say), the pact must be continually renewed, the letter of safe-conduct brought up to date." One way to bring our perceptions up to date, to renew them, is through art, which has a way, writes Shklovsky, "of pricking the conscience" and waking us from the deadening sleep of habit.

In response to an interviewer's question "What is the purpose of poetry?" poet Zbigniew Herbert replied, "To wake up!" It is the honest moment that pricks, moves us, gets the laugh. When we recover the sensation of life, we perceive our world anew, reverse our process of unseeing, and return, open-eyed, to wakefulness.

It's seldom the party I remember, but some small moment on the way. Such was the case one piercingly cold March night, walking through Clinton Hill, Brooklyn, with a friend, a poet originally from the Netherlands. I can't remember where we were headed; she had been staying with me in Brooklyn while she was in town for a few literary events, so I accompanied her to readings, drinks, spontaneous dancing in the back of the Half King. She is one of those rare people I became close friends with the moment we met, due to some ineffable sense of—what? resonance? recognition? I don't know the appropriate term for the waves that carry the energy I'm trying to describe, or even the kind of matter it must pass through to be perceived. But when I tried, falteringly, to articulate it to my friend during our walk, she immediately understood what I was grasping for and handed me a Dutch term vast enough to contain my slippery attempts. *Uitstraling*, which translates as "out-shining," means to glow, to radiate a kind of aura or charisma—although none of that is exactly right, she explained. It's difficult to pin down a definition of this sensation without leaning on phenomenological or loose terminology. But that doesn't matter much in the end, as words and thoughts become unnecessary in its presence. Certain feelings—a baby's sensation feeding at the breast, the twins encountering prime numbers—keep thoughts, language, and thinking at bay.

I have a framed photograph on the mantel in the front hallway of my home, a portrait of sorts, of the unanalyzable essence of a moment I wanted to capture while studying at Oxford. In discussing photographs, Barthes calls the part of an image we understand, and that we can connect to contexts of meaning that we know, the "studium," and he calls the part of an image that pierces us, that resonates with our interior to evoke strong feeling and prick our consciousness, the "punctum."

Barthes's punctum is similar to Joyce's idea of epiphany, "a sudden spiritual manifestation" that allows us to apprehend what we cannot access intentionally. Reading Virginia Woolf's *To the Lighthouse*, listening to music, smoking cigarettes in my sunlit room at Trinity College, I was suddenly seized by an acute sense of my being. I wanted to record the moment but realized, upon opening my notebook, that no words attached to the experience. So I took a picture. When people ask what the photograph is of, I say, "Happiness," even though I know that's not quite right. But what am I supposed to say—*holy intensity*?

Occasionally, while moving through the studium of existence, I am pricked by a sense of profound feeling, like the beam of light film director Krzysztof Kieślowski shines into his protagonists' eyes to indicate communion with another level of being. While reading, I sometimes stumble upon a passage so evocative it spills over the edge of my intellect, and the surplus is transformed into a bodily sensation that compels me to slam the book shut, stand up, walk around. Work that excites, rushes out of the intellect and into the body—what Borges calls "the aesthetic act, the thrill, the almost physical emotion that comes with each reading."

Meaning moves between body and mind: thinking can transform into feeling, a frustrated sensation can become a thought that is coped with through thinking, and psychic energy that is too overwhelming may be repressed, made unavailable for contemplation. An instinct, for Freud, is "a concept on the frontier between the mental and the somatic," the mind and the body, and what exists at this body-mind frontier also teeters between the rational and nonrational. Embodied knowledge, whether originating in the body or converted from mind to body, is most often communicated unconsciously—from one unconscious to another, bypassing reason—though it can also travel in the opposite direction and can be consciously converted through various processes, creative and psychoanalytic, into rational form.

"Martha, what is jumping?" Dancer and choreographer Martha Graham describes author and disability rights advocate Helen Keller asking her during a visit to her dance studio. Graham answered the question by having Keller place her hands on the hips of company dancer Merce Cunningham ("Merce, be very careful, I'm putting Helen's hands on your body") and asking him to jump. As he rose into the air, Keller's hands did, too, and as Graham recalled, "her expression changed from curiosity to one of joy." After Cunningham stopped jumping, Keller exclaimed, "Oh, how wonderful! How like thought! How like the mind it is!"

Intuition, the most familiar kind of embodied knowledge, often has the adjective *feminine* preceding it. Hysteria, marked by the conversion of feelings and thoughts into bodily symptoms, is generally seen as a feminine disorder (its etymological root is *hystericus*, meaning "from the womb") and carries a negative connotation associated with an emotional excess that obstructs reason—being *too much*. Even my beloved Joyce reportedly said, in response to being asked what he thought of writer Gertrude Stein, "I hate intellectual women." What is so threatening about this way of knowing?

"We have been raised," according to writer Audre Lorde, "to fear the *yes* within ourselves, our deepest cravings" because it threatens any system that calls upon us to prioritize external logic over internal knowledge. "The True Self comes from the aliveness of the body tissues and the working of body-functions," writes Winnicott of his version of the *yes* within ourselves, "including the heart's action and breathing." Trained to suppress the True Self and what Lorde calls the erotic power of "nonrational knowledge," we settle for lesser understanding, permitting essential meaning and emotion to be lost.

"A painting has to be the experience," writer Janet Malcolm quotes artist David Salle saying in *Forty-One False Starts*, "instead of pointing to it. I want to have and give *access to feeling*. That is the riskiest and only important way to connect art to the world—to make it alive. Everything else is just current events."

Access to feeling, a sense of aliveness, is a preoccupation of Malcolm's, though it appears cloaked in terms as various as *soul, essence, presence, insight, eroticism, animating impulse*, the *human*, and the *real*. It is not surprising to learn that Malcolm began her career as a poet. You can see the stirrings of this *feeling* stretching back over half a century to her first publication in the *New Yorker*, a poem titled "Thoughts on Living in a Shaker House." In the poem, she imagines a domestic tableau that places the occupations of "busy little souls" in contradistinction to "ordinary grief and cares," much as Salle opposes *feeling* to "current events" and Barthes separates the studium from the punctum.

But taking up the punctum, as Malcolm does, trying to articulate this nonrational sense of aliveness or sudden spiritual manifestation (*uitstraling?*)—easy to detect but embarrassingly difficult to verbalize—is risky, as Salle says. It's much safer to write about current events, the studium of recognizable griefs and cares, than to include in rigorous thinking this more numinous aspect of our being, even as most people recognize the emptiness they experience without it. I've always wondered why Malcolm's work, which, despite taking on high and low subject matter and maintaining access to the erotic ("Writing cannot be done in a state of desirelessness"), is celebrated for its intellectual rigor by the literary establishment rather than dismissed, as much work that is driven by internal logic tends to be.

"And by the way," writes Plath, "everything in life is writable about if you have the outgoing guts to do it, and the imagination to improvise. The worst enemy to creativity is self-doubt." I would add to self-doubt: anxiety around letting yourself be known, experiencing and expressing yourself as you are rather than an As-If version of who you would like to be (the creator of that great, dreary masterpiece everyone will merely pretend to read).

Instead of using guts and imagination to keep the erotic power of the *yes* alive inside themselves, many store it in a killing jar, then pin and frame behind glass what would not otherwise have lent itself to becoming a classifiable specimen attached to categorizable meaning. Critics, after all, tend to gravitate toward what they can write about (*What's your central idea?*), use familiar tools to cut into a work, and pull out what they already know—even if, in so doing, they kill it, as poet Marina Tsvetaeva explains:

> When, in response to the thing I offer, in which form has been vanquished, removed by means of rough drafts, I hear: "There are ten 'a' sounds, eighteen 'o's, assonances . . ." (I don't know the professional terms), I realise that all my rough drafts have been in vain, that's to say they've come to the surface again, and what was created is again destroyed. Dissection, but not of a corpse—of a live body. Murder.

The critic comes up against what Tsvetaeva describes as "the *calculability* of matter and the *incalculability* of spirit." The spirit cannot be apprehended from the outside, as an object might be: "To have an opinion of a thing, you must live in that thing and love it," she writes. For the reader to enter the work, the work must first enter them by way of their mirror neuron system, reach their unconscious, be experienced internally as though it belonged to them. "Read and love my things as if they were your own," she advises. "Then you are my judges."

The nonrational, incalculable spirit that connects us to the aliveness in the world and others is transmitted by way of unconscious communication, which Malcolm depicts in her book *Psychoanalysis: The Impossible Profession* through Aaron Green, a psychoanalyst she meets with for regular interviews about the psychoanalytic process. Green relays a vignette about feeling sleepy during a session with an analysand who was "defending herself against [the erotic transference] by making herself uninteresting and dreary." His sleepiness was an "unconscious" response because, though on the surface "her free association seemed to be full of the richest and deepest analytic material," it was, in fact, "shallow and hollow" and he "was bored because of what was missing—namely, the sap, the juice, the eroticism that is in everything and that makes for life and interest, that keeps us awake and alive." Someone who suppresses their eroticism will similarly communicate a certain hollowness, a milder version of an As-If personality, the "actor who is technically well trained but who lacks the necessary spark to make his impersonations true to life," in Deutsch's words.

Green's physical sensation had less to do with being tired than with—as I myself have experienced—colluding with the analysand to unsee something the analysand wants to keep hidden. Communications from the unconscious, the realm of the punctum, are often received through bodily sensations, like the "entirely sensual and non-intellectual" game with prime numbers that Sacks describes between the twins.

Perceiving an action or emotion of another, according to neurobiologist Vittorio Gallese, is equivalent to internally simulating it. The observer uses their own internal resources to experientially penetrate another's world by means of a process he terms "embodied simulation," which is driven by mirror mechanisms in the brain, including mirror neurons. Embodied simulation allows us to understand inter-subjectivity intercorporeally—to, quite literally, feel into the shape of another.

However, this penetrative "empathy" has the potential to be violent, as Saidiya Hartman explains, because the "projection of oneself into another in order to better understand that person" can result in a kind of obliteration that "fails to expand the space of the other but merely places the self in its stead." When a person's feelings penetrate another's borders—whether through embodied simulation, infectious laughter, or an attempt to walk in their shoes—the person whose shape is being felt into may experience what Hartman, in the context of a White person trying to understand the subject position of an enslaved person by making it their own, terms "a violence of identification." This "precariousness of empathy" is often overlooked because of the positive associations to empathy, which cause many to override their intuition with thought. In fact, empathy becomes precarious precisely when it is not driven by emotions—the body—but by the intellect.

An analyst attuned to an analysand, like a caregiver attuned to a baby, necessarily uses mirror mechanisms, their body—themselves as their instrument—to take in more than the verbal meaning within a communication. Yet this process must be enacted with attention and care. "Or," writes Bion, "putting it differently, the analyst needs to be able to listen not only to the words but also to the music, so that he can hear a remark which is not easily translated into black marks on paper." The same set of words can have "a different meaning when it is made in tones of sarcasm, or in terms of affection or understanding, or by a person who has actual experience of authority." To approach another human being solely with reason and the goal of pulling out a diagnosis—what you already know or what you want to discover—without taking in all levels of information, can be akin to dissecting a live body, indulging a murderous, obliterative spirit, much like the one Tsvetaeva attributes to critics in which a work of art or a person is treated like a vacant space that can be filled with the feelings, beliefs, or ideas of others.

One way of avoiding such violence is to remain receptive, feeling the feelings of the other inside yourself rather than projecting yourself into the other. Even while reading, when black marks on paper are all you can access, a different meaning is transmitted if you tune in to communications that target your body: the music of the writing, alternations of what philosopher Gilles Deleuze calls "style, with its succession of catatonias and accelerations," than if you take in a chain of dictionary definitions only. Sometimes even what we think of as most abstract—a number, for example—has its origin in the body (the decimal system emerged from counting on fingers). Writing that performs aesthetic acts, transmits emotion corporally, "feed[s]," in Deleuze's words, a "passionate conversation" by way of embodied communication that emits "atypical, almost animal traits of expression."

There is not always a connection between the meanings of the words used in a communication and the erotic, nonrational transmission that is received bodily. There's a place in *Psychoanalysis: The Impossible Profession* where Malcom suggests that Freud must have been turned on by the material of his young female patient Dora because psychoanalysts get turned on by sexual content: "Today's more sophisticated analysts have no compunction about admitting the stimulation they feel when a patient talks about sex; it is regarded as one of the ordinary occupational hazards of the work." I have found the opposite to be true, however counterintuitive. An analysand's material can be sexual without being erotic and erotic without being sexual. The words may be the same in each instance, but, as Bion reminds us, words add only one dimension to the overall communication and can sometimes pull in a different direction from a person's affect or feeling. An analyst must attend to the words, but also to the music, the way the mind moves, what is happening body to body.

For unconscious communication to work, the recipient must be open to receiving transmissions from others, but also have the receptivity to pick up on and process beta elements, emotional transmissions in their unprocessed, uncalibrated form. Unconscious communication involves the body and the intellect, and points to a more nuanced way of understanding than we can achieve through reason on its own. "An account of human reasoning based only upon abstract texts," explains philosopher Martha Nussbaum in *Upheavals of Thought: The Intelligence of Emotions*, ". . . is likely to prove too simple to offer us the kind of self-understanding we need." She therefore calls for us to "think of emotions as essential elements of human intelligence" and as "part of our reasoning capacity." Or, as Nietzsche writes, "There is more sagacity in thy body than in thy best wisdom."

This bodily wisdom is nevertheless rarely included in rigorous philosophical analyses. It's not clear whether that would even be possible, as subjecting what is alive to analytic reason risks killing it. That which "renders truth visible to the understanding," writes philosopher and poet Friedrich Schiller, "conceals it from the feelings; for, unhappily, understanding begins by destroying the object of inner sense before it can appropriate the object." In grasping "the spontaneous work of nature," the philosopher—much like the critic in Tsvetaeva's formulation—destroys the very aliveness they are trying to apprehend:

> Thus, in order to detain the fleeting apparition, [the philosopher] must enchain it in the fetters of rule, dissect its fair proportions into abstract notions, and preserve its living spirit in a fleshless skeleton of words. Is it surprising that natural feeling should not recognize itself in such a copy, and if in the report of the analyst the truth appears as paradox?

The translation of the nonrational into the rational enchains "feelings" and "inner sense"—the "living spirit"—into "fetters of rule," "a fleshless skeleton of words." It is far easier to calculate matter, talk about what is no longer alive, fixed, than to talk about the *incalculability* of the spirit, the unknown, that which keeps moving, refuses to behave, to sit still long enough to be pinned down.

It is risky to give way to the incalculable, to what is unknown in the world and also in oneself—particularly when seen by another. Once, upon greeting an analysand at the door of my office, I saw in her eyes that she was in a depressive episode. She spent most of the session re-counting her week in an upbeat voice—all facts, no feeling—until, near the end, she told me I looked sleepy. I had colluded with her in closing my eyes to what she didn't want me to see. I'm waiting for you to stop hiding how you're feeling, I said. With that honest statement, we both woke up. She admitted she had been extremely depressed. I saw that when I greeted you, I told her. Yes, she said. I saw you seeing it.

Philosopher Jacques Derrida is thrown into a metaphysical quandary one day after emerging from a shower and noticing his cat noticing his naked body (*What does it see?*). He likens the experience of being seen naked by an animal (his cat) and not being able to know how the animal cognizes his nakedness to "God's exposure to surprise," to the unknown, to the "promise" or "threat" implicit in the phrase "you'll see what you'll see." He is like Sartre's man at the peephole, except he cannot project himself into the mind of a cat as he would into that of a human being, because the act of projection would be conscious: he would know that what he was imagining was unknowable. Being faced with the incalculable, unable to anticipate what will happen, provokes in him "the dizziness one feels before the abyss open[s]." I used to ex-perience a similar sensation when my parents would say, You're going to get it! Not knowing what *it* was, I filled the abyss with my worst fears. Even when it's dreadful, the known will often feel more tolerable than the vertigo we experience on the precipice of the abyss.

At the same time, the unknown can be exciting, can offer a sense of possibility, spontaneity, or transformation. Derrida proposes this is the case for the poet, whom he imagines as a figure capable of sitting with unknowable animal thoughts: "for thinking concerning the ani-mal, if there is such a thing, derives from poetry." The difference be-tween philosophy and poetic thinking, he continues, is that poets or prophets, those "in the situation of poetry or prophecy," stand regu-larly before the incalculable abyss and "admit taking upon themselves the address of an animal that addresses them." Comedians, too, take upon themselves this animal address. In a stand-up routine, come-dian Sarah Silverman describes how to play a game she invented with her dog that sounds a lot like my daughters' game of Expressionless Face, only in an adult context: "When you're having sex, lock eyes with your dog. And then you see who looks away first." But what happens when you don't look away, when you accept the animal address? "After a solid minute of my dog and I locking eyes," she tweeted, "we both go to a pretty crazy place."

The animal address speaks to a nonrational, "crazy" part of ourselves that, positive or negative, reminds us that we are alive. The fleeting apparition of the living spirit—like the aliveness, sap, juice, and eroticism that Malcolm's work addresses—is often what our intuitive assessment of another person hinges on, as Malcolm explains in *The Journalist and the Murderer*. The narrative centers around the case of Jeffrey MacDonald (the alleged murderer of the title) versus Joe McGinniss (the journalist who wrote the best-selling true crime book *Fatal Vision*, based on the story of the alleged murderer), and the question of whether McGinniss upheld a clause in his contract that granted permissions "provided that the essential integrity of [MacDonald's] life story is maintained." The case hinged, in other words, on the jury getting at what, if anything, McGinniss did not maintain of MacDonald's "essential integrity," his core or essence— whether he had murdered the alleged murderer's aliveness in capturing his spirit in a fleshless skeleton of words.

In short, everyone is a poem. The jury needed to determine whether McGinniss had deliberately left out MacDonald's poetic essence, shut him up in prose. In focusing his analysis of MacDonald on externals—suggesting that MacDonald had "swallowed one too many diet pills and had therefore offed his family"—rather than on his inner world, McGinniss created "middle-class, unerotic pornography," destroyed his essential integrity by treating it as calculable matter, chaining it to a fixed, prototypical understanding. Similar to an analysand's sexual yet sapless material in a session, McGinniss's writing was criticized for conveying his representation of what happened through the unerotic pornography created when fleshless skeletons are manipulated into recognizable poses.

Facts, like words or sexual acts, don't, in and of themselves, carry emotional weight. Without the charge of emotion—a connection to a person's essence, True Self, or source—a communication is inevitably unerotic, incapable of moving anyone. As with the distinction between a true and a fake poem, the jury's verdict hinged on *feeling*, their ability to sense the sap at the "core of [the defendant's] being," to pick up on the quality of his animating impulse, which gets emitted like radio or light waves but with a frequency outside of measurement.

By unconsciously transmitting genuine feeling, defendants communicate to a jury that they are "'real' human beings" and not "soulless monsters." The jury saw in McGinniss "a strange absence of feeling," and his "apparent incapacity for feeling compassion" made it difficult for them to connect with him, for their mirror neurons to fire. His inability to feel empathy or elicit it in others then became the stand-in for the crime and the jury saw him as "guilty of a kind of soul murder."

Soul murder, a term significant in psychoanalysis, was also invoked by various playwrights in the nineteenth century, including Henrik Ibsen, who uses it to mean the destruction of another person's love for life. Soul murder targets a person's internal life and can be seen as a kind of *straling*-snuffing.

Foregrounding a person's internal reality over their external one, as the jury was asked to do, is a radical and controversial move. Many psychoanalysts subscribe to an approach that similarly focuses on psychic over objective reality. The ways in which external events become represented and embedded in the psyche are more important in the consulting room than a corroborated truth of what happened. (This is particularly true for children or childhood memories, during the phase of development when the interpretation of experience is limited to whatever tools are available at the time.) In understanding a person's patterns of thought, it is less helpful to look solely at what actually happened than to incorporate what a person experienced as having happened, their accompanying consciousness, as a way of enlisting other modes of perception that play into reality even as they are more difficult to articulate.

Poets, like many psychoanalysts, tend to focus less on the factual part of what happened and go for psychic reality instead—what happened *and* how it was represented internally—not to deny or mitigate reality but to incorporate levels of perception that most people pick up on but are unaccustomed to valuing as meaningful. The unconscious, like poetry, is most often communicated by way of bodily feeling—when we are *moved*—though that transmission is difficult to translate into rational understanding without destroying it, as Tsvetaeva and Schiller point out.

Psychoanalysts and artists—anyone, for that matter, who analyzes information—who are willing to enlist their unconscious minds, as well as their intuition, are most able to break ground, because intuition often leads to insight. Gut, or bodily feelings, which could be considered another mode of processing, are significant in analytic sessions, poetry, artworks, problem-solving, jury deliberations, predicting violence—perhaps every interpersonal interaction. Bodily sensations, as Bion describes, circumvent thinking and create other forms of knowledge that exist outside of words.

When you have *access to feeling*—the metaphorical breast in mouth—there's no need for thinking, just as in good films, according to Sontag, who calls for an erotics of art, "there is always a directness that entirely frees us from the itch to interpret." That directness, or out-shining, delivers us from our interpretive itch, because thinking that emerges to cope with thoughts is not necessary when the ability to feel has not been frustrated. When we are feeling, we experience within a different mode of cognition—one that allows us to incorporate systems of sensual thought, such as intuition, insight, or creativity. It is within this mode that we are able, as Walt Whitman writes, "to feel the puzzle of puzzles . . . that we call Being."

The twins Sacks writes about, who were able to access through numbers a sense of holy intensity, were eventually separated "for their own good," to prevent "their unhealthy communication" and "in order that they could come out and face the world . . . in an appropriate, socially acceptable way." Living in halfway houses, working "menial jobs," able to navigate the world under close supervision and with direction, they became "quasi-independent and socially acceptable." But, "deprived of their numerical 'communion' with each other"—that rare connection they thrived on—they lost "their strange numerical power, and with this the chief joy and sense of their lives." If that isn't *straling*-snuffing, then I don't know what is.

"I don't think that anyone can grow unless he really is accepted exactly as he is," says Fred Rogers, creator of *Mister Rogers' Neighborhood*, a television show that encouraged children to develop their inner lives. "In this country, anyway . . . a child is appreciated for what he *will* be, not for what he is. He *will be* a great consumer someday. And so the quicker we can get them to grow up, and the quicker we can get them out of the nest so that they will go out and buy . . . the better."

"Creative work in any established system of thought," writes Malcolm, "takes place at the boundaries of the system, where its powers of explanation are least developed and its vulnerability to outside attack is most marked." It is, of course, *risky* to throw yourself into the puzzle of puzzles, operate outside the demands and rewards of systems holding power, but the cost of not doing so is to make yourself vulnerable to inside attack, soul murder.

A communication from the soul, the unconscious—any spontaneous gesture from the True Self—that provokes feeling in the body not only will amplify rational thought but, because it will inevitably be encoded by the specific body it passes through, will have the potential to expand our modes of experiencing and relating to one another. This is not to say, of course, that emotions should not be subject to rational criticism, merely that operating on reason alone is like flying with only one of your engines.

Years ago, a woman approached me after a poetry reading I had given and chatted with me. As I listened to her, I found myself taking tiny steps backward, which she met with steps forward of roughly the same size. Though my instinct to move away should have made me decline to give her my email address when she asked for it, I, like so many others (women in particular), let a sense of propriety override my intuition. I recited the address quickly, hoping there would be a mistaken letter somewhere as she typed it into her phone.

The next day, I received a short email from her asking where she could find my work. I sent a formal but friendly response, to which she replied with a long personal email, including the news that she would soon be in New York and an invitation to meet. I wasn't interested in meeting or continuing the exchange and took a giant step back by putting off a response.

A couple of days later, her name appeared in my in-box. Immediately after I clicked on the message, the letters seemed to fly off the page toward me:

FFFFFFUUUUUUUUCCCCCCCCKKKKKK
YYYYYYYYOOOOOOOOOUUUUUUU!!!!!!

"No animal in the wild," writes security adviser Gavin de Becker, "suddenly overcome with fear, would spend any of its mental energy thinking, 'It's probably nothing.'" Instead of valuing our gut feelings, he continues, "we, in contrast to every other creature in nature, choose not to explore—and even to ignore—survival signals."

In response to reading a letter from McGinniss that MacDonald had covered "with a variety of savage marks," Malcolm "felt in the presence of a terrible anger and hatred and desire to do injury." She includes in her analysis not only the text but the feeling in her body as she reads it. Incorporating the erotic into the reading experience can cause the two-dimensional marks on the page—or screen, as with the email I received—to become animated into a live presence.

This animal address, which passes directly from one body to another, is also present in some of photographer E. J. Bellocq's works, as

Malcolm describes. A number of prints made and exhibited by photographer Lee Friedlander from glass-plate negatives found in one of Bellocq's drawers after his death, writes Malcolm in "The Real Thing," "derived from plates that [had] been defaced not by time and weather but by a deliberate hand." The faces of the subjects were covered, disturbingly, with "savage black scrawls . . . as if done by an angry child with access to India ink." In one print, Malcolm depicts how, "as the eye moves upward from the fair-skinned body, which the camera has tenderly modeled (and whose pubic and underarm hair it has recorded with a kind of reticent conscientiousness), to the blacked-out face, it recoils as if before a scene of rape." This image, literally defaced by violent marks, is, she concludes, "the real thing," accompanied by "the unwanted truths leaking out of [it]."

It is not easy to sit with the savage complexity of the real thing, to take in and record the unwanted truths leaking from it and not recoil. The way we manage embodied knowledge is connected to our handling of unwanted truths, much as hysteria shuttles into the body and out of conscious recognition what feels too difficult to confront. By trafficking in logical understanding, we short-circuit the erotic in exchange for intellectual currency—but with costs that extend far beyond closing our eyes to the full dimensionality of a truth, "the real thing."

When we move from the apprehension of specific details to the comprehension of an abstract idea, we shift from embodied to programmatic interpretation, from what the animal in us perceives to what we know, and risk locking the living spirit in a fleshless skeleton of words, unerotic pornography. To be comprehended through logic and reason is very different from being apprehended (*You feel me?*). Without tuning in to the frequency of unconscious communication, you lose access to the most meaningful, exhilarating, confounding, vulnerable, life-preserving, and courageous way to connect to yourself, others, and the world.

But also savage complexity.

I am the captain of my fate. Laughter is possible laughter is possible laughter is possible.

—SHIRLEY JACKSON

I must have turned my head in the direction of my lapel mic, because suddenly my volume shot up. As part of a panel on hoarding, along with another psychoanalyst and a memoirist, I was explaining the concept of *horror vacui* (fear of emptiness), pointing to its role in the aesthetics of the Victorian era (covering every surface with tchotchkes) and in sex, how some men who dread a sense of postcoital emptiness stave off—and this is when it happened—*ejacuLATION.*

The sudden surge of my voice came at me through the speakers as a kind of *horror vox*, a disconcerting eruption of my interior into the external world. That got really loud for a second, I observed matter-of-factly, then burst into a fit of uncontrollable laughter. I tried to compose myself, apologize—Sorry, I just had a juvenile moment—and return to the passage, but when I reached the word *ejaculation* again, I lost it, doubled over, put my head on the table before me. Seconds felt like hours as I tried, with little success, to pull myself together.

I had no idea why I was laughing, but the more I laughed, the more others in the room laughed with me. Attacks of laughter are contagious: another person's laughter—even if nonsensical—is enough of a stimulus to provoke your own. During one production of playwright David Mamet's *A Life in the Theatre*, in a scene in which an actor ate Chinese food onstage, "one piece of noodle went awry," according to critic Alexis Soloski in the *Guardian*, "and seemed to smack him in the face." He paused, then "slurped it up," causing the actor playing opposite him to break into a fit of convulsive laughter, "dro[p] his head to the table," then, "shoulders shaking . . . attemp[t] to hide himself behind his chair." Rather than express annoyance, the audience, like the one at my talk, joined in. Bystanders invariably get drawn into what Soloski calls "the joy of corpsing."

Corpsing is a British term for breaking into convulsive laughter and derives from the frequency with which a fit of laughter overtakes an actor playing a corpse onstage. Before bursting into laughter during my talk, I was, in a sense, playing dead, if you think of "dead" as symbolic of acting out of your socialized self, pushing emotions and spontaneous feelings underground.

We were sitting at a long table, as we might have at an academic conference, images and diagrams projected onto the wall behind us, while the audience, in organized rows, faced us in silence. As I presented my writing, one person directly before me scrolled and typed on her iPhone. Another stood up, walked loudly to the back of the room to get a drink, then returned to his seat to rummage through his bag. I suddenly became aware of my attempt to block out those actions and stay in role by pretending not to see what I was seeing.

"When you're acting," explains comedian Ricky Gervais, "you're not caught up in the moment. Anything can put you off. You're never not aware of your surroundings. So suddenly, one little thing will bring out the absurdity of what you're doing." The absurd is marked by a tension between the seriousness you attach to your life and the inherent meaninglessness that is revealed when you catch a glimpse of yourself from an outside perspective: "A man," writes Albert Camus in *The Myth of Sisyphus*, "is talking on the telephone behind a glass partition; you cannot hear him, but you see his incomprehensible dumb show: you wonder why he is alive." Tuning in to the quotidian, meaningless actions we perform on autopilot elicits a sense of the absurd, but when the ridiculous actor of that incomprehensible show is oneself, the absurdity intensifies to the extreme, and, like the indifferent universe around us, we "secrete the inhuman."

Corpsing, then, becomes a form of resistance, a way of refusing to play the inanimate body, objecting to the part you've been given by breaking character. Most often, we don't select the roles we find ourselves playing in daily life: our character is cast by a process we participate in without awareness. As we move through the world, we are drawn into social scripts, texts that govern interactions we are trained to reprise without conscious recognition. When we receive our cue—like the hypnotist's magic word—we take up our automatous position. Breaking character expresses a refusal to become an instrument in the production of a system that is invisible and indifferent to us.

Refusal to take your position in an established order disrupts the power structure of that order. The repeated objection of Herman Melville's character Bartleby when he's asked to perform a task by his employer ("I would prefer not to"), for example, or American football player Marshawn Lynch's repetition of the same nonanswer ("I'm thankful") to reporters' tedious postgame questions are, as Orwell says of jokes, tiny revolutions. Lynch, fed up with reporters' questions, at first refused to answer them. Yet because he was contractually obliged to attend press conferences—and faced a $50,000 fine if he did not—Lynch showed up and repeated an answer that had nothing to do with the question asked ("Thanks for asking," "I'm here so I won't get fined"). He fulfilled his contractual agreement without giving reporters what they wanted from him.

Tennis player Naomi Osaka announced on social media that to protect her mental health, she would not participate in press conferences for the 2021 French Open and was willing to accept the fines. When the French Open not only fined her but threatened her with expulsion, she shocked the athletic establishment by withdrawing from the tournament. "If the organisations think that they can just keep saying, 'Do press or you're gonna be fined,'" Osaka posted on her social media accounts, "and continue to ignore the mental health of the athletes that are the centerpiece of their cooperation [*sic*] then I just gotta laugh." This laughter, like the kind Orwell describes, expresses resistance—it says that she, like the actor cast as the dead body, refuses the role.

Had Bartleby said no to his boss's requests, or had Lynch or Osaka refused to stand before the press while remaining in the game, they would have played a recognizable role (rebel) and maintained the social order (*Because once they've got you violent, then they know how to handle you*). However, by responding in asyntactic ways—in poetry?—they broke agreed-upon codes and defamiliarized the social script before them. Lynch freed himself to speak on his own terms, nonverbally, through the game itself ("I'm just about that action"); Osaka stepped off the stage into her own script; while Bartleby, in preferring not to do whatever was asked of him, "den[ied]" his employer's "authority."

To refuse to play the part that is expected of you is to resist transferring power to whoever is invested in your taking up that role. The power another person has, explains trial lawyer Gerry Spence, is the power you give them: "*The power I face is always the power I perceive.*" The other's power, he says, speaking of psychological power, "is my perception of their power. Their power is *my* thought. The source of their power is, therefore, in *my* mind." If the power or authority a person expects another to grant them is withheld, the sense of deflation that ensues can make them feel, as Bartleby's employer put it, "disarmed," "impotent," and "unmanned."

A few winters ago, after noticing mouse droppings on a shelf in my pantry, I placed a sticky trap in the corner. I wanted to avoid the risks associated with other options: snapped fingers, poisoned food. The next day, rather than a mouse, I found droppings stuck in the trap's glue. When I caught sight of the droppings, I felt a surge of rage well up inside me, the same kind I sometimes experience when my daughters resist my authority. What infuriates me about them in those moments, I realized while standing in the pantry, is that they shit on my sticky trap.

A babysitter who quit working for us some years before the sticky-trap revelation described a similar frustration. She had asked my then five-year-old daughter to do something—I can't remember what—that she preferred not to do. The babysitter said, If you don't [whatever it was], I'll take away your cookies. My daughter replied, That's okay. Cookies aren't important.

"What does Melody want to tell her family, her mother, with this entrance?" an interviewer asks novelist Jacqueline Woodson on National Public Radio, referring to her sixteen-year-old protagonist's decision to have a Prince song play as she descends the stairs of her grandparents' Brooklyn brownstone at her coming-of-age party. "I think she wants to say," Woodson responds, "I'm here," [Woodson laughs] "and I am my own narrative."

Woodson's laughter—like Osaka's "I just gotta laugh"—was likely to have been elicited not by humor but by the recognition that her character refused the role that was expected of her. A cognitive satisfaction, explains evolutionary theorist Alastair Clarke in *The Pattern Recognition Theory of Humour*, accompanies completing a pattern, like when you place the last piece in a puzzle. When that piece not only fits but has been supplied by your own psyche, you experience a kind of *aha!* moment, a light switching on—the inverse of the deflation that accompanies a dispelled expectation. Recognition functions as revelation—the unveiling of a thought that had not quite made its way to consciousness—and is marked by laughter.

The process of humor, which includes a neurophysiological reward along with the laughter that marks it, is unconscious, Clarke says, "else we should all be able to explain its mechanism by simple analysis of what we think before we laugh." Laughter conveys metacommunicatively, outside of speech, something about a person's relationship to what is before them. A listener cannot know precisely what it was about imagining her protagonist saying, "I'm here, and I am my own narrative," that made Woodson laugh. Such laughter, as with a communication in clown or in psychoanalysis, is not elicited simply by thoughts and words but also by the music and emotion that accompany their expression. The laughter in Woodson's answer imparts erotic nonrational knowledge, what Shklovsky calls "the sensation of things as they are perceived." The emotion Woodson attaches to saying, "I am here, and I am my own narrative," is transmitted nonverbally to the listener through her laughter, which, like beta elements, can be metabolized by an alpha function and then connected to verbal meaning.

The meaning I perceived after processing Woodson's laughter within myself was a sense of awe at the courage it requires to resist the role that is expected of you and claim agency. Social scripts create a fixed interpersonal syntax. To be your own narrative is to operate outside that script, the sentence, and listen for the poem-self that is continuously being written, rather than default to putting forward a role that dutifully meets expectations. "The world will ask you who you are, and if you don't know," Carl Jung cautions, "the world will tell you."

Sixty percent of what we express is nonverbal, according to former FBI counterintelligence officer Joe Navarro. The most effective way to read someone, he discovered through his experience conducting interrogations, is to attend not only to what they say but to what accompanies their speech at the nonverbal level, as well as to the relationship between those two modes of transmitting information. In the therapeutic setting also, psychoanalyst Theo Dorpat explains, there is a "need to listen to both verbal and nonverbal (affective) communication in making the diagnosis of inauthentic communication"—expressions from a person's False Self. He refers to a vignette by Sacks about witnessing a group of patients with aphasia, which diminishes comprehension of verbal communications, watching a speech by former president Ronald Reagan on a TV in a neurology ward and roaring with "derisive laughter." They were able to listen through his words to the emotions expressed by his nonverbal communication:

> It is said that one cannot lie to an aphasic. Because the aphasic patient cannot grasp the meaning of the speaker's words, he or she cannot be deceived by them. But what the patient does understand is grasped with infallible precision, namely, the nonverbal communication and the emotional expression.

We leak truths from our bodies all the time.

"Have you ever noticed that you can often learn more about other people—more about how they feel, how it would feel to be them—by hearing them cough or make one of the innumerable inner noises, than by watching them for hours?": poet Elizabeth Bishop asks her friend the poet Donald E. Stanford in a letter:

> Sometimes if another person hiccups, particularly if you haven't been paying much attention to him, why you get a sudden sensation as if you were inside him—you know how he feels in the little aspects he never mentions, aspects which are, really, indescribable to another person and must be realized by that kind of intuition . . . that's what I quite often want to get into poetry.

Gaining access to another person's feelings through the sudden sensation of being inside them also describes the process that is propelled into action when your mirror neurons fire and you feel another person's feeling inside yourself. Poetry operates by "that kind of intuition," allowing you to foreground your sensory perceptions when feeling into the shape of another, rather than limiting understanding to what can be communicated through words and reason.

If you translate bodily, unconscious communication into logic, you risk reducing the dimensionality of what is being imparted to a single mode of understanding and become less likely to get at what Malcolm calls "the real thing." Subjecting understanding to reason, language, the sentence—its rules and regulations—is equivalent to being shut up in prose, taking up an interpretive position, which is another kind of scripted role, as it is governed, much like bodily processes, by codes.

Attempting to operate outside of language, rationality, and standardized modes of expression—saying, *I'm here, alive, charting my own narrative*—evokes a sense of intense pleasure that, like *la petite mort*, "the little death" that serves in French as a euphemism for orgasm, has a counterintuitive association with dying, as does, of course, corpsing (*I died laughing!*). A spontaneous fit of roaring laughter can, in fact, feel orgasmic. Certain pleasures rub against the edge of pain, whether physical (stitches in your side) or psychological (being transgressive, risking punishment), and it is precisely this adjacency of opposing emotions that amplifies sensorial intensity.

Corpsing relates, in this way, to *jouissance*, a term used by Lacan for a kind of pleasure so specific it defies translation. English speakers sometimes use inadequate words (*bliss, pleasure, enjoyment*), but generally stick to the French word, which has within it *jouir*—"to enjoy" (rights, things) and "to come" (*ejacuLATION*)—but also, as Lacan explains, "the sense in which the body experiences itself . . . at the level at which pain begins to appear" where "a whole dimension of the organism, which would otherwise remain veiled, can be experienced." The felt dimension of the organism unveiled, like Heidegger's *aletheia*—"being . . . stepped out into the unconcealedness of its being"—defamiliarizes existence so it is experienced as a sense of pleasure merely in *being* (alive, naked, for nothing) at the level of the body.

As does corpsing, *jouissance* has within it a force of resistance, that provocative, impish drive to burst free from external constraints also found within political action, poetry, and self-revelation. In explaining the complex psychology behind *jouissance*, Lacan borrows a scenario proposed by philosopher Immanuel Kant: a man is given the opportunity to spend the night with a woman he desires, in Lacan's terms, "unlawfully," on the condition that, upon exiting the room of lovemaking, he pass into an adjacent room in which he will be executed. For Kant, the pleasure of lovemaking is not worth the punishment of death, and anyone in his right mind would refuse this trade-off. However, "one only has to make a conceptual shift," counters Lacan, "and move the night spent with the lady from the category of pleasure to that of *jouissance*, given that *jouissance* implies precisely the acceptance of death—and there's no need for sublimation—for the example to be ruined." *Jouissance* shits on the sticky trap of practical reason.

"Birds feel something akin to pain (and fear) just before migration," writes poet Lorine Niedecker, and "nothing alleviates this feeling except flight (the rapid motion of wings)."

Thinking, as Bion reminds us, comes into existence to cope with thoughts, which, in turn, enter the mind when a yearned-for sensation has been thwarted. If the sensation is not thwarted, there is less of a need to think. Spontaneous outbursts of laughter express meaning outside of reason and, like *jouissance*, unveil a whole dimension of being and bodily aliveness that short-circuits logic.

Part of what makes an eruption of amplified being pleasurable, as in Kant's scenario, is the recklessness involved in expending drive energy unproductively, dangerously, without sublimation. Eroticism, as philosopher Georges Bataille defines it, "is assenting to life up to the point of death." *Jouissance* "is always in the nature of tension," according to Lacan, "in the nature of a forcing, of a spending, even of an exploit." When a raw impulse or drive is channeled directly from the unconscious, its urgent expression as pure energy often has an accompanying sense of *jouissance*. But, as with corpsing, this euphoric, even orgasmic, release of energy is nonrational, purposeless—like a dancer jumping.

Once a month, as Karen Blankfield writes in a *New York Times* article, David Wisnia and Helen Spitzer, lovers in Auschwitz, risked their lives by defying the rules of the camp to climb "on top of a makeshift ladder made up of packages of prisoners' clothing" into "a space amid hundreds of piles, just large enough to fit the two of them"—what became their "nook"—for thirty minutes of lovemaking ("Did you tell your wife what we did?" Spitzer asked when they met again for the first time seventy-two years later). Spitzer bribed fellow prisoners with food to keep a lookout for them. "She had loved him, she told him quietly [when they met again]. He had loved her, too, he said." These trysts, as I imagine them—involving agency, choice, pleasure, but also enormous risk—were moments of *jouissance*: life in the death camp.

What have we given?
My friend, blood shaking my heart
The awful daring of a moment's surrender
Which an age of prudence can never retract
By this, and this only, we have existed
Which is not to be found in our obituaries
Or in memories draped by the beneficent spider
Or under seals broken by the lean solicitor
In our empty rooms.

I return to this passage from T. S. Eliot's *The Waste Land* whenever I feel I've lost contact with the throbbing pulse of being. It is not the horizontal time of our life's narrative, its events and accomplishments, that determines the quality of our existence, but the vertical time of "a moment's surrender," its awful daring, that is experienced, like *jouissance*, at the level at which pain begins to appear.

La petite mort, the "death which lovers love," in Percy Bysshe Shelley's words, also pushes a person's sense of being to this threshold. In medieval times, the term referred to a loss of consciousness following sex. For centuries, death has been used metaphorically by poets to symbolize orgasm, a moment's surrender. "Eroticism," for Bataille, "unlike simple sexual activity, is a psychological quest independent of the natural goal: reproduction and the desire for children." Such an unsublimated expenditure of energy can be seen as wasteful: *la petite mort* is circumvented not only by men, as discussed in my talk, who want to avoid *horror vacui* emptiness after sex ("Suck on, suck on," writes Shelley, "I glow, I glow!"), but by others (athletes, artists) who don't want to squander their life force.

"I'm afraid of depleting my energy," Lady Gaga told an interviewer. "I have this weird thing that if I sleep with someone they're going to take my creativity from me through my vagina." Lady Gaga's worry that having sex will rob her of her glow is similar to Plato's warning in the *Laws* that laughter is a waste of wisdom:

For where waters, as we may say, are wasted by emission there must always be a balancing immission, and recall is the immission which makes waste of wisdom good. This is why there must be restraint of unseasonable laughter and tears and each of us must urge his fellow to consult decorum ...

Plato's strategy to resist a wasteful emission of laughter or tears is to counteract the impulse with an immission of decorum, to "recall" the rules ("unseasonable laughter and tears" should be restrained). Hammering in the "good" reinforces it so you become habituated to redirect the free flow of a spontaneous gesture from its natural course toward a socially sanctioned direction. But habit chains you to your vomit, as Beckett had it, so you attend to things as they are known rather than as they are perceived—the inverse of Shklovsky's call for defamiliarization, which is essentially a method of dehabitualization.

Sublimation offers another way of redirecting raw impulses or energies away from wasteful emission toward more acceptable (moral, civilized, valued) forms. However, you cannot sublimate something in the unconscious. An impulse must first be freed from repression, as Freud explains in a letter:

If we are not satisfied with saying, "Be moral and philosophical," it is because that is too cheap and has been said too often without being of any help. *Our art* consists in *making it possible* for people to be moral and to deal with their wishes philosophically. Sublimation, that is striving toward higher goals, is of course one of the best means of overcoming the urgency of our drives. But one can consider doing this only after psychoanalytic work has lifted the repressions.

If repressions are not lifted, you will not have conscious access to your wishes and drives and will be unable to choose the direction in which they are expressed, leaving open the possibility that they will be directed toward perverse, unethical, or socially unacceptable manifestations you may not be ready, able, or willing to manage.

The art of psychoanalysis, making the unconscious conscious, is a process of defamiliarization, making the familiar unfamiliar by bringing the invisible into visibility. When we can see the defamiliarized actions and behaviors, social scripts, that we repeat out of deadened habit, we resist falling into the rhythm of an endless walking song, like "members of the work crew," in Shklovsky's terms, lulled by their "necessary 'groaning together.'" We are free to step off the moving walkway.

By this, and this only, we have existed—

Aesthetic experience shares with *jouissance* a sense of urgency, directness. "Art reminds us," writes Nietzsche in a notebook, "of states of animal vigour," which are "on the one hand a surplus and overflow of flourishing corporeality into the world of images and wishes; on the other a rousing of the animal function through images and wishes of intensified life—a heightening of the feeling of life, a stimulus for it." Art recovers the urgency of our basic drives, our animal functions and animal vigor, intensifying life by way of corporeality. But what is the use of this heightened aliveness if it serves no purpose, leads to nothing, burns like an Independence Day sparkler: brightly, then out?

This brightness has its own value, as with the seemingly haphazard action painting of the mid-twentieth century for which artists harnessed the corporeal energy, movement, and sense of aliveness within themselves to place paint onto canvas. The process of Jackson Pollock, the most famous action painter, appears on video to be a kind of dance: he cross-steps around a massive canvas laid flat on the ground, brush in one hand, bucket of paint in the other, cigarette hanging from his mouth. "Does his action-painting," philosopher Slavoj Žižek asks, "not directly render this flow of pure becoming, the impersonal-unconscious life-energy . . . this field of pure intensities with no meaning to be unearthed by interpretation?" There is no need to interpret, to hanker after meaning when faced with the out-shining of impersonal, unconscious, nonrational life-energy, the glow of pure becoming, because you can *feel*.

"Joy," Nietzsche writes, "has no need of heirs or of children—Joy wants itself, wants eternity, the repetition of the same things, wants everything to remain eternally the same." Joy, like eroticism, is a "psychological quest," as Bataille has it, "independent of the natural goal": *jouissance* over procreation. Like the infant with a breast or bottle in its mouth, "the fulfilled lover," writes Barthes in *A Lover's Discourse*, "has no need to write, to transmit, to reproduce." To think. When we are reminded through art of our animal vigor, we don't need to sublimate, push ourselves toward productivity, or take the position of consumer. We need nothing more than an overflow of flourishing corporeality, the sensation of being present, alive, embodied.

◩

After Lev Glebovich Ganin, the main character in Vladimir Nabokov's first novel, *Mary*, discovers that a neighbor in his Berlin boardinghouse is married to his first love, Mary, he becomes swept up in an alternate reality of fantasies, memories, and desires far more thrilling than his actual life. Convinced that he and Mary are destined to be together, he plans a reunion by plotting to be the one to pick her up from the train station rather than her husband. After getting the unsuspecting man excessively drunk on the eve of Mary's arrival, Ganin tampers with his alarm clock so that he oversleeps. Once at the station, on the brink of the anticipated moment, Ganin realizes that "other than [his] image [of Mary] no Mary existed, nor could exist." He walks away before seeing her, to avoid disillusionment.

"A mandarin fell in love with a courtesan," writes Barthes, sketching a similar scenario. "'I shall be yours,' she told him, 'when you have spent a hundred nights waiting for me, sitting on a stool, in my garden, beneath my window.' But on the ninety-ninth night, the mandarin stood up, put his stool under his arm, and went away."

"As long as I did not meet him," writer Annie Ernaux says of the lover she yearns for obsessively in her memoir, *A Girl's Story*, "my dream remained intact." Dodging him was a way of avoiding "an encounter in which I might have the truth flung in my face, a truth suspected and just as soon dismissed."

Living a parallel life in fantasy gives one a way of maintaining Nietzschean joy, keeping things eternally the same. But to be sustained, the parallel life in the imagination must be split off from reality, the fulfillment of the lover achieved in fantasy rather than in the real.

Do you consider yourself an adult? my daughter asked one night during dinner. Yes, of course, I said. She burst out laughing, couldn't stop, had trouble remaining seated on her chair despite its being half-tucked under the table. What's so funny? I asked, suddenly unsure of my answer. I just . . . think—she struggled to get the words out—it's . . . funny that anyone . . . would consider . . . themselves an adult.

Why would anyone choose to be anything (adult, parent, authority) that requires them to take up a False Self role, stop the flow of pure becoming?

When you catch a glimpse of yourself from an outside perspective, you can see the gap that often exists between an idea and its reality, the seriousness with which you take your life and its fundamental absurdity, your story of self and imposter syndrome, authority and castration anxiety, fantasy and disillusionment. The space this gap opens often gets filled with negative emotion (rage, disempowerment, deflation, confusion around what is real). Common defenses against these uglier emotions—similar to the defense of sublimation, which redirects unacceptable expressions of energy toward socially sanctioned aims—are repression and disavowal. Both of these mechanisms disappear unwanted emotions: one by blocking them from entering consciousness, the other by expelling them after they have entered the psyche—as occurs with corpsing, which functions as a metaphysical sneeze.

Blocking out sensations that may destabilize your psychic equilibrium often means shutting out reality. It was precisely this defensive procedure that I was discussing in the context of hoarding when I corpsed on the panel. Trauma occurs, according to Freud, when someone is emotionally overloaded by an external event for which they were unprepared. Victims of trauma, which generally includes hoarders, become adept at preparedness in hopes that, by being prepared, they will protect themselves from further traumatization. No one will pull the rug out from under them, because they are standing on ten rugs and know it, since they put the rugs there themselves.

The so-called limbic system—which controls basic emotions and drives surrounding survival (safety, bodily impulses, memory, perception of the world)—is the area of the brain most affected by traumatic experiences. "When you're into your trauma," explains psychiatrist Bessel van der Kolk, "the left hemisphere"—the part of the brain that controls reason and insight—"disappears." When triggered, a traumatized person is not led by logical thinking but by their animal brain, the automatic reactions wired in the body through memories and experiences—erotic, nonrational knowledge.

Hoarders use external objects as vehicles of psychic management. They clutter-out thoughts and emotions—the unknown—that have the potential to overwhelm their psyches by filling their homes with objects that have known memories and feelings attached to them. When we hold on to objects, we are retaining the memories, dreams, emotions, potentialities that we project onto them, creating a parallel dreamworld of sorts—like that of Ganin, Barthes's mandarin, or the young Ernaux—that fills our space with curated objects and emotions to block anything unanticipated from coming to mind.

Much as Freud describes in dream-work, a splitting of the manifest and the latent content—the thing and the emotion that was once attached to it—occurs in the censoring and encoding of hoard work. What makes its way into the dream, into the hoard, keeps other highly charged emotions that have been detached from the object out of mind. The object, infused with emotion that the censor has granted entry, then keeps tolerable emotion flowing while holding other emotions the hoarder hasn't prepared for at bay.

A highly visual analysand I worked with needed to see something to think about it. What would happen, he wondered, if there were no objects? Would there be no thoughts? This, we realized, was part of a fear of internal emptiness—*horror vacui*—that fueled his compulsion to hold on to objects, even those that no longer had any use. A hoard wards off emptiness by keeping known thoughts concretely present through objects that come to stand in for them, while at the same time using those objects to fill empty spaces to protect against a flood of the unknown.

Aristotle believed there are no vacuums in nature because denser surrounding material will immediately rush in to fill any void. This rushing-in is, perhaps, at the heart of the *horror vacui* of a hoarder: if emptiness will necessarily become filled, then it is risky to leave any spaces through which thoughts and emotions that haven't been carefully curated can enter and potentially trigger retraumatization.

Non-hoarders also push back against the unknown. Answers to questions, like objects in a hoard, are, according to Bion, "space stoppers" that block curiosity. "*La réponse est le malheur de la question,*" he quotes writer and philosopher Maurice Blanchot saying, then elaborates: "The answer is the misfortune or disease of curiosity—it kills it. There is always a craving to slap in an answer so as to prevent any spread of the flood through the gap which exists." Answers force a shift from the limbic brain to the frontal lobe, the area that controls problem-solving and reasoning, redirecting emotions and bodily impulses in the direction of the already-known. Curiosity, on the other hand, can induce the vertigo Derrida describes as standing before an abyss of the unknown.

The flood, like the rushing-in avoided by hoarders, passes through a space, a vacuum, an absence, or a "nasty hole where one hasn't any knowledge at all," Bion elaborates:

> In certain physical situations there are ways in which the hole can be blocked in a more or less convincing manner: if you are aware that you are hungry you can put food in your mouth and hope that will, as it were, shut you up; a mother can stuff her breast into the baby's mouth—if she does it with feelings of anger and hostility that is a different state of affairs from doing it with love and affection. Even in the domain of mental curiosity, of wanting to know something about the universe in which we live, that hole can be blocked by premature and precocious answers.

The nasty hole provokes an "itch . . . to fill the gap" because the lack of control involved in being open to the universe—the unknown—is threatening. This nasty hole can also be filled by way of manic defenses—exercise, work, alcohol, socializing—that keep the mind busy with hoarded distractions that leave no pause, space, or aperture for dreaded or unfamiliar thoughts and feelings to enter.

Sometimes the mere facts of reality can feel overwhelming. Being closed-minded, with a rigid view of the world, and perverting the evidence before you so it does not challenge preexisting beliefs are other ways of slapping in answers to prevent any spread through a gap, to avoid a confrontation with information that may require a reevaluation of set beliefs and, with it, the discomfort that often accompanies change. This can happen "even with good people," a character in the Netflix miniseries *Unbelievable* tells her therapist after having been unjustly charged with lying for reporting her rape to the police—"even with people that you can kind of trust. If the truth is inconvenient, and if—if the truth doesn't, like, fit, they don't believe it." The truth is easier to disappear than to confront when inconvenient or misaligned with the narrative or script that has been invested in by you and others, particularly those in power. "To be truthful," writes Nietzsche, "means using the customary metaphors—in moral terms: the obligation to lie according to a fixed convention, to lie herd-like in a style obligatory for all." If you are not "truthful" in the moral, herd-determined way, you risk becoming "dispossess[ed]," as the protagonist of Joyce's *A Portrait of the Artist as a Young Man* describes when "he felt the world give the lie rudely to his phantasy."

It is a kind of dispossession to be stripped of your imagination and left with herd-determined truths, space-stopping answers: you lose your psychic property, what belongs to you at the emotional and intellectual level. In protecting against this manner of dispossession, a person can sometimes behave like a hoarder and protect their innermost thoughts and feelings—their True Self. A creator, in particular, nurtures their inner world, although that interior environment functions less like a hoarder's bunker than a "potential space," as Winnicott explains in relation to child development. A potential space provides an intermediate area between internal and external reality that helps a child separate from the primary parent in order to transition toward new attachments to people and the world. Reverie similarly carves out a potential space between waking and dreaming in which the mind is free to wander while remaining connected to conscious thought. Unlike a hoard, a potential space has openings through which the external world can enter, so that a person's interior exists beside external reality without the threat of being given the lie.

Belief in your illusion—that your teddy bear is real—is necessary in developing what Winnicott terms the "capacity to create." There is perhaps nothing more threatening to the act of creation than someone who thinks of themselves as an adult, authority, or expert stepping in to give the lie, point out a gap between who you are and who you strive to be. Free movement between real and imaginary worlds opens spaces through which we can come to understandings that reach beyond what we know, whether in mathematics, science, philosophy, art, or life. Near the end of *A Girl's Story*, Ernaux—who earlier in the narrative had blocked out realities that might fling truths in her face—describes searching online for the man from her past and finding a photograph of him in a conventional family scene:

> Nothing can be realer in itself than this photo, taken less than a year earlier, yet what strikes me most, dumbfounds me, is the unreality of what I see. The unreality of the present, of this rustic family portrait, set alongside the reality of the past, the summer of '58 in S, which I have worked for months to transpose from the state of image and sensation to that of words.
>
> How are we present in the existences of others, their memories, their ways of being, even their acts? There is a staggering imbalance between the influence those two nights with that man have had upon my life, and the nothingness of my presence in his.
>
> I do not envy him: I'm the one who is writing.

To be the one writing, "transpos[ing] from the state of image and sensation to that of words"—particularly when writing nonfiction—is to slip in and out of the imaginary world as we come to an understanding of the real that would not have been possible otherwise.

Potential spaces offer outlets we can plug into to restore our capacity for pleasure, reverie, improvisation, creative solutions, and play—which is the gateway to self-revelation and the unconscious. "When it seems least appropriate to play," primatologist Isabel Behncke explains through her study of bonobos, "it might be . . . most urgent." When we let the little one drive, the one who doesn't know how to drive, we find ourselves traveling along uncharted pathways. The low-stakes context—no one is judging or pointing out gaps—frees us to approach what might otherwise seem overwhelming. Through the use of processes of thought that creatively rearrange forms (metaphors, metonyms, jokes, artworks), we can stray from the rigidity of prototypes, impersonal scripts, and fixed conventions. Within the play of bonobos, you observe "the very evolutionary roots of human laughter, dance and ritual." Play develops trust, tolerance, resilience, and improvisational skills that help us manage unexpected circumstances. "Play is our adaptive wildcard,"

Behncke says: it offers a safe space in which we can approach the abyss, explore the unknown.

Centuries ago, Sufis were said to have constructed a room with precise dimensions that caused anyone who entered to begin to cry within forty-five seconds. Each visitor's response, as the mythology has it, was reliable, much like the reaction to program music with predictable chord changes and coded emotions (This is scary music, my then toddler daughter observed from the back seat about a classical piece in a minor key on the car radio).

Listening to a song and *getting it* is different from feeling moved, getting chills—as a surprising number of people report experiencing on hearing Adele's song "Someone Like You." The physical response to the song is so consistent, in fact, that it has been analyzed by psychologists. The sensation, similar to feeling moved by poetry, occurs at the bodily level, involving not only the firing of mirror neurons that may lead a listener to feel into the shape of the singer, but appoggiaturas, dissonant notes that disrupt the anticipated melody, then quickly resolve to consonant ones, creating a sensation of emotional yearning.

"Our brains are wired to pick up the music that we expect," explains professor of music psychology John Sloboda. "So when we're listening to music, our brain is constantly trying to guess what comes next. . . . When that chord is not quite what we expect, it gives you a little bit of an emotional *frisson*." An appoggiatura "taps into this very primitive system that we have which identifies emotion on the basis of a violation of expectancy."

To grant a dissonant note entry is to open yourself up to a primitive, amplified state of emotion provoked by something outside of yourself, outside of your control—the unknown—which is certainly a risk (precisely what the hoarder avoids by filling space) but also the only way to feel stirred, defamiliarized, awake, and thereby able to change and grow. This primitive system of picking up on dissonant factors is, in fact, evolutionary, in that it provides us with a way to adapt to variables in the environment.

When my daughters were six and four, they begged to watch the film *Pee-wee's Big Adventure*. Having seen clips of comedian Pee-wee Herman and heard snippets of his voice, they formed expectations about the film. Because they had not yet reached the stage of cognitive development the film requires, however, they missed much of the humor. During a classic scene, for example, in which Large Marge turns and makes an impossibly distorted and bizarre face at Pee-wee, my older daughter looked confusedly toward me, half smiling—as though she thought she should laugh but other feelings contravened—while the same scene disturbed my younger daughter to such a degree that, afraid to go to sleep at night, she asked over and over, How did Large Marge do that with her face?

"The sudden perception," according to Schopenhauer, "of the incongruity between a concept and the real objects which have been thought through in some relation"—the abstract and the concrete—evokes laughter, which acts as an expression of this incongruity. The greater the incongruity, the more violent the laughter will be. A change in a known pattern—through incongruity or, as with appoggiatura, dissonance—leads to surprise, according to Clarke, that serves the cognitive purpose of alerting us to new information about the world around us so we can adjust our perceptions. In this way, laughter has the potential to be an agent of change, of adaptation, "a corrective to invalid estimates of variables, or to defunct ideas and perceptions." Perhaps this is why Girard writes, "There is something profoundly subversive in all true comedy."

Blocking out reality, walking away the moment before fulfillment, staying inside the embrace of a hoard, whether literal or metaphorical, on the other hand, is a way of maintaining a feeling of consonance with an imaginary or stagnant reality that cannot exist in a changing world (*Okay, Boomer*). Is not refusing to take in correctives, to alter evidence in order to hold on to set ideas—as my professor did in insisting I was Scottish—a kind of mental hoarding? Perhaps that is why newspapers are among the most hoarded objects. Retaining artifacts that stand in for the mind-set of a particular period expresses a desire to keep a distant past present. Humor, like all aspects of culture, changes with the fears, preoccupations, codes, and taboos of a historical moment. Set jokes that do not tap into the current flowing beneath the surface will not have as their source the emotions of the cultural space-time they occupy, and they will not be funny—just as fixed truths and choices will dispossess a person from what most belongs to them: their internal world. Humor, like poetry and life, needs to move.

The dominant moves that jokes make, much like dreams, are condensation and displacement, which create low-stakes ways of expressing latent thoughts that may be too distressing to state directly. "No doubt," explains Freud, "just as watch-makers usually provide a particularly good movement with a similarly valuable case, so it may happen with jokes that the best achievements in the way of jokes are used as an envelope for thoughts of the greatest substance." Take this joke of his as an example:

> The *Schadchen* [Jewish marriage broker] had assured the suitor that the girl's father was no longer living. After the betrothal it emerged that the girl's father was still alive and was serving a prison sentence. The suitor protested to the *Schadchen*, who replied: "Well, what did I tell you? You surely don't call that living?"

The idea within the joke is that if you are not really living, you might as well be dead, which applies whether you are caged in a prison, a hoard, or a bad marriage. But it is an idea most people would feel uncomfortable hearing. In drawing a distinction between innocent jokes and those containing a provocative message, Freud explains, "Only jokes that serve a purpose run the risk of meeting with people who don't want to hear them." The most common purposes, he goes on to say, are aggressiveness, satire, defense, and exposure. Like a charged dream-thought escaping the dream censor, the thought within a joke, if not fully cloaked by humor, has the capacity to set off an alarm, jolt you out of sleep.

The pleasure or discomfort elicited by a joke containing a message will always be greater than what an innocent joke elicits, because it will be fueled by the energy released when the idea driving it—which, if provocative, would likely have been suppressed—breaks free from repression. The thought that slips out of suppression functions as a punch line, as in this joke recounted by Freud:

> The bridegroom was paying his first visit to the bride's house in the company of the broker, and while they were waiting in the *salon* for the family to appear, the broker drew attention to a cupboard with glass doors in which the finest set of silver plate was exhibited. "There! Look at that! You can see from these things how rich these people are."—"But," asked the suspicious young man, "mightn't it be possible that these fine things were only collected for the occasion—that they were borrowed to give the impression of wealth?"—"What an idea!" answered the broker protestingly. "Who do you think would lend these people anything?"

"Is it not a case of saying one thing and meaning another?" asks Freud. What is truly thought is rarely spoken, because it is "forbidden," and gets expressed only when it finds an opening, a nasty hole, to rush through in disguised form.

Freud goes on to say that the marriage broker "becomes comic because the truth escapes him as it were automatically." We are all subject to becoming comic in this way, but what Freud calls "tendentious jokes," ones that have a hidden message, "make possible the satisfaction of an instinct (whether lustful or hostile)" in a way that goes undetected. Tendentious jokes are suitable for roundabout attacks on "inferior and powerless people" and those "who are protected by internal inhibitions and external circumstances from direct disparagement"—those it would be inappropriate or risky to attack. A joke, in this way, can be used as a form of resistance that decenters power by upsetting the status quo in a disguised or seemingly benign manner.

Journalists and radio hosts cracked jokes about singer Nick Jonas after he performed at the 2020 Grammys with food in his teeth—not because there was anything funny about it (who hasn't had food in their teeth at one point or another?) but because he was exposed as a regular human being, which not only transformed him into an acceptable target but decentered the usual power structure, so that normal people were suddenly looking down on a celebrity.

When in face of someone or something that "lay[s] claim to authority and respect," even if it has been conjured only in thought, writes Freud, we speak differently, use different facial expressions, hold ourselves in a dignified way—all of which require an expenditure of energy. If we witness "the degradation of the sublime"—when the exalted is reduced to insignificance, to the commonplace—the energy that would have been directed toward maintaining a solemn mien is "discharged by laughter." Through its capacity to release and redirect energy, a tendentious joke can not only shift the emotional atmosphere but can reorganize power relations, move pieces around to reassemble our "puzzle of puzzles . . . that we call Being," as Whitman says.

"Only what [you] allow to be a joke *is* a joke," because, explains Freud, "without this internal agreement no one lets himself be mastered by . . . automatism which in these cases brings truth to light." Internal agreement—some part of you being okay with the truth being exposed—is felt when what slips out is, in psychological terms, "ego syntonic," in line with your values, beliefs, and ideas about who you are. When Trump mocked a disabled reporter on the campaign trail in 2015 ("the poor guy, you ought to see this guy"), people found it offensive rather than funny. In a video of his performance, only one person standing behind him—a blond woman—laughed.

The internal agreement that is revealed when a person snickers is what makes laughing at tendentious jokes—whether they are ableist, racist, sexist, or otherwise demeaning—so problematic. Laughter marks complicity, participation: "Our laughter is always the laughter of a group," writes Bergson. Through pattern recognition, the logic within the latent thought of a joke is completed by a piece supplied by the psyche of the person laughing, even if they were not previously aware that the piece was inside them. Laughter is one of the many nonverbal eruptions of a person's interior that reveal thoughts and feelings that most do not expose intentionally. Even bystander status and a moral self-concept—along with the ways in which they are signaled and branded—cannot shuttle back into hiding such eruptions from the unconscious.

I listened live to former secretary of state Colin Powell's speech to the UN in 2003 in which he presented false information to assert that Iraq had weapons of mass destruction, providing the basis for going to war. I was struck at the time by his verbal stumbles, which started only seconds after he began speaking and continued intermittently. "Iraq never had any intention of complying with this council's mandate," Powell said at one point. "Instead, Iraq planned to use the declaration to overwhelm us and overwhelm the inspectors with *lyu-u . . . useless* information." That he slipped on the word *useless* in describing the information Iraq was supplying during a speech that he knew was based on useless information is unsurprising. Powell, it seems, did not possess what Freud terms "internal agreement" with regard to his mission, as was revealed by his slips, which brought truth metacommunicatively to light—as does spontaneous laughter.

Was Powell not a kind of war broker, like the *Schadchen* of Freud's jokes, who must not say the truth aloud because his existence depends on exploiting it? The public, like the audience for a joke, gets that the sacredness of wars, like marriages, "after they have been contracted is grievously affected by the thought of what happened at the time when they were arranged," as Freud says. If the premise is faulty, what follows can only lead to grievous consequences.

When Trump ordered the assassination of Iranian military commander Qasem Soleimani just a few days into 2020, he pointed to the Iranian general's responsibility by proxy for the deaths of many American lives. Proxy killings are metonymic, and Soleimani himself is a metonym: one week later, Trump displaced his name with a title: "the world's top terrorist." I was in the gym the day after he was killed and overheard a conversation between two men lifting weights: It's complicated, the first said, because he was instrumental in getting rid of ISIS. Wait, the second interrupted. I thought he was a bad guy!

The assassination, which became displaced by a photograph of a blaze in the dark of night, created a spectacle of goodness setting fire to evil. The reasons Soleimani was a bad guy obscured what was beneath the smoke and flames: the foundational reason the assassination was ordered at that particular point in time. Instead of being given the premise that prompted and justified the killing, we were guided to look away toward all the man's evils and conclude that he deserved to die.

One of the strategies to convince others to buy into a dangerously illogical idea, according to political theorist Hannah Arendt in *The Origins of Totalitarianism*, is to create a diversion from the underlying premise with a display of logical thinking. The mind will imitate the logic of the thinking deduced from the premise—ending a terrorist's life means saving the lives of others—rather than question the premise itself, which would involve asking what, exactly, a terrorist is, whether the subject at hand fits that criterion, and if there is an imminent attack that needs to be stopped.

This form of psychological manipulation becomes even more effective when the logic deduced from the premise follows the thought process of an accepted theory, as Arendt points out that Adolf Hitler does with Charles Darwin's "idea of man as the product of a natural development which does not necessarily stop with the present species of human being." The premise would be that a human being (Hitler) can choose which race should survive and then speed up the process by organizing unnatural killings, much as Trump decides who deserves to die and justifies an assassination by hitching it to an idea of cosmic justice: bad things happen to bad people. An idea that is attached to an illogical premise will be problematic, no matter how logical the thinking deduced from the premise may be.

A premise shares a structural position with what Bayes termed "the source" and Winnicott describes as a wellspring of creative energy making up the True Self. If that wellspring does not have genuine emotion flowing through it but rather signals emotion that serves the purpose of manipulating others, the logic that follows will also be tainted because its purpose will be to conceal a piece of faulty reasoning. When a person twists a premise toward self-interest in a manner that is detached from internal reality and imposed from without for strategic purposes, they reveal themselves to be what Parker calls "a terrible actor," someone who needs "to indicate because they can never fully inhabit"—or, in the extreme, a stiff, a soulless dead body.

Nearly two decades after his speech to the UN, Powell said of Trump, "He lies about things. And he gets away with it because people will not hold him accountable." Trump fought back on Twitter with an I'm-rubber-you're-glue retort: "Colin Powell, a real stiff who was very responsible for getting us into the disastrous Middle East Wars, just announced he will be voting for another stiff, Sleepy Joe Biden. Didn't Powell say that Iraq had 'weapons of mass destruction'? They didn't, but off we went to WAR!"

When the media reported Trump's response to Powell's accusation that he lies all the time, it focused on his having called Powell "a real stiff" and not a liar. Thirteen hours later, Trump tweeted again about Powell's lies and the role they played in starting the war, as though he were repeating a punch line. Perhaps no one got it, because its message flew too close. When a liar whose lies are determining our present calls out another liar whose lies determined our past for calling him a liar, the joke is on us.

Power in politics, as in jokes, hinges on the politician's ability to reframe or pervert reality. President Trump called the 2019 impeachment hearings "a joke," though he was accused of, among other things, illegally withholding congressionally approved aid for Ukraine until Ukrainian president Volodymyr Zelensky—a former comedian—announced investigations into Biden and his son. During the first day of the hearings, as Republican congressman Jim Jordan twisted evidence in questioning diplomat William B. Taylor, who had been the acting ambassador for the US in Ukraine, it was visible on Taylor's face that he was trying not to laugh. He took on what psychoanalyst

Ernst Kris describes as "a somewhat artificial expression" in which "motility is shut off and . . . all play of the facial muscles is stopped in order to prevent them being seized by laughter."

It first became obvious that Taylor was holding back an outburst when Jordan began to sound like one of the marriage brokers in Freud's jokes who knows about "abuses" but "must not say them aloud, for . . . his existence depends on exploiting them." The joke becomes funny the moment the listener recognizes what the person in the marriage broker's position—here, Jordan—is up to and sees how they are rearranging information to create a spectacle of logical thinking that will obfuscate, for anyone not paying close attention, the premise hiding beneath the dramatic display.

The essence of a displacement joke, according to Freud, "lies in the diversion of the train of thought, the displacement of psychical emphasis on to a topic other than the opening one"—like Arendt's imitation of familiar logic (Darwin's theory of natural selection, for example) that distracts from a premise by displacing it. Here is a displacement joke he uses as example:

An impoverished individual borrowed 25 florins from a prosperous acquaintance, with many asseverations of his necessitous circumstances. The very same day his benefactor met him again in a restaurant with a plate of salmon mayonnaise in front of him. The benefactor reproached him: "What? You borrow money from me and then order yourself salmon mayonnaise? Is *that* what you've used my money for?" "I don't understand you," replied the object of the attack; "if I haven't any money I *can't* eat salmon mayonnaise, and if I have money I *mustn't* eat salmon mayonnaise. Well, then, when *am* I to eat salmon mayonnaise?"

This joke, as Freud explains, "presented us with a façade, in which a striking parade of logical thinking was exhibited; and . . . this logic was used to conceal a piece of faulty reasoning—namely, a displacement of the train of thought." As Arendt explains in relation to totalitarianism, the mind then focuses on the logic of the thinking deduced from the premise, rather than on the premise itself. The following joke presented by Freud also exposes the logical manipulation in faulty reasoning:

A gentleman entered a pastry-cook's shop and ordered a cake; but he soon brought it back and asked for a glass of liqueur instead. He drank it and began to leave without having paid. The proprietor detained him. "What do you want?" asked the customer.—"You've not paid for the liqueur."—"But I gave you the cake in exchange for it."—"You didn't pay for that either."—"But I hadn't eaten it."

This joke "has an appearance of logic about it," but one that is merely "a suitable façade for a piece of faulty reasoning." He "construct[s] a connection which did not exist between the giving back of the cake and the taking of the liqueur in its place," so there is the simulation of an exchange—he did not, after all, have his cake and liquor too—even if it "was not in reality valid."

Although the impeachment hearings were not "a joke," as Trump accused them of being, many moments exhibited joke structure. It was likely Jordan's faulty logic in questioning Taylor that led to his laughter:

Were you wrong when you said you had a clear understanding that President Zelensky had to commit to an investigation of the Bidens before the aid got released, and the aid got released, and he didn't commit to an investigation?

The logic within this question leaves out a crucial intermediary fact, which is that Trump released the aid to Ukraine only after a whistle-blower revealed that he had illegally withheld it for precisely the reason Jordan mentioned: to press Zelensky to investigate the Bidens. He was, like the man in the pastry-cook's shop, using the cake (the aid that was effectively Ukraine's, in that it had already been approved and earmarked by Congress) to pay for the liquor (an investigation of the Bidens), in hopes that the simulation of payment would oc-clude the unlawful bargain the whistle-blower exposed—Trump's at-tempt to exchange Ukraine's aid for something else he wanted from Ukraine—a fact that Jordan, Trump, and the entire Republican Party did not want to acknowledge or pay for.

Taylor, although undoubtedly perceiving the faulty reasoning in the above exchange, managed to contain his laughter, but at another point, when Jordan was questioning him, it slipped out of suppression. The setup for this moment occurred earlier, during the opening state-ments, making it what comedians refer to as a callback—a thought that resonates with a joke performed earlier in the set—when the top Republican member of the House Permanent Select Committee on Intelligence, Devin Nunes, portrayed the hearings as a "spectacle" produced by the Democrats: a "televised theatrical performance" that had been preceded by an "audition process," thereby setting the stage for witness accounts to be perceived as fictive. In addressing Taylor, who had specifically stated he was nonpartisan, as a "star witness" for the Democrats, Jordan accusing him of acting, playing a part to ad-vance a Democratic agenda while simultaneously calling back to and hammering in—with Platonic immission—Nunes's assertion that the hearings were nothing more than a theatrical performance.

Rather than adjust his understanding of Trump's actions based on the evidence before him, Jordan changed Taylor, as occurs in per-verse thinking, to cast him as an actor—much like the Israeli se-curity services' investigation did to Tamimi—providing him with a way of dismissing the evidence at hand by placing it in a fictional frame. Taylor's laughter was likely a reflexive method of dissociating from the role he was being placed into, the dishonest person he was made out to be, like a metaphysical sneeze that helped him return to a state of psychological homeostasis.

Manipulating reality so it matches up to the world you would like to see, like confining oneself in the bunker of a carefully curated hoard, is not really living, as the *Schadchen* said of the bride's imprisoned father. Performed to the extreme, a self-fashioned reality imposed onto a collective life would affect not only those choosing to retreat into it but also others in their orbit, as with the strategy of those described by the aide to Bush who spoke to Suskind as "history's actors"—Powell, Dick Cheney, now Trump—who exit the reality-based community and graft a fictitious world onto the actual one, a "phantasy" that gives the lie to the real. Living in a concrete reality in which we evaluate fact-based arguments is the only way we can move society forward, explains historian Heather Cox Richardson:

> Replacing facts with fiction means that as a society we cannot accurately evaluate new information, and then shape policy according to solid evidence. But the Trump administration's attempt to hide reality under their own narrative reveals a more immediate injury. You cannot make good decisions about your life or your future if someone keeps you in the dark about what is really going on, any more than you can make good business decisions if your partner is secretly cooking the books.

If false narratives, like simulations, come to be substitutes for the truth, if the evidence before us is not evaluated but twisted to confirm our desires or beliefs, then everything deduced from those fictionalized facts will be faulty or tainted, including our conscious choices. A discernible truth will no longer exist, and whoever has the most power, an army behind them, will get to dictate which fictional narrative— whose teddy bear—is real.

"What, then, is truth?" Nietzsche asks rhetorically:

> A mobile army of metaphors, metonyms, and anthropomorphisms—in short, a sum of human relations, which have been enhanced, transposed, and embellished poetically and rhetorically, and which after long use seem firm, canonical, and obligatory to a people: truths are illusions about which one has forgotten that this is what they are: metaphors which are worn out and without

sensuous power; coins which have lost their pictures and now matter only as metal, no longer as coins.

Metaphors that have lost their sensuous power, coins that lack faces—like numbers to the non-mathematician—detach from the emotional panelboard. Circulated among people for long enough, these emptied-out truths become like slices of processed American cheese wrapped in plastic, clean pieces of writing stripped of beta elements. Without bumps or snags, or any trace of sensuous power—the body—these truths, though they have social currency, will not only lack the power to move anyone, but may lead to the annihilative actions that are characteristic of those who exhibit, like McGinniss, a strange absence of feeling.

This mode of distortion is seen by some not as a loss but as an opportunity. In *Delirious New York*, architect Rem Koolhaas describes Salvador Dalí's "Paranoid-Critical Method" (PCM) as the conscious exploitation of the unconscious, a twisted or perverse relationship to concrete reality for creative purpose. He embraces the imaginary and uses it as a device to design the real. "I believe that the moment is at hand when, by a paranoiac and active advance of the mind," Koolhaas quotes Dalí saying, "it will be possible . . . to systematize confusion and thus help to discredit completely the world of reality." Koolhaas discusses through Dalí's PCM how paranoia came to be seen as a delirium of interpretation: "The paranoiac always hits the nail on the head, no matter where the hammer blows fall." The world then becomes, Koolhaas explains through the words of Dalí, who sounds much like the Bush aide discussing history's actors, "illustration and proof . . . to serve the reality of our mind." Paranoia, what Koolhaas calls "a shock of recognition that never ends," fabricates evidence for unprovable speculations and then grafts that evidence onto the world—which is one thing when it comes to art and another altogether where human lives are concerned.

During his presidency, Trump caged the public in a delirium of interpretation to "systematize" confusion and dismiss anyone bringing factual elements of reality to a discussion by characterizing them as attackers. Weeks into the coronavirus pandemic, when reporter Yamiche Alcindor, a Black journalist, asked Trump what responsibility he took for having disbanded the pandemic office—a move that caused the loss of valuable time during which steps could have been taken to prevent the virus's spread and acquire protective gear for health care workers—Trump responded with a chain of evasive displacements:

> I just think it's a nasty question, because what we've done is—and Tony [Anthony Fauci] has said numerous times that we've saved thousands of lives because of the quick closing. When you say "me," I didn't do it. We have a group of people I could ask, perhaps my administration, but I could perhaps ask Tony about that, because I don't know anything about it. You say we did that. I don't know anything about it.

A "nasty question" creates a "nasty hole" where one hasn't any knowledge at all ("I don't know anything about it. . . . I don't know anything about it"). Rather than open himself up to reflection, Trump fills the gap, hoards space stoppers in the form of metonymic figures onto whom he then displaces responsibility and knowledge: Tony, his administration, the reporter asking the question ("*You know*, people let people go. You used to be with a different newspaper than you are now").

Trump has a history of finding questions asked by non-White female reporters to be threatening. He told Weijia Jiang, an Asian American reporter asking a question about his response to the pandemic, to just relax and keep her voice down. He systematizes confusion, evades the problematic elements within his policy raised by reporters' questions, and instead furthers the logic of his own agenda ("We're doing a great job every day") to discredit questioning, curiosity, and the reality to which those forms of thinking lead.

The more the outside world is kept out, the easier it becomes to avoid correctives, ward off the admission of information perceived by the senses that is necessary to recognize concrete reality and to resist a paranoid delirium of perverse interpretation. The danger is equally acute when it comes to intimate relationships, as Freud writes to his fiancée in a letter:

> I don't want my letters to keep remaining unanswered, and I shall stop writing you altogether if you don't write back. Perpetual monologues apropos of a loved being, which are neither corrected nor nourished by that being, lead to erroneous notions concerning mutual relations, and make us strangers to each other when we meet again, so that we find things different from what, without realizing it, we imagined.

Without correction from the external world—in this case, a lover—Freud would be, like the main character of Nabokov's *Mary* or Trump of Great America, in a relationship with a beloved in his imagination and therefore perpetually vulnerable to being given the lie. An empty space opened by dissonance—like the pause after being struck by a provocation or a vacuum in nature—is subject to a rushing-in of surrounding matter. To open oneself to the unknown, to what is outside your conscious control or fixed story of self (*who you are*), can feel risky because you don't get to choose what matter will fill a gap, just as in psychoanalysis and clown you don't get to choose how you will be changed. At the same time, maintaining that openness is the only way to sustain genuine connections to others and to remain receptive to evidence in the external world.

When we are open, we allow ourselves to sit with animal thoughts, accept the animal address, tolerate uncertainties—as Keats describes in his idea of negative capability ("When man is capable of being in uncertainties, Mysteries, doubts, without any irritable reaching after fact & reason")—and the vulnerability associated with exposing ourselves to whatever may rush in to fill our yearning. What feels to some like a space of possibility, however, is experienced by others as an abyss, a "nasty hole" that needs answers, however falsely constructed, to function as space stoppers and keep reality from flooding in.

"What convinces masses are not facts, and not even invented facts, but only the consistency of the system of which they are presumably part," writes Arendt. This consistency is comforting, even if it is not reality-based (*We're doing a great job every day*), because "people," writes philosopher Richard J. Bernstein, "who feel that they have been neglected and forgotten yearn for a narrative—even an invented fictional one—that will make sense of the anxiety they are experiencing, and promises redemption." A narrative—including one made up of false space-stopping answers that kill curiosity—can feel soothing, as does a fetish or a parade of logical thinking, because it splits off the anxiety associated with nasty holes, what is incalculable and unknown, allowing people to tell themselves a more comfortable, programmatic story with predictable chord changes.

⅂

I'm going to ask you a question, my daughter, then age five, announced one evening while I was at the kitchen counter making dinner. If you don't tell the truth, you're going to get bad luck for the rest of your life.

Okay, I said, resting the knife on the cutting board and turning toward her. Let's hear it.

Is Santa real?

I paused.

For the rest of your life people are going to try to tell you what to believe. They'll even fight wars, throw people in jail for having beliefs that are different from their own. I told her, I want you to have a period in your life to learn to think freely, believe whatever it is you choose to believe without anyone stepping in to tell you what is or isn't real.

Okay, it's you, she said, and walked away.

A few days later, on the way home from school, my daughter's friend, who was coming over for a playdate, pulled an American Girl doll from her backpack and said, Santa gave this to me for Christmas.

Santa's not real, my daughter reported dispassionately. It's your mom and dad.

The friend looked at her, turned away, and stared blankly ahead. After a moment of silence that magically erased all that had come before, she added, This Christmas I'm going to ask Santa for a bed for my doll.

Looking at life through the lens of art allows you to enter a transitional space in which you can begin to imagine how you might live creatively, regain contact with the freedom and spontaneity of the True Self, without losing contact with fact-based reality. At the same time, in order to feel alive, to be your own narrative—with whatever extent of freedom—it is likely you will have to pay a price for frustrating the agendas of others, which is why creative work, as Malcolm tells us, takes place at the boundaries of the system.

It is easier for others, Bayes said, if you are less, because it maintains the social order, keeps things harmonic, leaves fewer openings for incongruent, dissonant factors. But if we don't open ourselves to information from the external world and tolerate the accompanying instability, we cannot know how to adapt to our environment, evolve.

"New literary forms," Anton Chekhov observes in a notebook, "always produce new forms of life and that is why they are so revolting to the conservative human mind." Roethke—who approached life phototropically ("I wish I could photosynthesize")—says, along similar lines, "When you begin to get good, you'll arouse the haters of life." Change is risky, uncomfortable. Even those who would like to revive, to maintain a flow of pure becoming, are likely to feel at least somewhat conservative, hoarder-like, and to crave a certain amount of stability to function in the social world. When we feel confident that we are living in a reliable universe governed by human and natural laws, we can worry less about being blindsided by disillusionment, chaos, or attack.

Our bodies, too, express a need for stability, which is why they are set up to vigilantly keep out or expel whatever enters our system that may throw off our homeostasis. Defensive procedures protecting us from irritants in the external world are seen at their most fundamental level in reflexive processes. Convulsive reactions (coughing, sneezing, diarrhea, vomiting, even laughing) expel foreign elements that enter our bodies and threaten our metabolic balance at the concrete level, while other responses protect our system's equilibrium at the emotional level—as happened to me when I corpsed on the panel, which I now see as a way of reflexively expelling some element that entered my psyche and threw me off-balance.

A spontaneous fit of laughter, in this way, can expel what upsets our homeostasis, both physiologically and metaphorically, as do tears, the primary purpose of which is to wash away foreign particles in the eyes, to cleanse. Laughter and tears are biologically entwined, managed by a laughter-and-crying control center thought to exist in the brain stem, which is why tears so often accompany fits of laughter. The bodily convulsions of laughter expel not material particles but emotional ones—beta elements—as when we cry for emotional reasons and "the eye," in Girard's terms, "is acting *metaphorically*."

The reflexive process of sneezing similarly serves a physiological function while also operating metaphorically. One of the many reasons bystanders, across the centuries, have offered sneezers blessings is the superstitious belief that the soul might escape through the nose and be claimed by the devil—which is not unlike the worry surrounding what your depths, or privates, might be subject to if laid bare.

Most people have a characteristic sneeze, an unchosen style for their convulsive expulsion of irritants that intrude upon them from the external world. As Bishop observes, a cough, hiccup, or other inner noise has the capacity to reveal "the little aspects [of a person they] rarely mentio[n]." Body-language analyst Patti Wood categorizes sneeze styles into character types that sound like back-page horoscopes. For example, the "Be Right" sneezer—"a deep thinker" who likes to read and "play by the rules"—is the most likely to cover their mouth; whereas the "Get It Done" sneezer—"forceful," "decisive," and resistant to being used unfairly by people—has an explosive sneeze that sprays into the distance.

Unsurprisingly, as Wood's approach is fairly stereotypical in its manner of breaking down gender-neutral bodily processes into types, men are predicted to be less likely to modify their sneezes, whereas women, she suggests, suppress or adjust the sound, often channeling it toward a high-pitched *choo*. The sound and intensity of a sneeze can express the level of perceived threat as well as the degree to which a person is willing to modify their instincts for the approval of others. Since reflexive actions communicate as effectively as speech, when someone edits their sneeze style, they are attempting to camouflage, even if unconsciously, unwanted truths that might leak out of suppression.

An outburst of laughter, according to Freud, is an eruption from the unconscious—a discharge of surplus energy—and, like a sneeze, cough, hiccup, or slip of the tongue, has the potential to expose raw, unedited aspects of a person's interior. The kind of spontaneous body-driven laughter that characterizes corpsing is termed Duchenne laughter, after the nineteenth-century neurologist. This form of laughter, like a sneeze, is often driven by emotions that break through censors and other inhibitory processes in disguised form to express deep-seated thoughts and beliefs that might not necessarily be in line with the image or persona one would like to project to others.

On a recent subway ride, a woman blew her nose so powerfully that everyone in the car could hear the heavy rasp of mucus being forced out. Many looked at her in disgust, perhaps hoping to shame her out of doing it again, whereas a man standing beside her sexualized the sound with a *Yeah!* A subway car is a great equalizer, holding together in shared space and time people from radically different backgrounds. Some cultures consider it rude for a person to blow their nose in public—to do anything, in fact, that allows their interiority to seep out and remind others of what is inside them.

Perhaps it is, in part, laughter's nonverbal revelatory capacity— like the sounds emitted from a person's interior—that has led certain cultures to regard an open-mouthed laugh as a form of indecent exposure. Although it is no longer the case in America, "the mouth opened for laughing" was once seen as vulgar, suggestive, "in the service of homosexual and feminine instinctual tendencies," according to psychoanalyst Kris, "used to seduce . . . in a feminine way." The notion that laughter could elicit sexual behavior is hundreds of years old: as twelfth-century philosopher Maimonides warns, "Laughter and levity bring about illicit sexual conduct." Poet Charles Baudelaire understands the maxim "The wise man never laughs but he trembles" to mean that "the Wise Man trembles because he has laughed. The Wise Man fears laughter as he fears the shows and vanities of this world, as he fears concupiscence. He pulls himself up on the brink of laughter as on the brink of temptation."

In the early chapters of *Anna Karenina*, Levin—the character based on Tolstoy—who has just traveled from the country to Moscow, is meeting a friend at a restaurant, where he observes the urban lifestyle of the other patrons with disdain. When a "painted Frenchwoman" bursts out in "genuine laughter," "he swiftly move[s] away from her, as if from some dirty place."

To express genuine laughter is to assert the internal world over the external—like Bartleby, Lynch, or the person who decides for themselves what has importance and determines their narrative accordingly. In a fit of laughter, you cannot help but appear as you are as opposed to a figure composure styles you to be. The emotions expressed in a fit of laughter are physiologically similar to a fit of crying, as Darwin observes:

> During excessive laughter the whole body is often thrown backward and shakes, or is almost convulsed; the respiration is much disturbed; the head and face become gorged with blood, with the veins distended; and the orbicular muscles are spasmodically contracted in order to protect the eyes. Tears are freely shed. . . . it is scarcely possible to point out any difference between the tear-stained face of a person after a paroxysm of excessive laughter and after a bitter crying-fit.

What is revealed in a paroxysm of laughter or crying, after stylization has been stripped away, is seen, from the centuries-old perspective, as obscene.

The open mouth of a fit of laughter, like a vacuum in space or a nasty hole, carries with it the risk of an uncurated thought or feeling rushing through. Ironically, the same freedom and spontaneity—the hallmark of Winnicott's True Self—are perceived in other contexts (clown, poetry) as beautiful. Spontaneous laughter breaks through a protective facade, places the body in a vulnerable position, and, since laughter is contagious, has the potential to operate seductively, lure bystanders' bodies to places their conscious mind may not choose to carry them, as Bataille explains:

> Seeing and hearing a man laugh I participate in his emotion from inside myself. This sensation felt inside me communicates itself to me and that is what makes me laugh: we have an immediate knowledge of the other person's laughter when we laugh ourselves or of excitement when we share it. That is why laughter or excitement or even yawning are not things: we cannot usually feel part of stone or board but we do feel part of the nakedness of the woman in our arms.

Another person's laughter, excitement, yawning, or nakedness communicates itself to us sensorially from within by way of mirror mechanisms in our brain. Defamiliarization, for Shklovsky, can achieve a similar effect, "recover the sensation of life" by spotlighting not the thing but the consciousness accompanying our apprehension of it, how it feels to us. Art, by targeting our emotions, can even lead us to feel part of the inanimate, "make the stone stony," in Shklovsky's words, by revealing objects to us "as they are perceived and not as they are known." It is not the stone, then, but the nakedness of the artist's perception of it as conveyed to us through the art that causes us to feel their feelings as our own.

"Stripping naked," Bataille says, "is the decisive action." Nakedness offers a form of "communication revealing a quest for a possible continuance of being beyond the confines of the self": we feel into the shape of others as they feel into our own. Our body connects with "a state of continuity through secret channels" outside of what can be known "that give us a feeling of obscenity," a sense of disquiet surrounding having our boundaries of self and self-possession destabilized. With Duchenne laughter, too, we strip down to a primal, unstylized state from which our body communicates with the bodies of others through secret channels where powers of explanation are least developed. We fall through a nasty hole into a vortex of laughter, excitement, or nakedness and take obscene pleasure in our corporeality, "poetic and divine though animal."

∧

Shortly after I moved to New York, I worked as a hostess at a restaurant in SoHo called Zoë. The other hostesses and I were instructed to answer the phone by reciting a scripted greeting that included inflecting our voices upward at the end: "Good evening. Zoë~." When someone passed through the door, we were told to greet them similarly, with a script, a smile, and, most important, that inflection: "Welcome to Zoë~." One of the owners would surreptitiously pick up the receiver in the office when we answered the phone at the hostess stand or call on an outside line pretending to be a customer in order to make sure we used the inflection. That inflection, I learned, was my job: it signaled to customers, at the unconscious level, the social script they were walking into, as well as the power position they were granted within it.

The restaurant, on Prince Street, was, for many, a stop on a shopping tour in a neighborhood that had become a tourist destination. Unlike the edgier East Village restaurants I had worked at, where my tips would increase the more inaccessible I seemed to be, my role at Zoë was to subordinate myself. Around the time I was working there, I came across a description of the restaurant in a magazine that opened with the phrase "Charmingly hosted." Our charm as hostesses was to amplify our customers' sense of importance, and the inflection was critical in that illusion. When you inflect your voice, your mouth opens reflexively, as when singing a high note. The only part of our skeleton we reveal to others is our teeth, so when we inflect our voices, smile, or laugh, we flash our interiors and, as do primates, signal our submission to others.

Inflecting my voice was a conscious and strategic way of transmitting a communication (submission) that would, in turn, unconsciously elicit a corresponding response (an amplified sense of power) in others. The ability to fake emotions voluntarily for strategic reasons evolved in human beings along with the development of our volitional prefrontal motor circuits, which allow us to control our expressions, voices, and breathing. We are able, in other words, to signal feelings we are not actually experiencing.

Most laughter, even if well intentioned, is similarly disingenuous, used to manipulate the emotional state of others, as is frequently done with a compliment or a white lie. Laughing to trigger the positive emotions we associate with laughter is characteristic of the other laughter category scientists use: non-Duchenne laughter. Non-Duchenne laughter is not expressive but imitates emotional expression, feigns the joy associated with genuine laughter, to influence other people, as Darwin explains:

> Laughter is frequently employed in a forced manner to conceal or mask some other state of mind, even anger. We often see persons laughing in order to conceal their shame or shyness. When a person purses up his mouth, as if to prevent the possibility of a smile, though there is nothing to excite one, or nothing to prevent its free indulgence, an affected, solemn, or pedantic expression is given; but of such hybrid expressions nothing more need here be said. In such cases the meaning of the laugh or smile is to show the offending person that he excites only amusement.

Whereas Duchenne laughter inadvertently expresses one's state of mind, non-Duchenne laughter is used to conceal or mask it.

Most of the laughter we express on a daily basis is not spontaneous or body driven, just as not all smiles, as Duchenne observes, are "put into play by the sweet emotions of the soul." Disconnected from the body, emotionless, and willfully used in social interactions as a communicative signal, non-Duchenne laughter transmits coded meaning to others, as when we "smile with our lips at the same time as being malcontented or when the soul is sad," in Duchenne's words. Non-Duchenne laughter—also called social laughter—is generated by the intellect, even if it is elicited subconsciously. We use this type of laughter to control interactions by consciously signaling expressions we hope will trigger corresponding responses in others. Laughter is an expressive behavior, as Kris explains, that is interpreted by observers by attending to a person's "unintentional reactions to stimuli and the signals he makes to his fellow men because only a part of his expressive behaviour is directed towards the other person, whereas the whole of it is perceived by the latter and serves the purposes of social contact." (We leak truths from our bodies all the time.)

Communication (*Nice to see you!*) is the primary objective driving non-Duchenne laughter, indicating to others how they should interpret interactions and the role they should play in the social script at hand. In a study, neurobiologist Robert Provine discovered that most laughter is unrelated to the content of what is being said. His team went out into the world, observed over a thousand instances of laughter, and found that, rather than laughing after jokes, "people laugh more often after such innocuous lines as 'I'll see you guys later' or 'Are you sure?'" In fact, he found, only 10 to 20 percent of pre-laugh comments were remotely funny: "Most laughter did not follow anything resembling a joke, storytelling, or other formal attempt at humor." Some typical statements leading to laughter were "I hope we all do well," "It was nice meeting you too," and "I think I'm done."

Ninety percent of the laughter we use on a daily basis has nothing to do with humor and is not body driven—our eyes don't tear up, our orbicularis oculi muscles may not contract, there are no stitches in our sides. Whereas non-Duchenne laughter is controlled and strategic, used to modulate interpersonal relationships, Duchenne laughter erupts in response to seemingly random stimuli, such as a wayward noodle smacking someone in the face. Because an outburst of spontaneous laughter marks an escape from the unconscious that expresses repressed instincts, thoughts, and emotions, it often seems to erupt in a form that feels alien to us and difficult to connect to our ideas about who we are.

◁

The narrator of the trailer for Roman Polanski's *Repulsion* describes the exposure of the main character's depths and her frenzied attempt to dissociate herself from what is disclosed: "Now the horrors from her twisted mind spill over into reality. . . . Now the nightmare terror from the depths of her imagination erupts into the solid world of everyday, and fact and fantasy are fused in a frantic fury of repulsion." Repulsion marks an uncomfortable resonance that is felt when inner thoughts and wishes that feel alien or too disturbing to acknowledge materialize before you in "the solid world of everyday."

Like disgust, repulsion develops later in human beings and is related to the repression of primal instincts, True Self spontaneous gestures, animal parts of ourselves we are trained to shuttle out of consciousness. In *Civilization and Its Discontents*, Freud discusses how human beings' upright stance distances us from our genitals, making us perceive the smells emanating from that region of the body as repulsive. Cleanliness became a marker of civilization and the socialization process. "We know that in the nursery things are different," remarks Freud. "The excreta arouse no disgust in children. They seem valuable to them as being a part of their own body which has come away from it."

As we develop, we learn to reroute our instincts to be in line with the dictates of civilization. Disgust then expresses the internalization of those social codes that deem our impulses, bodies, and animal aspects repellent: "Such a reversal of values would scarcely be possible if the substances that are expelled from the body were not doomed by their strong smells to share the fate which overtook olfactory stimuli after man adopted the erect posture," Freud writes. Consequently, anyone "who does not hide his excreta" becomes offensive to others and looked down upon as animalistic, a dog, "an animal whose dominant sense is that of smell . . . which has no horror of excrement, and . . . is not ashamed of its sexual functions."

Man's shame of his sexual functions, Derrida explains, referring to a literal man primarily, is connected to his erect posture and the shame that can accompany being seen: "There is a . . . sentiment of shame related to standing upright," to "erection in general and not only phallic surrection" but also "the face-to-face." We know through Sartre's man at the peephole that we do not need to see the face of the other seeing us to internalize the sense of having been seen. We project onto others—whether animal or human—the judgment we most fear, then see ourselves through that imagined perspective and try to adjust our behavior and wishes accordingly.

No matter how civilized we become, some inner wishes that take root in infancy, according to Freud, "can neither be destroyed nor inhibited," but continuously strive to be fulfilled. Because these wishes are often suppressed and exert their influence unconsciously, their fulfillment would contradict the rules and codes we develop through the socialization process and therefore lead to displeasure. When drives that are socially unacceptable are expressed, they often provoke guilt if we are alone and shame if there's a witness. Disgust comes later in development and is a sign that a person's primal wishes have been repressed and replaced with desires calibrated with expectations of others.

Being agreeable requires that we align ourselves with coded behaviors, inflect our voices and expressions with recognizable signals, disidentify with whatever might be seen within us as base. The incentive to detach from our messier parts is that we are more likely to gain admittance to the social world, even if it means operating at a less emotionally engaged register. A well-adjusted person learns to find compromises between impulses that are charged with the energy that fuels their life force—the throbbing pulse of being—and the desire to behave in a socially acceptable way.

The part of the mind that performs the work of suppressing impulses and feelings is what Freud terms the ego, and it regulates the negotiation between raw, nonrational, spontaneous energy from the id and the superego's sense of right and wrong. I explained the three elements within Freud's model of mind—the id, the ego, and the superego—to my children using an illustration that would be relatable to them at the time. I began, You see a child at the playground playing with a toy truck unlike anything you've seen before. Your id thinks, *I want it! I want that truck! I'm going to take it,* but your superego stops you: *It's not yours. You can't take it.* Your ego, the peacekeeper between your superego and your id, steps in to suggest a compromise: *You can't have that truck, because it belongs to someone else, but you can ask for one like it for your birthday.*

When my daughter was almost one, I took her to another child's first-birthday party. Most of the children were sitting on laps or wandering around pushing toy strollers with stuffed animals buckled in. Soon came the time for the cake, which had been made by a professional baker. Everyone herded into a room to sing "Happy Birthday." Once the children settled down, the birthday boy's mother walked slowly through the crowd toward a table, holding the perfect white cake at a level low enough for the children to see. As she passed us, my daughter reached out, swiped some icing, and put it in her mouth. The pleasure on her face, no doubt, contrasted starkly with the horror on mine.

Had she stopped to see the look on my face, the pleasure on hers might have curdled. Pleasure follows a similar trajectory to that of repulsion, in that we learn to repress our primal wishes. Sometimes we not only forgo the gratification of our wishes, but, in place of fulfilling them for ourselves, strive to satisfy the desires of others. Žižek describes Freud describing his young daughter fantasizing about eating strawberry cake because, in the past, "while voraciously eating a strawberry cake, the little girl noticed how her parents were deeply satisfied by seeing her fully enjoying it." The desire in her fantasy is not her own, Žižek explains, but that of her parents, and exposes "the original question of desire [which] is not directly 'What do I want?' but 'What do others want from me?'"—much like the infant who is affirmed for giving its mother what she wants rather than a spontaneous expression. The little girl's fantasy of eating a strawberry cake—which may, in fact, be Žižek's fantasy also, as I have yet to find this anecdote in Freud's writings—expresses the wish to see her parents' pleasure in watching her voraciously enjoy what they had given her rather than an id impulse to experience pleasure of her own in eating the cake.

The ego manages id impulses—spontaneous gestures (swiping the icing)—through a process explained by Freud in terms of hydraulics. Imagine a river flowing with great force that is stopped up by a dam. As the river pushes against the dam, two counteracting energies— the water's pressure and the dam's reaction force—cause tension to build. A suppressed emotion or impulse, like the river, pushes against the dam of repression, looking for an outlet. If the energy invested by the ego in the process of suppression is suddenly discharged, there's a sensation of pleasure that can range from relief to ecstasy, depending on the force of the impulse that has built up.

Surplus energy in the unconscious released as a titter, like an unthreatening splash over a small segment of the dam, reflects what Freud calls "a *comic* effect," a discharge of surplus unconscious energy. When the guard stationed to control our impulses leaves his post, however, what is ordinarily held back by the ego breaks through and a discharge of pent-up energy incites a sensation of pleasure that surpasses the comic and the rational and enters the territory of *jouissance*, which, like anything else expelled from a body, reeks of aliveness.

"I just hate normal human life," comedian and ventriloquist Nina Conti tells her therapist, played by Adam Meggido, during an episode of the improvised web series *In Therapy*. "It's so grim. It's so staid." The premise of the show is that Nina is seeking treatment to work through her need to split off her libidinous side and express it through a monkey puppet she has named Monkey. Initially, she says her aim in entering therapy is to give up Monkey. The therapist agrees that she has chosen a good goal and suggests they find a way for her to integrate Monkey into her sense of self. As time goes on, however, she realizes she would prefer to give up Nina than the part of herself she has identified with the puppet, because it is only through Monkey that she feels able to express her truth and to experience the joy accompanying its release from suppression.

The anticipation of shame or the ramifications associated with the slipping-out of truths that are regarded as unacceptable causes some to split off unwanted parts of themselves or to strengthen the dam stopping up their expression. The Bible (Colossians 3:5) calls on people to mortify their bodies and bodily urges: "Mortify therefore your members which are upon the earth: fornication, uncleanness, inordinate affection, evil concupiscence, and covetousness which is idolatry." The stakes in mortification get raised in another Biblical passage to a person's very survival: "For if ye live according to the flesh ye shall die, but if ye through the Spirit do mortify the deeds of the body ye shall live" (Romans 8:13). The force of an impulse determines how strong the dam or space stopper will need to be to counteract its pressure.

There do exist, however, those who are unwilling to stop up their earthly drives by mortifying the body, projecting them into an alter ego, or employing a guard engaged in the stringent enforcement of social codes. Psychoanalyst Catherine Millot, in her memoir about her affair with Lacan when she was twenty-eight and he was seventy, writes of "the farts and burps which Lacan, as a free man, did not restrain in public." The more liberated you are, the less willing you will be to suppress your impulses, play the part that is handed to you, subject yourself to the constraints expected of polite people. Lacan became "extremely impatient if he was forced to wait, even at a red light or a level crossing. If he was not served promptly in a restaurant, he soon obtained satisfaction by uttering a resounding cry or a sigh that resembled a cry." His frustration, she explains, "was aimed at the real . . . when 'little pegs don't fit into little holes.'" Lacan "shared with the Dadaists . . . their derision of the respectably conventional. . . . He particularly liked the famous adage: 'Once you've overstepped the mark, there are no more limits.'"

Spontaneous outbursts of laughter carry you over the mark into a joyful sensation of limitlessness, and, because of the positive associations attached to laughter, at a far lower social cost than farting, burping, or infidelity. Yet corpsing, the inverse of mortification, is risky. Most people are not as free as Lacan or cannot risk the freedom required to loosen control over themselves, and do so only in safe, low-stakes contexts. Although acceptable in Western societies, laughing with complete abandon—doubled over, stomach muscles aching, tears flowing—is relatively rare for adults, apart from in intimate settings, although recollections from childhood and adolescence are usually filled with such scenarios.

I remember waiting with friends one evening to be picked up outside a formal middle-school party when my slip suddenly began to slide down beneath my skirt. As I tried to pull it up, the slip tangled against my effort as though of its own volition. The more I wrestled, the more twisted and entangled it became, sliding only lower. My friends and I laughed uncontrollably, losing our balance, bouncing off one another like overheated molecules. When my friend's father pulled up in his car to collect us, we squeezed our unruly laughter into the small space, to his increasing annoyance—which, of course, only made us laugh harder. Attempts at suppressing laughter are kindling to its fire.

Objectively, there was nothing humorous in the scenario—I had borrowed the slip from my mother; the elastic was too loose. However, the exposure of the slip, like a slip of the tongue, represented the sudden revelation of something meant to be hidden (underwear, the fact that I was a child playing dress-up). Sudden exposure makes us laugh, like a jack-in-the-box surprise, particularly in conjunction with the incongruous impression of an object coming to life, as the slip seemed to do when wrestling with me. "You may laugh at an animal," Bergson explains, "but only because you have detected in it some human attitude or expression." Slapstick spotlights that fundamental vulnerability in all of us—our lack of control over our environment, even over our own bodies—and gives us the opportunity to look at ourselves in low-stakes contexts from a comfortable distance.

Much humor plays with our need to maintain a certain story about ourselves—as upstanding human beings, for example—which often involves suppressing primal instincts. When we try to keep impulses and bodily elements from being expressed, there's a breaking of the fourth wall, which is made up of social codes, and a flash of the human peeks out from beneath the actor's costume. Teenagers succumb to fits of laughter more easily because they've spent fewer years reinforcing their dams, and derision of the rules is, for them, the norm. Adults, on the other hand, tend to corpse when they feel safe enough to let their guard down: with family or friends from childhood, when judgment is not a concern, when their well-being won't be threatened, or when their ego functions have been compromised, as when they are sleep-deprived or drunk.

It makes sense that psychological regression would lead to more laughter, given that laughter is an escape from the unconscious and the infantile, according to Freud, is the unconscious's "source":

> The unconscious mental processes are no others than those which are solely produced during infancy. The thought which sinks into the unconscious for the purpose of wit-formation only revisits there the old homestead of the former playing with words. The thought is put back for a moment into the infantile state in order to regain in this way childish pleasure sources.

Adults exert energy to repress their infantile thoughts and impulses (*I just had a juvenile moment*), so when infantile material breaks through, it is often accompanied by a release of energy that is experienced as pleasurable.

A fit of Duchenne laughter operates outside the bounds of logic, propriety, and conscious desires and taps into "the source" to liberate a flow of pure becoming. Corpsing revolts against mortification, being made to play the dead body.

𝘟

An analysand relayed—with great shame—an anecdote about feeling a sudden, irrepressible urge to laugh at a funeral, as the body of his friend's father was being lowered into the ground. Compulsive laughter at funerals, Freud explains in a note on his case of an obsessional neurotic, "the Rat Man," is common and, like other reflexive outbursts (sneezing, coughing), expresses the need to expel a foreign element that threatens the system's well-being. For my analysand, the threat was metaphorical: the survival of his narrative of who he was (a sympathetic friend), which his laughter, if released, would have seemed to contradict.

A story of oneself, always on the verge of cracking, needs continuous structural reinforcement to be maintained. For example, when someone uses the phrase *I'm the kind of person who . . .*, what follows will inevitably be false, an expression of the automaton within telegraphing that the person speaking is what Parker calls a "terrible actor" who has "to indicate because they can never fully inhabit." Having a story of self is equivalent to seeing oneself from a third-person perspective, as a fixed object rather than a living human being in motion, a poem that is being written, even if it looks like a subject.

Much laughter, like the absurd, or even like castration anxiety, is born out of this tension between how a person believes they should feel—what would be in line with the character they are indicating—and the imp of genuine feeling that threatens to leap out from the wings and break the fourth wall to reveal the falsity of the production. There is a monkey in each of us that is always prepared to speak the truth.

The stronger the rule or the tighter the script before you, the greater the attempt will be to hold back spontaneous expressions—which, in turn, increases an impulse's force as it builds against the dam's resistance. An uncontrollable fit of laughter is then, however counterintuitive it may seem, most likely to erupt in a context in which it would be wildly inappropriate—as happened to me on the panel.

Because it is spontaneous, Duchenne laughter is nonstrategic, even anti-strategic. It often breaks free in ways that do not align with our beliefs about who we are and shows us to be most chaotic in the moments when we would most like to appear in control, like at a funeral.

The impulse to laugh arises when a perception resonates with something that already existed within our mind even if we were not aware of it. During our waking lives, according to psychoanalyst Jacob Arlow, a constant stream of data from the external world passing through our outer eye is met by a stream of data from our internal world, or inner eye, like two motion picture projectors flashing a continuous stream of images simultaneously from opposite sides of a translucent screen. One projector screens images from the outer world, while the other plays an unremitting stream of inner fantasy thought.

Each projector, as I imagine it, has a power knob that can be turned up or down. When sleeping, our internal projector is on high, particularly when we dream, while the external, even though we have our eyes closed, remains on (we know because we hear the car alarm outside our window, the dog scratching at the door). When we are focused on a practical task, such as setting up a wireless router, our external projector is on high, whereas our internal projector is set to low. These two streams of input—introversion and extroversion, the inner eye and the outer eye—are negotiated by the ego, whose job it is to judge, correlate, integrate, or discard the competing data.

The ego, therefore, operates in two directions, causing perception and fantasy thought to mingle, sometimes making it difficult to recognize the difference between what is before us and what we see, what is said and what we hear. Reality testing is the ability to distinguish between inner fantasy thought and outer reality, as a way of discerning whether something is coming from the external world or from our minds, as in Dalí's Paranoid-Critical Method. Experiences and memories from the past influence our perception of and response to our present reality and shape our expectations and interpretations. As Baudelaire explains in a notebook, "Feelings of contempt for other people's faces are the result of an eclipse of the actual image by the hallucination that arises from it."

The manner in which we process these two simultaneous projections, how we take things, has everything to do with what's on our minds, which determines whether an inner thought or feeling will resonate with an external perception to create a sensation similar to the *aha!* that is felt in pattern recognition. When someone says, *Don't take this the wrong way,* for example, they are basically saying, *Turn off the wrong—crazy—information transmitted by your internal projector and perceive solely from an external perspective belonging to me.*

Trump's inability to feel moved in the face of others' suffering likely results from his internal projector streaming at a much higher level than his external one. Upon meeting Nobel Peace Prize winner and Yazidi activist Nadia Murad, who was asking him to communicate with Kurdish and Iraqi leaders so Yazidis could return to their homeland after being driven out by ISIS, Trump seemed to be half listening, avoiding eye contact, indifferent to the trauma she relayed:

MURAD: They killed my mom, my six brothers, they left behind—
TRUMP: (*Interrupting*) Where are they now?
MURAD: They killed them. They are in the mass graves in Sinjar.
And I'm still fighting just to live in safety—
TRUMP: I know the area very well that you're talking about.

Murad tried to redirect the conversation toward important life-or-death matters, and Trump, unmoved by her account, slipped in a non sequitur:

"And you had the Nobel Prize? That's incredible. And they gave it to you for what reason? Maybe you can explain."

The conflict beneath Trump's response seems to be a sense of competition that makes him unable to empathize with the horrific experiences she describes, because they led to her being given a Nobel Prize he felt he should have received. As the *Washington Post* reported: "Trump has said that he deserves the Nobel Peace Prize for his work on Syria and North Korea and has lamented that President Barak Obama received the honor during his first year in office." Trump reverses Shklovsky's call, focuses on what he knows, what is already in his mind, over what he might perceive—keeping his external projector on standby—until all the world is a simulation supplanting the real and, like Mr. Arbitrary, he loses the ability to feel.

Even when spontaneous outbursts of laughter respond to external stimuli, they express internal conflicts and communicate unconscious meaning. The mourner who laughs at a funeral, Freud explains, is likely experiencing contradictory impulses: a consciously intended one (the desire to console) and a repressed one (some unacceptable thought or feeling) that pushes, like a river, for release. The unacceptable thought will be determined by the contents of each individual's particular unconscious.

My analysand's anxiety at the funeral turned out to be related to anxiety about his own mortality (*Glad it's him, not me!*). He came to understand that the literal mortification of the body being lowered into the ground before him made it feel threatening to shut off the motility of his facial muscles and play the corpse, as social roles demanded of him. The desire to console his friend and the impulse to reassure himself of his own vitality were in conflict, and in the end, the compulsion to laugh functioned as a way of disassociating both from the death before him and from an impulse that wasn't in line with his idea of who he was.

Contradictory impulses underpin much humor, particularly when an inappropriate or aggressive message is coupled with a safe, low-stakes scenario that softens the transgression or blow. The Benign Violation Theory of humor suggests there is a moral violation at the heart of everything we find funny. "A violation," says Peter McGraw, cocreator of the theory, "is anything that threatens the way you believe the world ought to be." A violation ranges from a concrete action, such as physical playfulness, to wordplay that defies linguistic norms. Tickling—a form of proto-humor that also exists in rats and apes—is a classic benign violation. One cannot tickle oneself, because the dynamics of the situation are too clearly understood, too safe. Some resistance or threat (*I'm gonna get you!*) is needed for it to work. On the other hand, if the threat is too great, the tickling will be perceived as an attack rather than as playful. If a stranger in a bar suddenly started tickling you, for example, you would likely experience it as an assault. (It's all too common for a parent to use tickling as a way of releasing aggression they feel toward their child in what appears, even to themselves, to be an acceptable—benign—way.)

There are three main scenarios, according to the theory, in which a violation is perceived as benign: if it's distant ("Comedy," quips writer Angela Carter, "is tragedy that happens to other people"); if the violated norm isn't one that transgresses a moral people believe in (for example, incest isn't funny); or if the violation can be seen from a different perspective that makes it okay (as with tickling or any other mock-attack). If a violation causes harm or is too disturbing, the scenario will not be read as humorous.

An old woman slipping on ice and breaking her hip is clearly not funny. In order for another's fall to be funny, you must first ascertain that the person who fell wasn't injured. A violation can also be recast as benign when the consequences reinforce the predictability of the universe or societal morals so that a person gets what they deserve. If a robber who snatches the purse of an old lady who slipped on ice later slips themselves, it is funny even they do get hurt, because, in a just universe, they had it coming. A benign violation requires, in this sense, a certain degree of openness to transgression, the dissonant note. Otherwise, it would be difficult to find any violation funny, regardless of the ethical stature of its victim.

Recently, walking along Broadway in New York, I saw a woman, coffee cup in hand, slip on ice and fall. As I moved toward her to see if she needed help, she began to howl with laughter—a non-Duchenne signal that she was okay (*I've got this!*). Without thinking, I averted my eyes and crossed to the other side of the street to give her space to regain the dignity that accompanies composure.

"When we laugh at someone falling over," says medical anthropologist Ann Hale, "it's not the process of falling that tickles our funny bone but the attempt to stay upright." Falling exposes a failure to maintain a posture, a story of self, that indicates that you are not subject to basic vulnerabilities, like gravity, befalling anyone with a body. That story is destabilized even further if you take into account Freud's notion that the upright gait of human beings distances them from their shameful prehistoric origins, which placed the head and the genitals in proximity. It is the attempt, then, to remain not only upright but *upstanding*, civilized, distanced from our origins—particularly when amplified by resistance, such as ice, high heels, or a primal drive—that makes for comedy.

Inversely, when a person becomes so distanced from their human qualities that they begin to appear machinelike, they can also be comic. Bergson sees the essence of humor as "any substitution whatsoever of the artificial for the natural," when a person looks "mechanical," or doesn't seem alive: "We laugh every time a person gives us the impression of being a thing." During a press conference in November 2020, as Giuliani attempted to cast doubt on the presidential election that had been lost by his client, Donald Trump, a brown liquid with the appearance of motor oil began to trickle from above his ear, across his face, and toward his mouth. He seemed, quite literally, to secrete the inhuman. The visual effect of his robotic repetition of untruths seemingly causing a repulsive fluid to seep through his mask was—to those who were watching the press conference live—less funny than uncanny.

The uncanny induces a feeling of derealization, the psyche's way of rejecting external reality, keeping a sense of what feels metaphysically wrong outside of the self. There was, in fact, a pervasive feeling that much was not as it should have been during Trump's presidency, particularly when Trump refused to concede the results of the 2020 election and his supporters stormed the Capitol in a riotous attempt to stop Congress from formalizing Biden's victory. Basic laws governing how we relate to one another safely were continually defied, most flagrantly by the authorities who were supposedly in office to protect us and our constitutional rights. As the Benign Violation Theory of humor demonstrates, a situation cannot be funny if it is threatening. Because that period in history was decidedly unsafe, it was often difficult to interpret even structurally humorous scenarios as funny.

Only from a safe distance, played back on YouTube or on news shows with commentary, did Giuliani's press conference make me laugh. After the substance was reported to be makeup that had been applied to darken his gray hair and conceal his vulnerability to aging, he appeared human again, and the metaphysically disturbing aspect dissipated.

Even with a new administration in office that is capable of conveying a reliable facade—a consistent narrative of the system—I continue to feel wary of what might slip out at any moment to throw our collective lives off-balance, reveal a nasty hole that destabilizes our sense of democracy and who we are. People, too, are unknowns. No matter how well you believe you know another person, you can never fully grasp what's in their head.

I entered through the back door of the Cape Cod cottage. There was sand stuck to the bottoms of my sneakers from a run through the dunes, and I wanted to minimize the mess. I walked straight into the bathroom, skipping my after-run stretch, and turned the shower on. As I stepped beneath the spraying water, I heard my daughter's voice, her quick footsteps growing louder as they approached, and the swelling note of the ungreased hinge of the bathroom door swinging open.

Through the mottled shower door, I could see her shadow disrobing, building a pile of dark matter on the floor. Move over, she said, opening the door, stepping in, and positioning herself at the center of the stall to hog the spray.

Her little body was covered with what looked like war paint but was probably a combination of sand and mud. She saw me noticing and said, We found this really cool clay pit at the beach. She is a child who loves to get dirty, to hold a jellyfish until it drips between her fingers—a child who loves *The Magic School Bus* books merely because in them Miss Frizzle cries, "Take chances! Make mistakes! Get messy!"

Why don't you let me finish, I said, and then I'll leave the entire stall to you? Okay, she agreed, stepping aside.

As I put my head under the spigot, I felt a little water trickle from my ear. Finally, my ear's draining! I said aloud. I had felt as though water had been trapped in my ear since my morning shower, when shampoo suds had seemed to fill my ear canal as I rinsed my hair. Periodically throughout the day, I had experienced a sensation of pressure and had hopped on one foot with my ear tilted downward, trying to release it.

Suddenly, my daughter was screaming in horror: There's a spider crawling out of your ear! There's a spider crawling out of your ear!

In a split second, I knew exactly what had happened. While taking a shower that morning, I had caught a glimpse of a large brown spider spinning a web in the upper left corner of the stall. After a blink, it was gone. I assumed it had hidden from the water and me, and I had gone on with my day.

I started slapping my head, threw the shower door open, and we both leaped out. My daughter, still screaming, looked like an inverted exclamation point: mouth agape, lanky body taut with fear. I looked around for the spider, which had been knocked to the floor, ripped off a piece of toilet paper, picked it up, squeezed it, and tossed it into the garbage can. Then, thinking again, I picked it up, threw it into the toilet, flushed, and turned back to my daughter, who was staring, watching me closely.

Children take cues from their parents when interpreting the world. It's not simply what happens to a person that influences their psyche, but how it is worked through and who is around to help. During World War II, for example, many families living in London sent their children to the country to protect them from air raids. They might have been safer at the physical level, but in a study that compared the psychological effects of war on the children who stayed in London and those who had been evacuated, Freud's daughter Anna Freud discovered that the children on the whole were much "less upset by bombing than by evacuation to the country as a protection against it." She attributes this surprising finding to the fact that "love for the parents is so great that it is a far greater shock for a child to be suddenly separated from its mother than to have a house collapse on top of it." (I think, with stomach-dropping horror, of the children separated from their parents at the United States border with Mexico.)

Oliver Sacks, one of those children who were evacuated, writes of the time he spent in the country as one of the great traumas of his life, particularly "the horribleness of the school [which was] made all the worse by the sense that we had been abandoned by our families, left to rot in this awful place as an inexplicable punishment for something we had done." Trauma, again, occurs when something from the outside world overwhelms a person and their capacity to process an experience. If a trusted person is emotionally available to help metabolize an experience, to process beta elements, there is a chance the traumatic impact can be minimized.

Tragically, Sacks's school protected the external lives of students but destroyed their internal lives. The school was "run by a sadistic headmaster whose chief pleasure in life seemed to be beating the bottoms of the little boys under his control." Sacks writes of his brother, Michael, who had been sent away with him to the same school, eventually becoming psychotic as a result. "If this is happening to his body," his aunt said to his parents during a visit, after noticing his bruises, "what is happening to his mind?" The parents "seemed surprised, said they had noticed nothing amiss, that they thought Michael was enjoying school, had no problems," was "fine." They weren't able or willing to be there for him, and offset his trauma by cushioning whatever crossed the threshold of what he could handle.

At the same time, there can be a danger in overcushioning experiences so that a person no longer has access to their own emotions. The company that bioengineers androids in Ridley Scott's film *Blade Runner* also manufactures "implants," memories placed in the internal projectors of high-level androids ("replicants") that act as cushions to mute their reactions. "If we gift them the past," explains Dr. Eldon Tyrell, head of the company, "we create a cushion or pillow for their emotions and consequently we can control them better." The implants lead the replicants to recognize rather than to cognize data streaming from their external projectors to shape how they take things—not to protect against trauma, but for the corporation to manipulate them from within.

Containing the memories of other people, the implants serve as reference points that keep the replicants from being struck by their own emotions. The data projected onto the translucent screen of their minds from the external world calls up the projection of an interior thought or feeling emerging from an implant, someone else's memory, rather than from their own fantasy thought or experience. By framing not only a replicant's sense of self but also how they interpret encounters—spiders are scary, love is meaningful—the implants control them by manipulating the thought processes that lead to action.

We are all like replicants in that we internalize the memories, ideas, and beliefs of others—data that is effectively implanted within us to shape how we should take things. When I was in kindergarten, for example, my father told me a story from his school days. One afternoon, his teacher asked him to stay after class. Assuming he had done something wrong and was about to be punished, he was terrified. But instead, he had won an award! A few months later, when my teacher asked to speak to me after class, I, like my father, was terrified. Then I remembered his story and thought, I've won an award! Alas, I was in trouble.

Stories, from personal anecdotes to myths and fables, function as implants, which is why many children's books strategically narrativize confusing feelings and experiences to provide their young readers with reference points to cushion encounters that might otherwise feel overwhelming. A tantrum, much like trauma, often results from an encounter with a feeling or thought that the child does not have the tools to process. Passing along memories, stories, and beliefs is a way of learning about the world, especially the difficult aspects, secondhand, and of creating, by way of expectations that shape our interpretations, a communal history that prepares us for a collective present and future. These teachings are particularly important where unnatural power dynamics are forcibly imposed, as George Tillman Jr. portrays in the opening scene of his film *The Hate U Give*, which shows a Black father explaining to his children how to behave if they are pulled over by the police—where to place their hands, how to speak. Survival, as the film so poignantly shows us, does not often involve expressing oneself freely.

In some ways it can be seen as a privilege to focus on soul murder, resisting mortification, and staying emotionally alive, even though it is a basic right. Survival, physical and psychological, can involve anything from giving others what they want from you to following an implanted script to hiding among dead bodies (literal and figurative). When our encounters trigger implants rather than sensations, our experiences will not necessarily be connected to our feelings, the emotional panelboard, and will have a quality of deadness to them. Improvisation requires being open to data streaming from the external projector and remaining awake to our surroundings, while also tuning in to how that information mingles on the translucent screen with interior data so that we can gather enough intelligence to be able to choose how to act. After all, some threats are impossible to anticipate. To recover genuine emotional responsiveness—to taste the cake, protect a child, feel alive—it is helpful to be in an environment, as with tickling, in which we feel safe or confident enough to risk going off script.

In 1999, two artists, Paul Kaiser and Shelley Eshkar, made a video installation, *Ghostcatching*, using Bill T. Jones's dancing, in which the dancer's physical body is separated from his movements and taken out of the video images, so what remains is a visual representation of motion in color and light.

I remember watching a late-night news segment warning people against eating the bowls of free nuts put out in bars. People come back from the bathroom, the anchorman explained, not having washed their hands, and then reach into the bowl—the same bowl you will innocently reach into minutes later—and contaminate it. They had proof: they had gone into a bar and shined a special light on the nuts. "And now let's see what we discovered!" the anchorman said. "Remember, the light is going to make everything that has bacteria on it turn a fluorescent green. Here we go. Oh, man! Look at that! You can't even see the nuts anymore!" Everything was illuminated, like a clump of glow-in-the-dark slime.

The color and light surrounding our being are always there, but we are trained to focus on the body, the visible. We aren't taught to value the more numinous levels of experience, but to tune in to the external, narrative elements—the script—and push down other perceptions. Our experience moving through the world takes on a similar structure. Washington Square Park in New York, for example, has a burial field beneath it containing an estimated twenty thousand corpses. Without knowing this, as you cross the park and walk through groups of tourists taking pictures, people sunning themselves, street musicians performing for crowds, you may receive a transmission from that other level that you *feel* without necessarily being conscious of what you're feeling. Tuning in to instinctive, animal-brain perceptions is critical not only in survival (*If something feels off, it is*), but also in training yourself to take in the evidence before you rather than your own projections (expectations, beliefs) so you don't end up chained to a stagnant reality.

What would it take to learn to see the world through a ghostly lens, to cast a special light on it that momentarily removes the physicality, the narrative story line, and reveals instead the virtual level of kinetic shifts—a lens that illuminates not the spider or the ear (data from the external projector), but the imprint left on the observer witnessing the movement out of the ear?

In psychoanalytic terms, this might be thought of as tuning in to communications from the unconscious. When I see something particularly disturbing, I often think, That will definitely make its way into my dreams tonight. But somehow I am never right. We cannot predict what images will enter our psyche, what will hook or snag. Moments pile up like nuts—but which ones will glow?

My daughter became suspicious of me. What if the spider crawled into your mind? Quick! What's one thousand times ninety-six?

Ninety-six thousand, I told her, adding that there is a wall that blocks the ear canal from the brain, so the spider had nowhere to go.

What if it laid eggs in there, like that friend of yours who had a bump on his foot that burst in the shower and a hundred baby spiders crawled out?

That was in the jungle in a faraway country, and they weren't spiders, I lied, feeling guilty for having shared such a thing with her. They were Ichi.

There's no such thing as Ichi. You're making it up.

Am not.

Are too.

When I put her to bed, she asked, How do I know you're my mother and not a zombie pretending to be my mother? Because I'm so wildly flawed, I told her. If I were pretending to be your mother, I'd memorize all the lines and be sure to do everything perfectly.

For days, she couldn't look at me without saying in a monotone, A spider crawled out of your ear. She began to tell the story to everyone—the woman at the fruit stand, strangers at the beach. After a week, she had turned my slip of the ear into a joke: What's for dinner, Spiderwoman?

Joking involves improvisation, the rearrangement of elements in concrete reality into new configurations that shift the perspective on a situation so the person making the joke has mastery over an experience that was once out of their control. In psychological terms, it's a way of flipping passive into active—a common defense against trauma.

Many stand-up comedians, in fact, do just this: transform trauma into humor. Comedy, as the saying goes, is tragedy plus time. Now with Twitter and other social media platforms, as well as late-night shows that digest the news at day's end, time is no longer the crucial ingredient. It is *aletheia*, unveiling, honesty.

"Good evening. Hello. I have cancer," comedian Tig Notaro famously began a set at a Los Angeles club in 2012, a week after finding out she had breast cancer. "How are you? Hi, how are you? Is everybody having a good time? I have cancer." The audience wasn't sure how to respond. They were primed to have a specific kind of reaction simply because of the context they were in but were suddenly having another. "It's weird because with humor, the equation is tragedy plus time equals comedy," she continued, improvising as she went on. "I am just at tragedy right now." As in clown, the audience laughed not because she was funny but because she was honest. By the time I listened to the recording of her performance, I knew what to expect. I had been primed: expectations cushioned my response. I can only imagine what the experience of the live audience must have been.

Humor, like trauma, is often perceived in the face of a violation of expectancy—a spider crawling out of an ear, an appoggiatura.

Developmentally, a person needs to have achieved a certain level of cognitive ability to have a set of expectations about how things go and to identify whether a violation is dangerous or benign—which explains, in part, my daughters' struggles with grasping the humor in Large Marge's impossible image. When a young child sees someone pull a face, it is more likely to be perceived as comic if the person making the face is familiar, because the pattern, as Clarke explains, "is not the visual pattern adumbrated by the distorted facial features, but the pattern of repetition produced by the similar face-puller in different contexts." If the face-puller is unfamiliar (Large Marge), the situation will be perceived as unsafe and will therefore lead to "disorientation and potential upset."

Benign violations are dependent on the tension created by opposing signals, contradictory impulses, resolved through a kind of canceling-out that produces a feeling of relief experienced pleasurably as a comic effect. Freud saw a multitude of instances of such humor in his case study of the Rat Man, whose name was drawn from his main obsession, a fear of rats, specifically a horrific form of rat torture that he worried would befall his father or girlfriend if he didn't follow specific rituals to stop it. The Rat Man's feelings, as with many obsessionals, were often double, contradictory, so that a conscious fear would compensate for a repressed wish that felt unacceptable, such as wanting to protect someone whom he also (unconsciously) wanted to harm.

The classic example of this kind of contradictory impulse from the Rat Man case is when Freud's patient protectively removed a stone from the middle of a road along which his girlfriend's carriage was soon to travel, then returned to place the stone back in the same spot, where it could have caused an accident, expressing his ambivalence (love and hate) toward her. This ambivalence toward people the Rat Man loved was often made visible on his face when he imagined harm befalling them, and is described by Freud as "a very strange, composite expression" that could be interpreted only as one "of horror at pleasure of his own of which he himself was unaware."

The contrary impulse to do and undo, know and unknow, allows horror and pleasure to coexist in split form. The attempt to counter an unacceptable thought or feeling (hostility) with its opposite (love) aims to neutralize the objectionable element so it will not be exposed, even to oneself. A composite expression like the Rat Man's—visible to others, invisible to the self—is most often the result.

There's a photo of my older daughter looking down sweetly at her new-born sister as she hugs her with such intensity that the baby's face contorts in pain. The photo is an example of what Freud terms a reaction formation, a "counter-forc[e] such as shame, disgust and morality . . . that rises like [a dam] to oppose the . . . instincts." My daughter's unconscious wish (to destroy) was counteracted with an opposing force (to love), which allowed both impulses to be expressed while also (slightly) concealing the unconscious wish. My daughter attempted to neutralize her murderous rage against her new sister, who had stolen everyone's attention, by loving her to death.

A reaction formation is much like Lynch's approach to satisfying the demands of his contract by showing up before reporters but resisting the role they expected him to take up through his evasive nonanswers to their questions. Lynch's compromise resolves an interpersonal conflict, while many reaction formations, like that of my daughter, are intrapsychic, between different parts of the mind.

An unsuccessful reaction formation—like a dream censor that fails to keep a charged emotion from entering a dream—will often express what was meant to be held down in a metonymic form that creates kinetic shifts (reverberations from beneath the surface, the ghostly light) that will be perceptible outside of language. If the irrepressible conflict is both interpersonal and intrapsychic, its force is likely to build in intensity and eventually burst through whatever guard has been stationed to restrain it.

Emotion that is discharged without being processed—the task of Bion's alpha function—often takes the form of Duchenne laughter, as my analysand feared might occur at the funeral and as Freud describes the Rat Man worrying he might succumb to in a dream:

He dreamt that my mother was dead; he was anxious to offer me his condolences, but was afraid that in doing so he might break into *an impertinent laugh*, as he had repeatedly done on similar occasions in the past. He preferred, therefore, to leave a card on me with "p.c." written on it; but as he was writing them the letters turned into "p.f."

The abbreviations "p.c." and "p.f." are, according to the translator's footnote, "customary abbreviations for *'pour condoler'* and *'pour féliciter,'*" condolences and felicitations. As a protective measure against "break[ing] into *an impertinent laugh*," he wrote a card, but by switching "c" to "f," the impulse nevertheless broke through, and, rather than condolences, he offered felicitations (*Congratulations on your mother's death!*). Freud explains in a footnote that "this dream provides the explanation of the compulsive laughter which so often occurs on mournful occasions and which is regarded as such an unaccountable phenomenon."

Spontaneous laughter, like the humor in a benign violation, is frequently born of contradictory emotions. An unconscious thought or wish in a dream that could upset and potentially wake the sleeper often gets expressed in disguised form, including an opposite emotion or impulse. Freud understands the Rat Man's dream by using his theory of wish-fulfillment—every dream hides an unconscious wish—which, in this case, would be to express hostility, and with it the pleasure of letting a truth slip out of suppression. Two opposing impulses within the Rat Man of equal strength—love and hate—were pushing for release. Hostility broke through his attempt to be caring, neutralized it, and both impulses, as in the photo of my daughter hugging her sister, achieved satisfaction simultaneously.

Being hostile to someone who is attending to your needs—like a child displeasing a parent, an analysand offending their analyst—can be risky because it can lead them to withdraw their care. Concealing such an impulse by writing a card instead of speaking freely would be a way of mitigating that risk. If you don't reverse or mortify your urges, they are likely to build up and exert increasing pressure toward release, and alternate methods of managing their expressive force will need to be mobilized to hold them down. Even when you appear to have been successful at tucking away an impulse, it can suddenly break free from suppression—like my slip—or emerge from an opening in an alien, repulsive, strange, horrific, yet sometimes pleasurable form. It felt much better, for example, to be outside the formal venue wrestling with my slip in a fit of ridiculous juvenile laughter than on the inside mortifying my aliveness in order to appear grown-up. Even the spider crawling out of my ear was accompanied by relief when the pressure was released.

When the Rat Man prayed, "something always inserted itself into his pious phrases and turned them into their opposite. . . . For instance, if he said, 'May God protect him,' an evil spirit would hurriedly insert a 'not.'" Freud calls this reversal "an inverted Balaam," referencing the diviner in the Torah who would try to curse believers and end up blessing them instead. An American middle schooler, on the other hand, would call it a "Not Joke": *May God protect him . . . Not!*

The basic structure of a Not Joke is an affirmative statement followed by a negation: *You're pretty . . . Not!* There is no humor in the content of the joke; rather, it's a simple way to liberate an unacceptable, usually hostile, impulse, thought, or feeling from suppression under the guise of a compliment. On the surface, the negation appears to be a reversal that delivers hostility in the form of a joke, making the aggression seem harmless.

But jokes that express hostility can be quite complex because they have been disguised to escape the detection of individual and collective superegos. Inside a joking envelope, the message appears innocent, as though there were nothing more to it than its neutral container, as seems to be the case with the manifest content of a dream. Framing a hostile statement in a fictive form—either by pouring it into the structure of a joke or merely by claiming it wasn't meant the way the addressee took it—offers a socially acceptable way of releasing aggression that might break through in unacceptable ways if suppressed for too long.

It is the emotional exposure of the victim of a Not Joke that makes the joke. During the brief moment when affection is expressed (*You're pretty*), the target of the joke will experience a corresponding feeling (pleasure) that will be visible to onlookers and will function, retroactively, as the punch line. If the affectionate and aggressive impulses do not balance each other out, the scenario will not feel benign, and the target, sensing attack, will raise their guard.

Objecting to being made the butt of a joke, like refusing to be cast in a role—*I am my own narrative*—can have social consequences. Since joking, like tickling and non-Duchenne laughter, is associated with positive feelings, it is generally assumed to be good-natured and therefore easy to pass off as play (*Just joking!*). Empathy similarly signals compassion in social exchanges, even as it is precarious, as Hartman cautions, due to its capacity to become "violent" when driven by the intellect and not the body. The incentive to override intuition and accept an expression, gesture, or violation as benign is knowing that not doing so is an easy way to become ostracized from a group. Enlisting non-Duchenne laughter and taking the joke indicates flexibility, the ability to go with the flow, roll with it, loosen up, laugh things off.

In my seventh-grade English class, a note was passed to me from the back of the room. I unfolded the small, ripped-off square of notebook paper, scanned to the bottom to identify its author, and read on. The note, from a boy named Paul, contained a question followed by a threat: Do you want to go out with me? If the answer is no, don't tell anyone because if you tell, I'll say it was a joke.

When I turned to the back of the room to see if I could read sincerity on Paul's face, his friend—who was in on the note-passing—was nodding and mouthing, with a caricature of a serious face, It's for real! Yet I had no way of being certain—how can we know anything for certain, when meaning proliferates, is doubled, shifted, all the time? Besides, I thought, why involve a friend if you're trying to keep things quiet? I didn't know how to take it.

When I recall my teenage years, most memories rest beneath the hovering fear that I would take things the wrong way—along with the sense that, all of a sudden, the circumstances could shift (*Will you go out with me? . . . Not!*) and I would be revealed to possess the fatal flaw of misinterpretation. In adolescence, mistaking the meaning of others is a constant source of humiliation and dread that is only intensified if you are marked by something nonnormative (looking different, coming from a different culture, having a foreign name), making it even more crucial not to stand out, not to risk getting snipped. Fitting in is most readily achieved by grasping the codes and behaving in line with their dictates to signal your part in a group. Jokes attempt to work through and master the anxiety around navigating social codes and taking things the right way, which is so fundamental to trying to find a place in the social world.

Taking someone literally, assuming they mean what they say, *You're pretty. Do you want to go out with me?* is a form of inelasticity, a sign that you are grasping only one level of a communication and are not taking in all the information before you. Attending to things as they are perceived rather than known is necessary in order to apprehend when to adapt and evolve in our ever-changing world. The inelastic, literalizing figure—such as a foreigner—is a ripe subject for humor, as Baron Cohen reveals through his use of foreign characters in his undercover comedy. Sticking to dictionary definitions and limiting yourself to logic makes you rigid. Literalizing can make the literalizer the fool, and foreigners who cling to their dictionaries and guides because they do not fully grasp the connotations or codes of the culture they have stepped into become, in their attempt to comprehend, quite naturally inflexible and unable to adapt to new circumstances.

"Foreigners are funny," writes Orwell, describing one of the two political assumptions of British weekly papers written for boys in the twentieth century. The other assumption, he writes in the essay "Boys'

Weeklies," was that "nothing ever changes." The essay critiques the set of beliefs these publications "pumped into" adolescent readers: "that the major problems of our time do not exist, that there is nothing wrong with *laissez-faire* capitalism, that foreigners are un-important comics and that the British Empire is a sort of charity-concern which will last for ever." (These beliefs of the 1940s are strikingly similar to Trump's, not only in their nostalgia, classism, and patriotism, but also because, as with totalitarian logic's suppression of the premise, the real meaning of any struggle is kept out of sight and a colorful parade of logic is put in its place.)

The stories in the weeklies were about "wildly thrilling and romantic," "posh public school" life (private school to Americans) and were read more often and for a longer period by "the boys at very cheap private schools" and the "working-class boys" whom the weeklies are "obviously . . . aimed at," as opposed to the boys whose lives were the purported basis for the characters. The weeklies implanted beliefs and codes into their readers during the difficult, identity-forming period of adolescence to teach them what to strive for, so they could interpret things in a way that was strategic for the ruling class. Adopting an assigned position in a fixed class system is exchanged for the promise of belonging. But like a hat attached to an invisible string in a vaudeville routine, the dream of belonging gets yanked away each time it appears within reach, because "*all* fiction from the novels in the mushroom libraries downwards [was] censored in the interests of the ruling class."

Laughing at foreigners, then, is an easy way of demonstrating that you belong, are part of a national identity that views "foreigners [as] comics who are put there for us to laugh at . . . [and who are] classified in much the same way as insects." Laughter at foreigners conceals a latent thought, which, if expressed directly, would clearly be hostile, such as the command/expression now omnipresent in the United States "Go back to where you came from." In a 2019 tweet, Trump said four minority congresswomen should "go back and help fix the totally broken and crime infested places from which they came" instead of "loudly and viciously telling the people of the United States" how to run the government. Only one of the women was born outside the United States, but Trump was not interested in this reality. His goal was merely to mark them as Other and subordinate them to the status of foreigners, so that the public would distrust them. When we treat another being as inferior—try to disappear them—our underlying goal is to evacuate a threat to our boundaries of self that destabilizes the story we tell ourselves and others about who we are.

On the first day of my college biology class, the professor informed us that what we think of as our interior is really part of the external world. He used the example of our digestive system, which, replete with bacteria, is arguably the external environment housed within our bodies with two openings at either end. I later became fixated on a parallel metaphorical boundary we place around the mind. There is no region in the body you can point to that contains it—the mind is within our bodies and is relational, encompasses our perception of experiences and those experiences themselves, what we feel and what fires when we witness the feeling of others. The mind, quantum entangled with the universe around it, is everywhere, spread across our bodies and beyond.

How, then, do we create the boundaries that are necessary in preserving an illusion of a stable self, that resist the obscenity, as Bataille has it, that results from having that self-possession shaken—stop a spider, foreigner, from crawling into or out of our ear?

Non-Duchenne or social laughter—always, according to Bergson, the laughter of a group—is perhaps one way to create such a boundary in that it signals to us to perceive meaning that is not necessarily there. Group identity is similarly constructed through a signaling process in which disidentification with someone outside the group implies the presence of group characteristics that indicate belonging, as writer Ralph Ellison explains in an American context:

> Since the beginning of the nation, white Americans have suffered from a deep inner uncertainty as to who they really are. One of the ways that has been used to simplify the answer has been to

seize upon the presence of black Americans and use them as a marker, a symbol of limits, a metaphor for the "outsider." Many whites could look at the social position of blacks and feel that color formed an easy and reliable gauge for determining to what extent one was or was not American. Perhaps that is why one of the first epithets that many European immigrants learned when they got off the boat was the term [N-word]—it made them feel instantly American. But this is tricky magic. Despite his racial difference and social status, something indisputably American about Negroes not only raised doubts about the white man's value system, but aroused the troubling suspicion that whatever else the true American is, he is also somehow black.

The instability of defining an Other to indirectly delineate the self—identification through disidentification, like using negative space to create the perception of a subject—is counteracted with a stringent enforcement of the outsider's image to keep the subject's identity (insider, White) in relief.

Racism, in this way, is a form of perversion: the evidence in the world relating to other human beings becomes twisted to avoid the psychic pain involved in accepting what is before you as reality and having that reality demand that you adjust your beliefs about others and yourself. One of the costs of what seems protective—patrolling the boundaries of the self and the beliefs that cast the lines delineating it into relief—is a loss of the very sense of selfhood those acts of reality-twisting attempt to preserve.

Because one often cannot bear to tolerate the conflicting views of others or of the self in their full complexity, the defense mechanism of splitting is used to polarize a person into all-good, then all-bad. Someone who splits in this way will generally alternate between perspectives so one side of a split does not confront the other and both versions of reality can remain true (hag, beautiful woman). It is this lack of confrontation between the two sides of a split that allows a person to simultaneously know and unknow something, as Freud explains in his idea of fetishism, as long as both sides are not held in the conscious mind at the same time.

The compartmentalization that results from splitting, though it eases any pain around having to adjust one's thinking, leads to a "breakdown of the self," explains philosopher Pedro Alexis Tabensky in the context of racism, in that "racist subjects are guided by psychic forces that are largely out of their sights and out of their control, meaning that their agency is compromised." They become subject to their "passions, guided largely by protective mechanisms that block them from being able properly to understand the distorting protective function of their racist beliefs." In other words, the split-off beliefs that are held out of consciousness nevertheless exert influence from their exiled position, so that a person who splits is directed by forces that are housed within their psyches but unknown to them. If you do not make the unconscious conscious, you will be guided by psychic forces out of your sight and out of your control. You cannot be captain of your fate—of your own narrative.

We are all entangled with the world around us. A self that is severed from others and its environment will have limited energy entering or leaving its system and will become depleted. Aligning one's beliefs with a reality that has been self-fashioned and imposed onto the world—as the Bush aide describes "history's actors" doing—means losing contact with the flow of energy that maintains life and eventually emptying out. This internal emptiness "accounts for the uncanny sense one gets," writes Tabensky, "when talking to a paradigmatic racist—similar to the feeling one gets when talking to religious fundamentalists or the paranoid delusional—that there is nobody there doing the talking." Although they may be "emitting sounds, gesturing—generally parroting rational behaviour," as with a person possessing an As-If personality, they do not communicate "in the sphere of the rational *where beliefs face the tribunal of evidence*" (my emphasis). Racist thinking maintains a split between beliefs and evidence, systematizes confusion, like Dalí's PCM, to discredit the world of reality so that, as in paranoia and perverse thinking—which twists evidence to fit beliefs—it always hits the nail on the head, no matter where the hammer falls.

During the 2020 protests following the murder of George Floyd, as discussions around racial inequality became more frequent and more nuanced in the media and on the streets, "color," in Ellison's terms, ceased to be "an easy and reliable gauge for determining to what extent one was or was not American" (*Go back to where you came from*). The "metaphor for the 'outsider'" began to break down, and as a result, the "deep inner uncertainty" Ellison says that "white Americans have suffered" about "who they really are" intensified.

Trump needed a new enemy and chose a barrage of undelineated ones—"radical-left criminals," "Antifa," "anarchists," "terrorists," "thugs"—that he fought with corresponding unidentifiable enforcers, such as the federal agents commanded by the Department of Homeland Security that cropped up at protests without uniforms, badges, or other ways of being identified by role. They were sent, according to Trump, to "restore public safety" to "cities run by liberal Democrats," such as Portland, Oregon, whose politicians, as he stated mendaciously, have "for decades . . . put the interests of criminals above the rights of law-abiding citizens." Safety, for him, would have been achieved ideologically, by reestablishing a metaphor for the outsider that would offer a more certain sense of self, however false.

The violence Trump expressed could be interpreted in Lacanian terms as "aggressivity," the manic aggression imposed on the Other and the world by someone who feels that their idea of self is being challenged. The federal officers, behaving like law enforcement officials yet without an attachment to the law or its insignia, hopped out of unmarked vans, heads covered in robotic-looking protective gear, and detained people arbitrarily, destabilizing expectations surrounding the order of things. This systematization of confusion was performed to create not art, as was Dalí's aim in developing his PCM, but a new reality in which people were not meant to see what they saw, knew what they know.

A friend of mine observed that her husband has the habit of yawning immediately before telling a lie. His yawn is likely an attempt to subdue his anxiety about lying, much like dogs yawn before a fight to calm both themselves and their opponents. Non-Duchenne laughter can similarly signal an emotion that may not be genuinely present to mask or hide a feeling. If you incorporate laughter into speech that isn't humorous, you can get away with saying—or communicating—attitudes, emotions, or opinions that would defy basic social mores if stated directly.

Another friend has the habit of laughing in a single burst (*ha!*) before saying something hostile: Ha! You don't want to hear my thoughts on that. Ha! I'm not saying it was your fault. My friend turns to non-Duchenne laughter—as most of us do at one point or another—to manipulate the way others might take her comments and to evade responsibility for her aggression by passing it off as humor.

The attempt to preemptively unsay what is about to be said, undo what is about to be done, is central to the literary trope known as litotes, a double negative, as in *That's not half-bad*. The assertion remains intact—*That's half-bad*—but the negation preceding it renounces accountability for the hostility that is about to come. *It's not that I don't want to hang out with you*, for instance, communicates an assertion (I don't want to hang out with you), but only after the speaker has negated it to signal that they are not saying what you are about to hear. Litotes offers another way of telling a person not to take something the wrong way, but in a form that is less reality-bending, in that it implicitly acknowledges that they will, of course, take it that way (who wouldn't?), even as they are being directed not to do what is most intuitive. (*No animal in the wild, suddenly overcome with fear, would spend any of its mental energy thinking, It's probably nothing.*)

A statement that is unmade immediately before being made, like a Not Joke, is devised to say and unsay something, affirm and negate, slip in a "p.c." to neutralize a "p.f." Like the Rat Man's conflict between hostility and affection, litotes often expresses contradictory emotions, safeguarding against how others will respond to what is being said by reversing it, thereby transmitting and erasing a message simultaneously, like writing in disappearing ink.

Litotes is a device used by master manipulators, the Iagos of the world. Iago, the deceitful character in Shakespeare's *Othello*, propels into motion his plot to "abuse Othello's ear"—to convince him that his wife, Desdemona, is having an affair with Cassio—by, like my friend, preceding his first insidious comment with a laugh: "Ha! I like not that." The statement, made in the face of Cassio and Desdemona parting ways, is meant, like most non-Duchenne laughter, to say something without saying it.

The violation, or the insidious part—what his laughter attempts to preemptively undo—is his pointing with suspicion at Desdemona and Cassio having been together (*I don't like that*). When Othello asks for clarification—"What dost thou say?"—Iago negates, then points again, but in an obscured way: "Nothing, my lord: or if—I know not what." Iago denies knowledge of what he is spotlighting, to distract from the fact that it is his hand doing the pointing, planting the seed of suspicion:

OTHELLO: Was not that Cassio parted from my wife?
IAGO: Cassio, my lord! No, sure, I cannot think it,
That he would steal away so guilty-like,
Seeing you coming.

No, sure. I cannot think it. Litotes—*I cannot think what I will simultaneously assert* ("That he would steal away so guilty-like, / Seeing you coming")—delivers a substantive thought that cannot be put forth directly, like the message within a tendentious joke or the latent content of a dream image, which is constructed to avert waking its recipient to the manipulations that obscure the premise beneath the surface. Iago disabuses Othello's ear while simultaneously obfuscating his part in the abuse through metacommunicative signals to ensure Othello takes his communication the right way—which is to say, incorrectly.

Not Jokes are far less complex than Iago's machinations; nevertheless, they, too, shift frames of reference to obfuscate a message that is delivered and retracted at the same time. It is the moment when emotion is exposed that creates a joke. Exposure makes the joke, functions as a punch line, which is why acting disaffected is cool, protects against the expression of the very emotion that might make you vulnerable to becoming a target. There are various caveats that call upon us to turn our emotional knobs to standby: *Don't take this the wrong way; No offense, but* . . . These caveats give the person who is preparing to deliver a hurtful message a way of disavowing responsibility for the aggression that is about to come, reversing hostility before it has been expressed.

If the target admits to perceiving hostility and takes offense, the insult is redoubled—*Can't you take a joke?* They will be exposed a second time as inelastic, not knowing how to take things, to interpret properly, which is a cognitive failing particularly embarrassing to adolescents and people invested in maintaining a public image. Only by not stepping into the role that you have been cued to adopt are you able to expose—defamiliarize—the setup.

In 1985, when actor Eddie Murphy was a guest on *The Dick Cavett Show*, Dick Cavett asked Murphy, "Have you read Mark Twain?" After Murphy replied, "Not a drop," Cavett told him it was a shame. "You'd love [*The Adventures of*] *Huckleberry Finn*," he continued, then asked, "Are you offended by the [N-word]?" In asking the question, Cavett didn't just say the word but drew out its component sounds in a lilting way, with an affected accent, seeming to signify that the word was being spoken in a voice that was not his own. Murphy responded to Cavett's attempt to say and unsay the word simultaneously, disown his speech:

> MURPHY: Why . . . Where'd that come from?
> CAVETT: Did I say that?
> MURPHY: He's, like, possessed.
> CAVETT: It's just that there's a big flap in various parts of the country where people want that great American novel

142

> [*The Adventures of Huckleberry Finn*] taken off the shelves
> because of the [N-word]. [N-word] Jim is a character—
> MURPHY: I thought you were going to say there are various parts
> of the country where they enjoy hearing someone say that on
> television. This is cable. They're sitting in Memphis like this:
> *I like that Cavett boy.* [Applause] *Did you see him say [N-word]*
> *right in front of him? I like it. [N-word] is sitting two inches away.*

Through improvisation, Murphy reattached the word—which had become a detached, free-floating, racist particle Cavett likely assumed would attach, electron-like, to Murphy—back onto Cavett, exposing the racism as Cavett's, to the applause of the audience. Improvisation, resilience, letting things bounce off you, keeps the projections of others from getting beneath your surface.

Cavett then tried to brush off the violence of the word, which had reattached to him: "No, you know me better than that. I mean, the fact that I've done shows with George Wallace, Lester Maddox, and yet we're friends, and I think that's what America's all about." Neither Murphy nor the audience bought it, resulting in silence where he had expected to hear laughter—a horrible sensation for a performer. "I've always wanted to see that on a show," he continued. "You know, no applause on a show." Cavett recuperated slightly by admitting he had flopped, which, as Bayes taught us in clown school, leads the audience to hate you a little less.

Life and society, according to Bergson, require of us "a constantly alert attention that discerns the outlines of the present situation, together with a certain elasticity of mind and body to enable ourselves to adapt in consequence." You need to be able to remain "constantly alert," awake, so that rather than act out of habit, assuming you already understand the situation you are in and how people will respond, you interpret in the present and make a conscious choice about how you are going to behave. Like a shark, you have to keep moving.

Unlike animals' instincts, which, according to psychoanalyst Richard Sterba, are "rigidly fixated in the genes and lead to automatic survival functioning when set into motion," human drives "are characterized by their plasticity which enables them to some extent to be satisfied by substitute aims and objects." We are capable of overriding instincts and working toward aims that have nothing to do with automatic survival functioning (*It's probably nothing*). This "transformability" gives the psyche a way of directing the powerful energy sources of the mind toward "creative productivity and thinking power," as with sublimation—redirecting energy toward higher goals—and reaction formation, neutralizing an impulse with its opposite. We can even think our way out of unacceptable impulses, such as the sadism of a White person not only "say[ing N-word] right in front of" a Black person, as Murphy called out Cavett for doing, but "lik[ing] it." Impulses are sublimated, neutralized, or repressed—transformed—in order to keep our story of self intact and maintain relationships, even when it means overriding impulses and intuition.

As the show went on, Cavett sacrificed his idea of himself to allow an authentic conversation to take place. He ended up standing onstage like a performer before Murphy, who remained seated. Cavett then wrestled with his slip, which fell lower and lower as he invited Black nonactors, including Murphy's uncle, onto the stage to interact with him—a move meant to redeem himself but which only exposed more of his racism. Yet he rolled with it. In the end, Cavett saved the show by being elastic, letting the little one drive, even as it revealed him not to be the person he thought he was. Murphy nearly fell off his seat with laughter.

To take in reality and look from a fact-based perspective at your ideas about your life, at the eye-twitching rituals and procedures that uphold them, is to bring out, as Gervais puts it, "the absurdity of what you're doing." When you are honest, even if it means revealing your absurd ideas about life, an authentic conversation can take place, which, as in clown, makes the audience laugh.

Inelasticity—not adjusting your ideas or beliefs to the evidence before you—also makes the audience laugh, though in a different way. When a person reveals the gap between their idea about their life and its reality but nevertheless sticks to the idea and refuses to adapt it to the situation before them, the audience recognizes the perverse machinations necessary to uphold the split, remain upright. Their laughter is provoked by what Bergson describes as "mechanical inelasticity, just where one would expect to find the wide-awake adaptability and the living pliableness of a human being." Othello was susceptible to Iago's manipulations because a man who does not heed suspicions and trusts his wife out of habit, believes their contract over the living evidence before him (even when manipulated), has the potential to become laughable in his blind rigidity.

Appearing disaffected may protect you from exposing the emotion that makes you a target for discourse-shifting jokes, but it can also put you at risk for becoming laughable in the mechanically inelastic way that Bergson describes. Anna Karenina's husband, Karenin, for example, after finding out that his wife is having an affair, continues to move through the social world as though nothing had happened. In maintaining the same stiff, inelastic behavior he had exhibited before their marriage broke down, he becomes like a child who tries to hide by covering their eyes or an adult hoarding old newspapers to deny the passage of time and the changes that ensue. Karenin's mechanical inelasticity, his inability to adapt to changing circumstances and his lack of transformability led to his becoming a laughingstock to others in his social milieu.

The term *laughingstock* itself appears to be etymologically rooted in a kind of inelasticity. The word *stock*, meaning "tree trunk," first entered the English language from German. The term refers to a person who is treated as the direct object of an action, as opposed to an agent of action themselves. Being wooden, immobile, unable to bend—improvise or adapt—makes one particularly susceptible to becoming the butt of a joke. (A "butt" is similarly rooted in immobility, in that it once referred to a mound of earth used as a target in archery practice.)

The more elastic you are, the better you will be able to adjust to the different roles social scripts call into being—literally, to fit in. But to be elastic, you must be able to pick up on cues indicating how and in which direction you should bend. Marc Segar's "Coping: A Survival

Guide for People with Asperger Syndrome" offers strategies for knowing how to take things, particularly when it comes to social situations in which people do not mean what they say.

Social survival, he advises, involves flexibility, such as translating humor into "constructive criticism." He describes the humor of "non-autistic people" as often having to do with "finding clever ways of pointing out faults in other people and causing them embarrassment." This embarrassment, he explains, is a form of subordination: "In the eyes of many zoologists, humor is a human replacement for the violence which animals use on each other to establish an order of dominance (the pecking order)." He then warns the reader, "No-one talks about the pecking order of which they are a part." You are to silently take up the role you've been given, *make do*, like a good soldier, bending to fit its parameters.

Learning how to take things, which includes not feeling uplifted by compliments or demeaned by hostile remarks—staying in character, playing it cool—trains us to suppress the fatal flaw of emotion so we can avoid becoming the punch line of others' jokes. In order to laugh, to find a Not Joke funny, or to merely take a joke, "we must," Bergson tells us, "for the moment, put our affection out of court."

Aristotle, in his *Poetics*, explains how a tragedy can not only put our emotion out of court but evacuate it by way of catharsis, which, he argues, can be used to reinforce moral structures. He developed his theory as a defense against Plato's call to banish poetry—lyric, epic, dramatic—from the Republic out of fear that it would weaken the guards by making them too emotional to perform their duties. To Aristotle, emotion itself isn't dangerous. If poetry—which includes plays—is composed with a set structure, like the room the Sufis constructed, it can stir up select emotions and evacuate them in a guided way. In fact, if the emotions are stirred up and released within the framed boundaries of his blueprint, he says, poetry can even provide a moral function.

At the center of Aristotle's formula for tragedy is a tragic hero, who must be basically good, according to agreed-upon morals, but with a fatal flaw. His basic goodness makes him relatable. If the hero were bad, his downfall would be expected, because in a moral universe, bad things happen to bad people (as with Trump's justification for killing a person he labels a terrorist). If, on the other hand, he was basically good without a fatal flaw, his downfall would reflect the kind of injustice that preoccupies Ivan in "The Grand Inquisitor" section of Fyodor Dostoevsky's novel *The Brothers Karamazov*—if there is a God, how can there also be innocent suffering? By making the hero basically good with a fatal flaw, the audience identifies with him but also accepts his downfall because it is justified (*If you do bad things, bad things will happen to you*)—as with the robber who slips on the ice while stealing an old lady's purse.

The structure of the narrative must include a twist of fate and the audience's recognition that the hero's downfall has occurred as a result of his tragic flaw. Because the hero is basically good, audience members feel into his shape and experience what is happening to him within themselves by way of neural mirroring. Or, as Kant puts it: "the misfortune of others stirs sympathetic sentiments in the bosom of the onlooker and allows his magnanimous heart to beat for the need of others. He is gently moved and feels the dignity of his own nature." Because of their identification with the hero and the "sympathetic sentiments" it stirs, the audience feels fear (*That could happen to me!*) in witnessing his downfall. With the subsequent recognition that the hero's tragic flaw, such as hubris, led to his twist of fate, however, the onlooker experiences pity, a distancing emotion, and disidentifies with the hero through the recognition that what happened to him won't happen to them so long as they follow the moral dictates of society.

The buildup of fear and pity, intensified by the tension created by their contradictory pulls of identification and disidentification, is then cathartically expelled when audience members learn, through the trajectory their emotions follow, that if they are morally good and don't possess the fatal flaw that led to the hero's downfall, they will be fine.

Whereas tragedy, which, in Aristotle's words, "reduces the soul's emotions of [pity and] terror by means of compassion and dread," has "pain as its mother," comedy, which produces catharsis "by means of pleasure and laughter," "has laughter . . . as its mother." In Aristotle's theory of comedy, characters are "inferior to ourselves . . . somehow in error in soul or body"; they are types, mere placeholders whom we observe from a comfortable distance. Without interiority, they become As-If characters, prototypical, so that fear (*That could happen to me!*) rooted in identification is not elicited by their foibles, and whatever befalls them is easy for us to accept, because we have already disidentified with them.

But for our laughter—the telos of comedy—to release psychic energy in a manner parallel to the catharsis in tragedy, it must still tap into our emotional panelboard. Girard interprets the catharsis of Aristotle's theory of tragedy as "purg[ing] the body of its bad 'humours,'" both in terms of "religious purification" and "medical purgation." What gets evacuated in a structured way in viewing a tragedy is released in a less moralistic way in comedy because it taps less into the socialized part of us and more into our unconscious. The nonrational, uncalibrated emotions that slip out unintentionally in the form of laughter or parapraxes are related to those Plato finds dangerous because, like jokes, they have the capacity to upset the established order.

There are, of course, times when our impulses need to be kept in check, as Plato calls for—we do, after all, live in a communal world—and most ego functions are oriented toward that end. At the same time, there is a danger in acting according to a script or formula with mechanical inelasticity rather than making conscious choices that respond instinctively to the reality before us. Even those who act with volition may eventually fall into a set habit of making the same choices and become a type, like a comic character expressing the inelasticity that Bergson flags as ripe for humor. If the bulk of our hours are spent playing a part in an incomprehensible show—living behind glass, instincts on mute—we risk losing contact with our interior and begin to secrete the inhuman, like mechanical automatons dissociated from the animal part within us.

"Most people are disgusted," writes Nussbaum, "by drinking from a glass into which they themselves have spit, although they are not sensitive to the saliva in their own mouths." The idea behind disgust, she continues, is that the self will be contaminated if it takes in something thought of as repellent—even if the substance originated within one's own body. Secretions, what Freud calls "excreta," that we share with animals are the main contaminants—mucus, urine, feces, semen—and "in all cultures an essential mark of human dignity is the ability to wash and to dispose of wastes."

Anyone who is denied control over the borders of their own body and interior becomes dehumanized—think of the "untouchables" in India, she suggests, or people in concentration camps ("In Auschwitz," writer Primo Levi explains, "'to eat' was rendered as *fressen*, a verb which in good German is applied only to animals"). Seeing someone as inhuman makes it easier to disidentify from whatever it is in them we fear is in ourselves as well but don't want to acknowledge because it would feel too threatening to our survival, psychic or literal.

Repulsion expresses our desire to distance ourselves, as Polanski's film suggests, from what we are afraid could erupt from our own bodies as a way of "ward[ing] off both animality in general and the mortality that is so prominent in our loathing of our animality," as Nussbaum puts it. It's not only our mortality, our animality, that repulsion helps us dissociate from, but the fact that we are embodied and that our animal bodies, only partly under our control, sometimes function in ways we have not commanded, as though they possessed their own volition, like my slip.

During my talk, when my volume shot up, it seemed as though my voice had erupted into the concrete world and was then projected back at me as an external object. Even though it originates within a body, a voice often becomes object-like in this way, particularly when it has passed through a machine to be amplified or recorded. Once externalized, objectified, a person's voice ceases to be their own and becomes a component of concrete reality, which perhaps explains why hearing your recorded voice played back can be disturbing.

Taking your voice back in after it has left your body is a lot like drinking your own saliva from a glass, although the ear, unlike the mouth, does not have lips that can close or muscles capable of spitting out. Because it is difficult to enlist repulsion to block out or regurgitate sound after it has entered our body, an uncanny sensation arises instead.

Freud uses the term *uncanny* to describe a circumstance in which the familiar becomes defamiliarized in a way that makes the real feel unreal. In German, the word for "uncanny" is *unheimlich*, or "unhoused," and my voice was, indeed, unhoused when I heard it outside my body, my speech appearing to travel not from the inside out but from the outside in, as Cavett pretended the N-word had done, prompting Murphy to call him "possessed."

An uncanny sensation is amplified when it is projected through a mechanical, inanimate object, such as speakers, earbuds, or a computer. When the self that has become not-self reenters the body as a foreign object that appears to have come to life, what might otherwise feel violating or intrusive may be experienced as a metaphysical crisis that leads to a sense of derealization, confusion around what is inside and what is outside, self and other—what is real.

Corpsing was likely my bodily attempt to expel the unhoused feeling of crisis that was provoked. The voice, psychologist Paul Ekman explains, is an "emotion signal system, equal in importance to facial expression" that "rarely gives false emotional messages," and that "very few of us can convincingly simulate." Laughter offers an escape from stressful situations by flipping them, shifting the atmosphere from negative to positive emotion, expulsion to *ejacuLATION*. Whatever I was feeling, my fit of Duchenne laughter, like an inverted Balaam or a Not Joke, was able to reverse.

The alien voice-object became most disconcerting when it was suddenly amplified on the word *ejaculation*, which Derrida connects to shame associated with "standing upright" and with "erection in general and not only phallic surrection . . . the face-to-face." There was an interpersonal element to my laughter, not only in relation to the audience with whom I was face-to-face, but with those to the side of me as well.

When I met with the other participants ahead of time to discuss the format for the panel, the organizer suggested that she open with remarks, that the author of the book we had gathered to discuss speak, and that I respond to what the author said. I felt nervous about having to respond on the spot, as the author was not planning to read a passage from the book or discuss something specific enough that I would be able to prepare a response ahead of time. I expressed my concern to the organizer and she told me not to worry. I could simply write and present to the audience whatever I wanted to say in relation to the book and to hoarding more generally. My mind was at ease.

In her introduction to the audience on the evening of the event, however, the organizer presented a format that matched her original plan: I was to be a respondent. I felt panicked, confused. Should I follow the setup I had prepared for, the one we had agreed upon, or change course? I worried I would look foolish reading a talk rather than responding, but also knew it would be difficult to respond on the spot.

As I deliberated over what to do, I felt as I had in high school when, in the midst of taking the standardized test for college admission, my bra came undone. Should I fasten my bra, I wondered, or keep going? I had the habit of fastening my bra at the front of my body, then twisting it to the back, which meant I would have to go to the bathroom if I were to fasten it in my habitual manner. I could, however, try to fasten the hooks at the back and stay in my seat—how hard could it be?—or continue taking the test braless. As I weighed my options, I became like the Rat Man removing the stone from the middle of the road and placing it back again.

I picked up my pen and pretended to take notes, then put it back down. By the time it was my turn to speak on the panel, I was gripped by anxiety over what to do. I had planned on playing one role but had suddenly been cast in another. I knew that what I had prepared would be more interesting than what I might come up with while buzzing with anxiety, so I decided to follow the plan we had agreed upon and read what I had written.

I began to read, but my mind strayed from the text. I imagined how odd it must seem for a respondent to take on the role of presenter, play the wrong part in the production, read from the wrong script. I began to doubt my decision, which only increased my anxiety. My river of emotion pushed with insistence against my dam of composure until it finally broke free. I can't say exactly what made me break into laughter when I did—I suspect it wasn't simply the mic's sound or the word it amplified. As Clarke says, humor is "unconscious, else we should all be able to explain its mechanism by simple analysis of what we think before we laugh."

Regardless of origin, my corpsing elicited the *jouissance* associated with breaking character, refusing to take the position that had been imposed on me, charting my own narrative, letting the costume of stylization fall to the floor. While laughing, I let myself stay offtrack a bit, improvise, remain elastic, alive. My psychological state shifted from an anxious fluctuation between options to an open field of clarity and light.

Duchenne laughter places the mind in an alternate cognitive space in which two things that usually can't be comprehended simultaneously—the hag and the beautiful woman—come into view at the same time. Our perception operates by binocular rivalry: each eye sends data to a different side of the brain, and our attention shifts between these two sets of data constantly but imperceptibly. As with splitting—when we hold two things in mind in separate compartments, know and unknow—binocular rivalry permits us to perceive from two angles, two sides of the same coin, in quick succession, without ever holding both in view at the same time. When we laugh, that illusion is lost, and information from both of our brain's hemispheres registers concurrently.

With the suspension of binocular rivalry comes a respite from the tension created by keeping contradictory impulses apart, from the energy that needs to be exerted in order to maintain a split. As with repression, when energy that is being used to hold emotions in their separate compartments is liberated, its release is often experienced as *jouissance*, and "a whole dimension of the organism, which would otherwise remain veiled, can be experienced," as Lacan says.

In contrast to a benign violation, which takes ethics into consideration, *jouissance* breaks from systems of rational thought, shits on the sticky trap of practical reason, so that good and bad, life and death, similarly cease to be held in their binary compartments. The suspension of binocular rivalry accompanying laughter transports one beyond pleasure to a state of "being . . . stepped out into the unconcealedness of its being," as Heidegger puts it: an expression of pure energy.

Corpsing, writes poet David Marriott, is "a kind of excess of body over representation" that discloses rules, morals, and propriety as "artificial and theatrical." My laughter on the panel not only broke character, revealed the artificiality of the setup, but demonstrated a refusal to play the part I had been assigned. Laughter threatens authority— the authority of others, but also of the self. It functions as a higher power that exerts greater control than a human being could possess, as philosopher Samuel Weber explains:

> Laughter is dangerous to the guardians of the state, as to all good men, because of its tendency to get out of hand. This tendency, in turn, derives from the peculiar relation of laughter to the "subject": one does not laugh the way one walks or speaks; it is not an act that the subject performs (or avoids) at will. Rather than deciding or choosing to laugh, "one abandons oneself to" it, and it is this necessity of self-abandonment no doubt, that explains why the "condition" of laughter would tend to be "violent," as well as to provoke "a violent reaction."

In abandoning myself to laughter, letting be, the mood and structure of the event changed, even though that was not my subjective intention.

Once I admitted things had gone awry—*sorry, I just had a juvenile moment*—acknowledged my failure rather than continue to deliberate which approach would best hide my discomfort around the role that had been imposed on me, I was resuscitated. "If it's going badly and you admit it," Bayes reminded us, "you're alive"; whereas "if you pretend it's okay when we know it isn't, we hate you a little bit. If you're bad and you admit it, we love you again."

Only with wide-awake adaptability and the living pliableness of a human being—movement—will you connect with yourself and give others a way to connect with you. Corpsing stripped me of the script and suspended my binocular rivalry so I could stop playing the dead body, feel present and alive. Laughter shakes us out of our deadness.

One must still have chaos in oneself to be able to give birth to a dancing star.

—FRIEDRICH NIETZSCHE

A 1962 *Candid Camera* episode has actors follow a subject into an elevator and turn to face the rear. The subject notices everyone around him acting in unison, following an unfamiliar protocol, and he himself slowly turns, falls in line, and faces the back as well.

One episode of the Japanese version of *Candid Camera* shows a running crowd approaching a solitary walker from the opposite direction. The crowd disperses, spreading out around the walker, who, now engulfed by the throng, turns to face the same direction as the others and begins to run. The people in the crowd—which the subject now, in effect, leads—continue running at the same pace. They all continue to run in unison, though there is no discernible threat.

In another Japanese candid camera clip, a crowd spreads out around a man so that he is in the midst of the throng when someone calls out what sounds like a warning. Everyone ducks, crouches on the ground, and covers their head. The subject instinctively ducks, too, a mere fraction of a second later.

The instinct to fall in line is primal, which is why it carries across cultures even as humor does not. Humor is shaped by cultural codes and scripts, how an individual reacts to the particular expectations and demands others place on them as well as to the threat of unbelonging, which dissuades them from choosing to be their own narrative. "Catching people in the act of being themselves"—existential shame—

was, as producer Allen Funt puts it, the goal of *Candid Camera*. Sometimes being yourself involves what Weber calls "self-abandonment": abandoning what you think of as your self and letting what is most alien in you, the unconscious, step through.

Another Japanese candid camera video involves a port-o-potty prank at what appears to be a park of some kind. Three public port-o-potties are rigged so that ten seconds after someone enters and locks the door, the floor—with the toilet and the person using it—shoots through the ceiling, and what should be contained within walls is exposed on an elevated stage for everyone to see. (This is supposed to be funny? my daughter asked, taking the dog into her lap and turning away from my computer screen.)

Part of what is so disturbing about seeing or thinking about someone on the toilet is that, in our daily lives, we edit out the essential animal within—the inevitable shitting and pissing—and deal instead with abstracted images of one another that have cropped-out physicality, as Žižek explains:

> When we deal with another person, phenomenologically, which is to say the way that we experience them, we erase, abstract from the image of the other person or partner certain features which are simply too embarrassing to be kept in mind all the time. I talk to you—of course, rationally, I know you are defecating, you are sweating, not to mention other things—but, quite literally, when I interact with you, this is not part of the image I have of you. So when I deal with you, I am basically not dealing with the real you. I am dealing with the virtual image of you. And this image has reality in the sense that it nonetheless structures the way I am dealing with you.

The virtual images we have of one another have reality—like Bion's beta elements—because they structure our interpersonal relationships (much like the idea of Whiteness). The exposure of a stranger's interior on camera appears uncanny because what is usually erased bursts through the virtual image and, like hearing your own voice projected through a machine, destabilizes your perception of what is real. The more machinic the uncanny quality, the more it will resonate with the fundamental impersonal animal in each of us.

All this information is assessed in a split second when we experience another person or witness a prank. If the violation within a prank is benign, it will be perceived as humorous. When the audience experiences a sense of identification with the person being duped, a part of the self resonates with the part that is revealed in the other and pattern recognition ensues. The reward for the recognition (laughter) serves a critical function: it expresses assurance that what we are identifying with is being observed from a comfortable distance, in the same way pity does in Aristotle's theory of tragedy.

This distance, however, is illusory. In comedy, the "laughing spectator," writes Girard, is often included because "as this spectator laughs, he falls into the very trap which has already swallowed his victim and he becomes laughable in his turn." Girard describes a man standing on ice seeing another person slip and, as he laughs at the other person slipping, slips himself. There is no way to distance himself from the trap that swallowed his victim—the tension between an attempt to remain upright and gravity's pull—or to avoid exposing in himself the precise thing that was laughable in the first place, because that trap is inside him as well. It is inside all of us.

Whereas tragedy centers around subjective aspects of the individual, even as their destinies may be in the hands of the gods, comedy reveals impersonal structural patterns that we are all subject to and that, in Girard's words, "deny the sovereignty of the individual more radically than either god or destiny." Because laughter is not an act performed by will, as Weber writes, its peculiar relation to the subject is that it unveils a fundamental lack of autonomy. It speaks through us, the way collective and individual unconsciouses do, which is why psychoanalysts call on us to take control over our lives by making the unconscious conscious. We can then make deliberate choices, become our own narratives, and direct our lives.

It is disturbing to imagine oneself as an actor drawn into the script of another director, a person who unconsciously takes a position (turns to face the back, ducks)—to accept that, regardless of our subjective experience, we may not be as individual as we imagine. At the same time, the instinct to mimic behavior, step into sameness, also has an evolutionary purpose. Mirroring another's actions, emotions, or gestures plays a role in survival.

The Japanese subject acts on an instinct that protects his bodily survival—undoubtedly sensing a threat compelling the others to flee—while the American in the elevator adjusts his behavior to fit in with the group, exhibiting an instinct for social survival. Both the fleeing Japanese man and the American in the elevator are engaged in isopraxic behavior, which is a form of mirroring rooted in the feeling that sameness leads to safety. Falling in line helps you to avoid notice and avoid becoming a target yourself. Following protocol or social codes and ceasing to be an individual by taking a position that allows you to merge into a larger configuration and become invisible are both self-protective measures.

"A crowd," explains social psychologist Gustave Le Bon, "thinks in images, and the image itself immediately calls up a series of other images, having no logical connection with the first." Crowds are like dreams, like poetry: the conscious personality of an individual in a crowd, according to Le Bon, recedes, while the unconscious personality is awakened:

> We see, then, that the disappearance of the conscious personality, the predominance of the unconscious personality, the turning by means of suggestion and contagion of feelings and ideas in an identical direction, the tendency immediately to transform the suggested ideas into acts; these, we see, are the principal characteristics of the individual forming part of a crowd.

When that unconscious personality dominates, it becomes difficult to draw a distinction between the self that we know and the alien within.

We receive our cue and find ourselves "turning by means of suggestion and contagion," running madly with no idea why, turning to fall in line, take our position, play an assigned role in an invisible script.

When something outside of us resonates with an element in our unconscious, a humorous effect is produced by way of pattern recognition. We all have elements in our depths we are not aware of, that feel foreign and that can subject us to the same kind of exposure we witness in others. Following social codes enables us to effectively hide in a crowd, appear prototypical, airbrushed, so our potentially disturbing parts recede and we avoid exposure. Putting forward a False Self allows us to tuck away all the aspects of ourselves we don't want others to see, even if it also means remaining silent, complicit, or asleep.

Sitting with my father in the family room one day during a college break, I noticed his socks: black and gray with a geometric pattern that appeared three-dimensional, as bathroom tiles sometimes do when held in view for a sustained period. I love your socks! I told him. Rather than thank me, he took the pair off his feet and extended them toward me. They're yours, he said. In Arab culture, if you openly admire something belonging to another person, you must be prepared for it to be handed over to you. If you say the dish someone ordered in a restaurant looks good, they will pass it over. The more you resist, the more insistent they will become.

This unspoken code around generosity is pushed to the extreme in an Egyptian candid camera episode. A subject at a lunch counter of a restaurant faces the dilemma of choosing how to respond when a stranger starts eating off their plate. One person moves the plate closer as an offering, another moves it away, while yet another becomes so irritated that he leans over his plate protectively to block the actor from taking more food. The response of each, as with all choices, reveals something about their character that following prescribed behavior can conceal.

Humor is culturally specific. Iraqi candid camera is radically different from the American, Japanese, and even Egyptian versions. The title of an Iraqi candid camera show that ran in 2010, *Put Him in Bucca*, has a double entendre in Arabic: the first meaning is "to put him in Camp Bucca" (a detention camp that was in operation from 2003 to 2009), and the second is "to rob him," raising the question of what is stolen when our lives are inserted into another's fictional frame, particularly one imposed by an occupying force overriding the local population's customary way of life.

In one episode, a well-known comedian is stopped at a staged checkpoint that mimics actual checkpoints familiar to anyone in Iraq during that time. A soldier tells the comedian there is a bomb beneath his car that is about to go off and accuses the comedian of being a terrorist. The comedian hops out of the car, takes his shoes off, and runs, panicked, to an area far from the car. The audience, along with everyone involved, knows the scene is staged, that he was stopped arbitrarily, that there is no real danger, that the violation is benign. "The imagination is sometimes said to be tickled by a ludicrous idea," writes Darwin, "and this so-called tickling of the mind is curiously analogous with that of the body." But for some, the threat of being arbitrarily stopped at a checkpoint and accused of a crime they didn't commit that might land them in the hell of a detention camp would not be a benign violation, a tickle. When something is too much like a real threat in daily life, it is less funny than it is potentially triggering.

The audience member that laughs presumably does so cathartically—out of identification (*That could happen to me!*) and the pity that arises alongside the recognition of being at a safe distance (*It's a fictional scenario on television*). Seeing a celebrity with food in his metaphysical teeth, having done nothing wrong except reveal his fundamental animal, allows the viewer to transfer the empathy they feel toward the prank's miscast victim onto themselves—onto all of us. It's hard to be human.

But as with the man at the peephole, the way you are seen can infiltrate your sense of self. Iraqis have long been mistaken as the enemy of the West, invaders, terrorists, the supposed perpetrators of 9/11—a "paranoid construction," in psychoanalyst M. Fakhry Davids's terms, that identifies the Muslim as the enemy. This way of thinking defends against anxiety and "protects us all from the fear of annihilation, which the 9/11 attacks (and again the 7/7/2005 ones here in London) brought forcibly to the surface." Much as perverse thinking twists reality to fit an idea, a paranoid construction hits the nail on the head—finds its evidence, catches the criminal—no matter where the hammer falls. Laughter provides a means of expulsion, a way for the target to evacuate, to spit out, the identity or paranoid construction projected onto them and break character, refuse the role.

Still, it is difficult for me as an American, despite my Iraqi heritage, to find the episode funny. Unlike laughter, humor rarely crosses cultural borders.

A man stood on a street corner in Madrid, bottle of wine in hand, laughing hysterically, half tripping over his own feet as his body lurched in different directions. Alcohol was the clear trigger for this fit—there was nothing humorous about the situation. Nevertheless, passersby, including myself, joined in his hilarity. Laughter, even when nonsensical, is infectious.

In 1962, an epidemic of laughter ripped through a girls' boarding school in East Africa. More than half the students were afflicted, their laughter lasting from minutes to hours to days. The school had to be shut down for a period, though that measure didn't keep the laughter from being transmitted across villages, traveling from body to body.

The sounds within a laugh have an evolutionary purpose. Professor of psychology Joanne Bachorowski collected over thirty thousand laughs and analyzed the communications within the variations she discovered. A glottal whistle, she explains to the host of *Radiolab* in the episode "Laughter," sounds like a wheeze and "seems to really say, 'Hey, pay attention to me!'" Other laughs change pitch. "Acoustically extreme laughter" is hard to process, but nonetheless has the capacity to "tweak us emotionally," Bachorowski explains: "Humans have the ability to produce a sound that makes other people feel good. And so if we can do that then they're most likely to feel positively towards us, and behave positively towards us. Ultimately, we want to shape their behavior towards us."

We use laughter much like a con man does confidence: we give our good feeling to others so they will give us their good feeling in return. Voiced laughter, which has a tonal, songlike quality, provokes more positive feeling than does unvoiced laughter, which is less musical and consists mostly of grunts and snorts. Different kinds of laughter also signal and reinforce power positioning: people, one of the *Radiolab* hosts adds, "laugh louder and more extremely around their boss" in an attempt to induce good feelings and positive regard.

Laughter can also be a tool in trying to feel safe. "Are You Actually Funny," writer Katharine Coldiron recently wrote on Twitter, "or So Creepy That Women Laugh Nervously at Your Comments for Their Own Safety? A Pamphlet for Men." The massive number of likes and retweets she received reflects how resonant this particular use of laughter is. Positively influencing the feelings of a man who seems threatening by amplifying his sense of power is strategically similar to the owners of the restaurant I worked at instructing me and the other hostesses to inflect our voices when greeting customers and answering the phone. Charm, too, is a metacommunicative signal used to influence the emotions and behavior of others in both innocent and manipulative ways.

Signaling interpersonal feeling that is not necessarily present is characteristic of non-Duchenne laughter and is also biologically wired in animals as a way of managing others in contexts where survival is at stake. Metacommunication signals a power position, most often submission—tucking a tail between the legs, showing some belly—to communicate peaceful intent and avert attack.

Emotions, like unconscious communication, are transmitted bodily through more ways than those managed by mirror mechanisms in the brain, although mirror neurons have also been found in the brains of songbirds and macaques. Pheromones signal everything from sexual attraction to alarm (the "ranke smell" of an injured bee, Charles Butler wrote in the seventeenth century, indicates the need to mobilize defenses against an enemy presence). Scents that are not biologically produced also have the power to elicit emotional states, as do tastes (Proust's madeleine). According to a recent BBC article, an amusement park created a special Halloween attraction that "uses specially-crafted smells like 'wood smoke' and 'rotting flesh' to manipulate customers' emotions." The company manufacturing those scents also creates "smells of yesteryear to help dementia patients." The part of the brain that controls memory and is responsible for connecting scents to emotion is part of the limbic system, which oversees bodily functions that ensure survival.

Biologically wired responses to different kinds of laughter—like smells and musical sounds—can be manipulated in unconscious ways, as is often the case with non-Duchenne laughter, and in conscious ways, as with the implants placed in replicants to shape their behavior in *Blade Runner* or the use of a laugh track.

The laugh track—recorded laughter that plays during a TV show to induce laughter in audience members—was designed to manipulate biologically wired responses to calculated advantage. Popular in American television from the 1950s through the 1970s, it was originally invented by Charley Douglass, a sound engineer who noticed that live audiences could not be relied on to laugh at desired moments and were sometimes distracting or disruptive when they laughed at undesired moments. His Laff Box was created as a corrective. It played recorded laughter to sweeten moments when the audience didn't laugh but should have, and to desweeten or mute moments when laughter occurred in undesirable ways or went on too long.

Laugh tracks are, for the most part, a thing of the past, and when they are used in contemporary shows, they often signal to the audience how to take things. In *The Jamie Kennedy Experiment*, a modern candid camera television show that aired from 2002 to 2004, laughter appeared to be used to sweeten moments that raised ethical concerns. A potential violation within the scenario was countered with laughter that seemed to be coming from a person who was being violated. For example, if a woman was put in a compromising position, a loud, "voiced," songlike female laugh would lead the laughter. In a skit in which Kennedy plays a yoga instructor, while a woman demonstrates a downward dog position, he stands behind her and holds her hips in a sexual stance (doggy position). As he does so, an acoustically extreme female laugh breaks out. The laugh, signaling a joyful feeling, indicates to the audience—its female members in particular—that it is okay for women to overlook the scene's misogynistic elements (*Relax; don't take it the wrong way*) and enjoy the fun.

Chappelle's Show, which was prerecorded before an audience, used the laughter of real audience members in place of a laugh track. However, in one skit, "Dudes' Night Out," a laugh track was used to compensate for the audience's not having sweetened where sweetening had been expected. The episode, as the title suggests, is about a group of dudes who go out drinking. Unlike the jovial male-bonding portrayed in beer commercials, however, the episode is "honest," as Chappelle says in the stand-up portion of his show, about the reality that "drinking beer brings the animal out in somebody."

The response of real-life dude drinkers in the audience would inevitably be complicated. What were they to do with any resonance with their interior fantasy thoughts, memories, and images that might have been called up by way of pattern recognition while watching the drunk characters get into senseless fights, vomit, cry, shit in the street, feel a desire to hook up with a broad range of people ("a mouth's a mouth, man")? Perhaps the skit was not sufficiently Aristotelian, in that it lacked a built-in distance that would allow the viewer to disidentify with what they saw on the screen. Without a guarantee that what was happening to the characters would not—had not—happened to them, the episode ran the risk of hitting too close to home and provoking emotions that cross-circuit laughter, including the implicit transphobia, which disturbs in yet another cross-circuiting way. By overriding the viewer's gut reaction with canned laughter, however, the producers were able to provide a corrective, both by inserting another audience between the viewer and the characters to push them back a row, and by indicating how the skit should be taken.

Having someone help you work through an experience—as Anna Freud underscored in discussing the advantage of children who were not evacuated over those who were separated from their parents—helps you process overwhelming feelings that can lead to traumatizing, retraumatizing, disturbing, or just plain uncomfortable reactions. The first agent for laughers at Central Casting was Lisette St. Claire, according to the same episode of *Radiolab*, who was searching for audience members for the 1990s sitcom *The Nanny* because the star, Fran Drescher, was not comfortable being in a room with complete strangers after having been assaulted in her home by armed robbers. While screening people in front of select audience members, St. Claire had the idea of choosing people who not only seemed safe but had sweetening laughs. She then began casting them on other shows as well, transforming the act of laughing into a profession.

Knowing the laugh sounds of the audience members and the corresponding set of communications they will transmit is a way of curating the emotional atmosphere of a studio, much like a hoarder does in filling their hoard with objects that have predictable emotions attached. Like the chorus in a tragedy, laughers influence how the audience understands the actions onstage. Leaving few openings, nasty holes, for something unexpected to rush in is a way of protecting against the unknown—understandable in a posttraumatic context.

Pizza in Auschwitz, a 2008 Israeli documentary, follows the return of seventy-four-year-old Holocaust survivor Danny Chanoch to Poland and the death camps of his childhood with his two adult children. Danny is a cheerful person who wants to remember but not to mourn. Being placed in the physical atmosphere of his past and taking in the sensory data (sights, smells, beta elements, sounds) of its emotional architecture is like walking into a massive, mythic room like the one constructed by Sufis, except in Danny's case the emotions brought up are unpredictable, out of his—and anyone's—control.

At one point during the journey, the family visits the school Danny went to as a child before the war broke out, a visit he had made with his wife some years earlier. His daughter, Miri, asks, "Why come here again?" He responds, "To feel like I'm in the first grade and that I can continue to the second grade. I'm angry. Angry that someone intervened in my life. And took away the joy of studying in a school that overlooks a river and a green mountain. It's sad, no?" Someone in the background says, "Very sad."

"Sad that they took me from school and killed my mommy and my daddy," he continues.

"Danny, why don't you cry? What happened to you is horrible."

"Forget it."

"What would happen if you cried?"

"I despise people who cry and are hungry or are tired. I would have achieved nothing with tears. Let me tell you something: Where should I have cried? In Birkenau? To Mengele? To my parents who weren't there? Who should I have cried to? In Birkenau, on the ramp, the crying ended. In Birkenau, after removing the clothes from the dead, those killed with Zyklon B gas, and passing the 'selections'; you get over it. After Birkenau, you'll change, he'll change, everybody changes."

Near the end of the film, Danny visits Birkenau, where the crying ended. He wants to show the camp to his children and spend the night there with them. While walking around, rain begins to fall and they retreat into his old barrack sooner than planned. Two young German men also duck into the barrack to get out of the rain. Danny begins to tell them his story in a characteristically lighthearted way, lists the camps he was placed in, then suddenly yells, "Idiots! Sadistic idiots! . . . This is your people! These are your people!" Miri says gently, "Dad, don't yell at them." One of the young men tries to defend himself—not everyone participated, he says—and Danny, who has once again composed himself, shifts his tone and brings the conversation to a close: "Anyhow, I don't want to ruin your vacation." They end on a polite but strained note.

Because the film is a documentary, there is no script, and without a script, there are no emotional guardrails. Danny stands before his old bunk, says he's going to bed, imitates the voice of a Kapo yelling an order in German, and gets into bed. As he lies there, he begins to regress. Time dissolves: it's difficult for the viewer to tell whether he is recounting memories or reliving them. His daughter brings over a slice of pizza and hands it to him. "What's this?" he asks.

"A slice of pizza," she tells him. "Pizza from Auschwitz."

He eats lying down. "This is the first time I've had pizza on this bunk," he says. "It never occurred to me before. What fun."

Danny then seems to fluctuate between the adult character we've been watching for the bulk of the film and a disintegrated, childlike version of himself, reliving the horror as he lies on his bunk, one hand on his forehead in a fainting position, recollecting devastating details and anecdotes from a child's perspective.

After a few minutes, he sits up, looks at his children as though they were strangers, and tells them he doesn't understand them—their worries, their hungers. His daughter, offended, says he's crossed a line. "There is no line," he says. The viewer senses this as well. "Once you've overstepped the mark," as Lacan has it, "there are no more limits." But in the context of a death camp, the horror of a limitless world is terrifying.

Miri tries to bring her father back to the side of order and logic. He is trying to make her and her brother feel guilty, she explains, for not having gone through the horror he experienced and for not wanting to simulate it, as Danny would like. As she is speaking, she is interrupted by her phone's ring. It's her young daughter. We can't hear the little girl but can tell she is asking her mother questions you would expect from a child, such as, *Where are you?* "With Grandpa, filming," Miri answers.

"In his barrack," Danny adds from the background.

She continues to speak to her daughter (*How are you, sweetie?*), while Danny, from his bunk, tries to join the conversation with an air of perverse nostalgia, "Tell her Grandpa lived here. . . . Tell her we're in Grandpa's house."

Miri doesn't relay Danny's comments—which are clearly as unsettling to her as they are to the viewer—but eventually she hands him the phone with the caveat that he is not to say where he is. He obeys, speaks to his granddaughter sweetly from the bunk, and then says to his wife with disturbing cheer. "We're here in the barrack having a nice conversation. In the barrack and everything's cool, eating and drink."

His son sighs and rolls his eyes. "Are we going soon?" Miri moans. "I can't take it anymore." She insists she needs to leave immediately, "this very minute." Danny suggests she wait outside, then stands up and says reflectively, "I think the séance may not have gone so well; I thought we would come here free of human needs—"

"Oh, shit," Miri cuts in, standing abruptly. "I sat in the Coca-Cola!" Her brother and the crew laugh.

Humor has the capacity to break through an interpersonal impasse, as Andy Bichlbaum of the prankster activist group the Yes Men explains:

> If you're angry about something, you rant. But pushing facts down people's throats doesn't work. Humor can really sideswipe this problem. It's like there's a wall between [you] and a person and if you make a joke, it's a crack in the wall.

"Facts don't change people's minds," says Silverman, along the same lines. "You've never changed someone's mind by arguing." Rather, "laughter lifts the barriers," Bakhtin proclaims, "and opens the way to freedom." Miri intuitively understands this use of laughter and jokes but needs to make more cracks—crack more jokes—before she can reach her father, who continues reflecting on the séance.

"Dad, stop it!" She cuts him off, nearly in tears. "I want to go now." He smiles. She tells him he can't re-create the past, and she doesn't want to go on to the next camps, to continue the "tortuous" journey.

Her vehement plea is punctuated with humor: "I don't know anyone else who spent the night in Jerkenau." Everyone laughs. She wants to leave, go to a hotel, get rid of the "lice" and "filth," but Danny objects. "I'm sorry," he says. "I don't want to go. You can go. I'm staying." He sits back down on his bunk, which prompts Miri to make an impassioned speech:

> Your life was damaged, in the cruelest way possible. Nothing is as cruel as this. Nothing. And we don't really understand you, and never will. . . . But you know what, you should be happy. Imagine if we had to endure the same things you did and then we'd all understand each other. Is that what you want? Rejoice in the fact that you're surrounded by sane people who'll never understand you but will always love you. So you have Yudkeh and Mushkeh and Bulkeh with whom you can trade Holocaust horror stories. But would you like to live with Yudkeh? Would you like to wake up in the morning with Bulkeh? No! You're lucky to wake up in the morning with Mom, who says, "Danny, let's have some coffee or go for a walk."

Everyone breaks into laughter, especially Danny, who laughs in a full-bodied Duchenne way. "If we weren't at Birkenau, you never would have said that!" he tells Miri with pleasure. Birkenau continues, all these years later, to be the place where crying stops. There is no script for an encounter with the limitless realm or the "tragic laughter," writes academic Jacqueline Bussie, "that occurs in the moments when we most expect tears."

"Revolt is not a solution," says writer Elie Wiesel, "neither is submission. Remains laughter, metaphysical laughter." Miri managed to bring her father out of his fluctuation between the past and the present, the hag and the beautiful woman, with jokes. When Danny laughs, his emotional version of binocular rivalry appears to have been suspended, and the parts of life that trauma keeps from touching achieve metaphysical integration momentarily.

"Laughter is one way of coping with the incomprehensible," writes Žižek. When emotions are high, they are most infectious, and the chance that something will go awry increases. Following prescribed protocols helps to avoid scenarios in which genuine emotion leads people into uncharted emotional territory, as happened with Danny and his children in the barrack. Professional mourners—people paid to help ignite the contagion of tears and grief at funerals—cue others to take their position in an invisible script by effectively implanting chosen emotions into the neural mirror mechanisms of others so they participate in the cued emotions, as Bataille describes it, from inside themselves. The professionals choreograph the emotional contagion of a group so something unanticipated won't burst through, as my analysand feared.

These hired mourners have been around for centuries and, like Freud's marriage brokers, are easy targets for humor. Kant recounts a joke about professional mourners in *The Critique of Judgment*:

> Take the case of the heir of a wealthy relative being minded to make preparations for having the funeral obsequies on a most imposing scale, but complaining that things would not go right for him, because (as he said) "the more money I give my mourners to look sad, the more pleased they look."

We laugh at this tale, Kant explains, because "we had an expectation which is suddenly reduced to nothing." Structurally, that sounds a lot like Schopenhauer's incongruity theory of humor (that "the sudden perception of the incongruity between a concept and the real objects which have been thought through in some relation" causes laughter) and also like castration anxiety, which is triggered by the apprehension of a gap between who one wants to be ("a concept") and who they are ("the real object"). For me to laugh, however, the "tale" would need a lot of sweetening—particularly after the anecdote directly preceding it in the same passage:

Suppose that some one tells the following story: An Indian at an Englishman's table in Surat saw a bottle of ale opened, and all the beer turned into froth and flowing out. The repeated exclamations of the Indian showed his great astonishment. "Well, what is so wonderful in that?" asked the Englishman. "Oh, I'm not surprised myself," said the Indian, "at its getting out, but at how you ever managed to get it all in." At this we laugh, and it gives us hearty pleasure. This is not because we think ourselves, maybe, more quick-witted than this ignorant Indian, or because our understanding here brings to our notice any other ground of delight. It is rather that the bubble of our expectation was extended to the full and suddenly went off into nothing.

Multiple factors go into my not finding the above story humorous, but perhaps the most powerful is that I do not identify with the "we" that thinks itself maybe "more quick-witted than this ignorant Indian." My bubble of expectation, developed through a combination of my personal circumstances and the historical moment—cultural space-time—that I exist in, is very different from Kant's. So different, in fact, that in reading the above passage, I was left with an emotional *something* rather than "nothing," making a humorous response impossible (as was the case when I felt disturbed by the apparent transphobia in Chappelle's "Dudes' Night Out"). Without the audience's internal agreement, you would need a laugh track or an army behind you, as Nietzsche has it, to make them laugh. "Laughter," Bergson writes, "has no greater foe than emotion."

But what kind of laughter was Bergson discussing? Certainly not the full range. The analysand who felt an urge to laugh at the funeral of his friend's father was experiencing many emotions, most of them contradictory, creating a tension between the pressure of the impulse and the reaction force of the social codes stopping it up, which undoubtedly amplified its drive. Had he broken into a hysterical fit of laughter, everyone around him would have been horrified. Even so, their horror might not have been enough for them to be able to prevent themselves from joining in. The body, seduced even by a spectacle that the intellect rejects, revolts against the will.

Duchenne laughter, in this way, is a form of parapraxis that reveals the unconscious. As with the "chestburster scene" in *Alien*, in which a reptilian creature bursts out of actor John Hurt's body, sometimes it seems a foreign part of our personality breaks free, escapes repression, and runs wild, as though it had a life of its own. If analyzed with the same methodology you would use for a slip of the tongue or a dream, this feral part of ourselves can help us gain valuable insight into our psyches. Perhaps corpsing, like Le Bon says of crowds, causes the disappearance of the conscious personality and the predominance of the unconscious. The problem is that releasing the unconscious, even in the form of laughter—which generally has positive associations— means also sitting with the savage complexity of the real thing.

The premise of laughter yoga, by contrast, is the fake thing. Proponents assert that because the body can't tell the difference between real and fake laughter, simulated and genuine laughter will lead to the same benefits. But when I gave it a try in the basement of an office building in Midtown Manhattan with ten or so people in their sixties and beyond, my body wasn't fooled. In fact, I found being in a room full of strangers laughing with their mouths only to be so off-putting that I shut down entirely.

We began with some breathing and chanting exercises using the sound "ha" and were then told to walk around and make eye contact with one another while (fake) laughing. When I looked into the eyes of someone making laugh sounds without any contraction of the orbicularis oculi, I felt involuntary suspicion. Instinct, as Lecoq says of the body, knows things about which the mind is ignorant. If genuine laughter could be consciously controlled, I wouldn't have laughed along with the man on the street corner in Madrid, and the girls in East Africa could have been ordered to stop laughing and the entire epidemic would have been averted.

Fake it till you make it—line up your external chips and your internal ones will eventually fall in line—is a maxim that matches up with non-Duchenne laughter, whereas it is Duchenne laughter that studies indicate leads to the health benefits laughter yoga is after. When we laugh, our pulse, blood pressure, and breathing increase and deliver more oxygen to our tissues. Our muscles are stretched, and endorphins, the feel-good hormones, are released. We use laughter to discharge energy that has been wound up into anxiety or stress, much as dogs shake as a way of discharging fear or aggression. And, perhaps most psychologically significant, when binocular rivalry and its psychic counterpart, vertical splitting, are momentarily suspended, a brief sense of clarity and wholeness—*jouissance*—is felt.

People often mistake non-Duchenne laughter for Duchenne laughter. In 2020, during the pandemic, I came across an article published in the *New York Times*, "Laughter May Be Effective Medicine for These Trying Times," that seems to mix up Duchenne and non-Duchenne laughter in potentially problematic ways. The article, written by Richard Schiffman, suggests that laughter and smiles can give people a different perspective on the "bad things" that happen to them:

> Dr. [George] Bonanno interviewed young women who had been sexually abused and noted their facial expressions. "Those who managed to laugh or smile at moments during their interview were more likely to be doing better two years later than those who had not," he said. "Humor keeps negative emotions in check and gives us a different perspective, allowing us to see some of the bad things that happen to us as a challenge rather than a threat."

What does it mean, from a male researcher's perspective, for a woman who has suffered sexual abuse to "[do] better"? Has she made herself more agreeable by laughing and smiling more, "keep[ing her] negative emotions in check," giving others what they want from her in viewing her assault "as a challenge rather than a threat"? Is it not possible that laughter and smiles provide these women with a way of shielding themselves, as most victims of trauma do, from repeat attacks, retraumatization (*Are You Actually Funny or So Creepy That Women Laugh Nervously at Your Comments for Their Own Safety*)?

Along the same lines, the author quotes Dr. Kari Phillips as saying that humor between patients and doctors is helpful because it "results in better patient satisfaction and empowerment, and it helps people feel more warmth in their connection with the doctor." Perhaps the patients, naked beneath their hospital gowns, are trying to modulate their vulnerability by managing the doctor's feelings toward them, as the Rat Man tried to do in his dream about Freud's mother dying by writing a condolence card rather than risking the impertinent laughter he feared would accompany speech. What's more, the doctors themselves may feel uncomfortable. After all, it's not easy to sit with the naked complexity of human vulnerability, take in and record the unwanted truths leaking out of it. Non-Duchenne laughter elicits positive feeling, but at the risk of displacing what needs attention with coded signals, including friendliness and submission. Everything I knew about trauma, emotional vulnerability, laughter, and power caused me to question the article's logic—and suspect that the approach of the yoga class was misguided.

The laughter yoga teacher announced, Now we're in Tokyo, being served hot soup. He mimed cupping a bowl of soup in his hands, lifting it to his mouth, and burning his tongue. Ouch! Ha-ha-ha! Ho-ho-ho! We were then instructed to walk around pretending to fill our invisible bowls with hot soup, bring them to our mouths, burn our tongues (*Ouch!*), and laugh: Ha-ha-ha! Ho-ho-ho!

What's funny about being burned? I wondered, picturing the woman who had slipped on ice on Broadway laughing to signal she was okay. Before I was able to consider the question, the exercise ended, and, as at the end of every exercise, we threw our hands in the air and said, Yay! Ha-ha-ha! Ho-ho-ho!

Is anyone here good with computers? the teacher asked. An older woman stepped forward. I am! she said. I'm good at breaking them every time. She launched into a rehearsed routine about feeling so frustrated with her computer that she picked up a hammer: I hit it on the left [*miming a blow*]. I hit it on the right [*miming a blow*]. And I hit it on top [*miming a massive blow*]. We were then led to imaginatively hit a computer on the left, on the right, and on the top. Yay! Ha-ha-ha! Ho-ho-ho!

The older woman, still leading us from the circle's center, then invited us to the Metropolitan Museum of Art for a special exhibit on the Ming dynasty. Each of us is allowed to hold a precious vase, she told us. Just as you pick yours up [*cue to pick up imaginary vase*], the school bell rings! She pretended to drop her vase, and we all followed, dropping ours as well. Yay! Ha-ha-ha! Ho-ho-ho!

Laughing authentically at these scenarios would be easiest for someone who identified with the prototypes being presented (*This is what makes you laugh*) rather than with a person who turns inward and plays true to their "own gnomes and demons," as Plath puts it. This is precisely the balance a professional mourner needs to strike to make themselves cry at the funeral of a stranger, as one explains:

> Naturally, since I don't know the deceased, it can be hard to work up too many tears about them. Some professional mourners I know can cry on cue like a toddler at Toys 'R' Us, but most of us keep a supply of tools to help us jerk out some tears on command. For example, if we know the person's occupation, we try to find the saddest or most depressing movie involving that profession and use that as a baseline.

Because the job of a professional mourner is to control the response of the crowd, they must model the kind of crying that will calibrate collective emotion in the desired direction. At the same time, the crying must be real to trigger genuine tears in others.

In clown school, Bayes suggested we imagine that the internal images we reach for when making ourselves laugh or cry were painted in watercolor. Space could then be left for expansion, for unexpected emotion to rush in spontaneously. The job of a clown, to "get all up in your humanity and celebrate . . . your elastic connection to emotion," is similar to what is asked of an analysand in psychoanalysis, to bend in the direction your mind and emotions take you. In 1930, Martha Graham premiered *Lamentation*, a solo dance performed by a seated figure, wearing a restrictive purple robe, whom her company website describes as essentially painted in watercolor; "neither human nor animal, neither male nor female [but] grief itself." Dance, too, can be a mode of animal address. After the premiere, a woman in the audience reportedly said the dance made her recognize that "grief was a dignified and valid emotion, and that [she] could yield to it without shame"—precisely the kind of response a professional mourner is hired to suppress and redirect.

To guide real mourners toward prototypical behavior (crying, expressing the saddest, most depressing emotions), a professional mourner needs to use rational triggers and leave no space or openings for uncurated responses, like the laughter that nearly overtook my analysand at the funeral of his friend's father. Professional mourners would not be necessary if strong, raw emotions were not susceptible to taking unexpected forms.

I had trouble grasping why the stories recounted during the laughter yoga class, which would ideally have been a space for free play, left no such openings for unanticipated responses, genuine emotion, the firing of mirror neurons. The scenarios—fleshless skeletons of words that didn't target the body—were utterly unerotic. Each involved the destruction of a precious object that stood in for a world from which we were assumed to feel excluded. There was a dated, *Looney Tunes* quality to the anecdotes that expressed an urge to retaliate against whoever we imagined was holding us down, as when Bugs Bunny, in the role of a concert pianist onstage, shoots an audience member whose incessant coughing makes it impossible for him to stay focused on the piece he is trying to play.

"The idea that I would somehow borrow somebody's gun, waltz into Biden's inauguration like some Looney Tunes character and somehow line up all senators and execute a firing squad on them, I think is a pretty ridiculous idea," said conspiracy theorist Brendan Hunt during a 2021 trial that found him guilty of threatening to "slaughter" members of Congress ("If anybody has a gun," wrote Hunt, "give me it. I'll go there myself and shoot them and kill them"). He claimed his videos and social media propaganda ("KILL YOUR

SENATORS") were just jokes, and that his time in jail had helped him realize his need to "readjust what I think is humorous." (Many *Looney Tunes* cartoons have, in fact, been readjusted in recent decades because of the violence, racism, and sexism they depict.)

At the end of the laughter yoga class, the instructor told us to walk around in a circle and—if we were feeling it—embrace people. He immediately headed toward me, open-armed. I'm not the hugging type, I said, retracting like pill bug. I was tired of playing along.

We were then invited into a circle for sharing time. Someone said, I love to laugh! The instructor smiled, nodding. I feel relaxed and joyful, someone else said. Hearing others laugh made me laugh even harder, the woman beside me added. They were rushing to say what the instructor wanted to hear, I thought cynically. "However spontaneous it seems," Bergson writes, "laughter always implies a kind of secret freemasonry, or even complicity, with other laughers, real or imaginary." Suddenly, he turned to me. What about you? he asked in a tone that seemed calculated to sound neutral but came off as taut. You had some reservations.

My heart started beating quickly and I broke into a sweat. What was I afraid of?

▲

As I walked out of the Guggenheim Museum with my daughters one day, we passed a man drawing caricatures for two dollars. My daughters begged (*Please! Please!*) to sit together for a portrait. After five minutes of sketching, the artist handed the sheet of paper to us, took my money, and turned away. The girls looked at the drawing together. The younger one said to her sister, You look so much better, noting that her head appeared as large as her sister's torso and head combined. My older daughter, fixated on an enormous mole on one cheek, disagreed. Do I really have a mole on my face? she asked. I looked, never having noticed it before, and told her she did, though it was much smaller in reality than in the portrait. That mole, of course, then bothered her for years.

It is the act of rendering visible some deep-seated, previously unacknowledged feature, emotion, inclination, or fear and magnifying it to unmistakable proportions that makes art forms like caricature and satire successful. As metaphors do, caricatures cause hidden similarities between disparate elements to come into relief. It is this element of unveiling that is central: if whatever is exposed were readily available for perception, the artful aspect would be absent.

President Trump employs the techniques of a caricaturist and the manipulative tactics of Iago in planting insidious associations in the minds of others. He has created hundreds of demeaning monikers for institutions, news outlets, television programs, and public figures, mostly politicians (Sleepy Joe, Pocahontas, Wild Bill, Crooked Hillary, Fat Jerry). Trump's nicknames are not meant to reveal deep-seated characteristics, but, like metonyms, to displace individuals with his associations, indicating to others how certain figures should be taken—mostly in pejorative ways. (Alfred E. Neuman for Pete Buttigieg is kind of funny, a friend admitted sheepishly, ashamed at what finding one of Trump's nicknames resonant might reveal about him and his unconscious, the alien within.)

During a 2019 campaign rally in Minneapolis, Trump parodied the affair between former FBI lawyer Lisa Page and FBI agent Peter Strzok: "I love you, Peter. I love you, too, Lisa." Trump resented them because they had exchanged private text messages that were pro–Hillary Clinton during the period leading up to the 2016 election, while they were both investigating Clinton's use of a private email server. Although the two, removed from the FBI investigation after the messages came to light, were not accused of breaking any laws, Trump nonetheless retaliated against them, demeaning Page in characteristically misogynist ways for having had an affair. His parody culminated with an imitation of Peter Strzok (presumably) having an orgasm while repeating Page's name ("Lisa. Lisa. Oh, God, I love you, Lisa").

As I watched Trump deride Page on my computer screen, my eyes moved toward the individuals behind him, who were all laughing. I noticed that the laughter was particularly dramatic among the women, two of whom had their heads thrown back orgasmically. Eight of the twelve all-White laughers standing behind him were women, six of them blond. Perhaps it was a conscious strategy to place Trump in front of more women than men, more blondes than brunettes, at a rally during which he ridiculed (slut-shamed?) Lisa Page, much like Kennedy's laugh track was led by a loud female laugh during a scene in which a woman was put in a sexually compromising position. Their laughter, their participation, gives his anticipated audience (White people who prefer blondes?) permission to laugh.

Are the people placed behind political figures at rallies the modern-day versions of professional laughers? And why do scenarios involving such laughter seem so frequently to have a sexually demeaned woman at the center of their frame?

Freud had a name for the laughter Dr. Christine Blasey Ford remembered between Brett Kavanaugh and his friend Mark Judge. It was smut: sexual aggression posing as play. Ford testified at a Senate Judiciary Committee hearing assessing Kavanaugh's nomination to the Supreme Court. In one of the most poignant parts of her testimony, Ford alleged that Kavanaugh had assaulted her when they were teenagers, saying that the most searing aspect of the assault was "the uproarious laughter between the two and their having fun at my expense."

According to Freud, smut is a scenario that calls for three people: there's the one who is being sexually aggressive (Kavanaugh), a second who is taken as the object of the aggression (Ford), and a third who witnesses the scene and laughs (Judge). That laughter is the crucial element, as it is the goal: in smut, the focus is on producing pleasure in a third-party bystander. Smut can play a part in sexual assault (as Ford describes in Kavanaugh's case), as well as in the redistribution of power, and can also be sublimated into the form of a verbal joke.

Smut gives people a way of being aggressive while simultaneously disguising their aggression, much like litotes. It's the ambiguity that makes it particularly insidious. Is it really a violation? Or is it only a joke, something the target should be able to laugh off? A similar dynamic is described in the recollections of soldiers at Abu Ghraib, who often used smut as a way of breaking detainees. In a letter home, Sabrina Harman, a soldier at Abu Ghraib, writes the following:

> I walk down stairs after blowing the whistle and beating on the cells with an asp to find "the taxicab driver" handcuffed backwards to his window naked with his underwear over his head and face. He looked like Jesus Christ. At first I had to laugh so I went on and grabbed the camera and took a picture. One of the guys took my asp and started "poking" at his dick. Again I thought, okay that's funny then it hit me, that's a form of molestation.

The image of a man with his underwear over his face is incongruent—it mixes up bodily regions and functions (*You don't eat where you shit*)—and Harman "had to laugh." She thought, "That's funny." But as the situation escalated, "it hit [her], that's a form of molestation." It's exactly this sort of situation that provides a fertile ground for smut. Contradictory signals—violence and fun, as with the Rat Man's "p.c." that turned to "p.f."—can scramble a person's ability to interpret what's happening. It makes the benign funnier, as with tickling. But it also makes the malicious more dangerous, able to be passed off as play: think of the "boys will be boys" argument. ("He was funny," Lynndie England, another soldier involved in the abuses at Abu Ghraib, says of ringleader Charles Graner, "the jokester.")

What's particular about smut is that its aggression is triangulated and doesn't work without the third element, the bystander's laughter. It creates an incentive for the aggressor: the greater the bystander's expression of pleasure, the greater the ability of the aggressor to disguise his aggression.

Triangulation in relationships offers people a way of concealing their emotions, even from themselves, by metonymically displacing them.

When someone sleeps with their best friend's partner, for example, they can safely express their desire for their friend by proxy. This dynamic is particularly common between straight friends who, fearing their homoerotic desire, find themselves both sleeping with the same person instead of with each other.

Part of what adds to the confusion of the triangulated scenario in smut is that the bystander can just as easily slide toward a different angle of the triangle and identify with the unsettled reaction of the object, as Harman did. Ford's portrayal of Judge seems to indicate that even as she clocked his laughter, she sensed some ambivalence—he "was urging Brett on, although at times he told Brett to stop" and she "made eye contact with [him] and thought he might try to help [her], but he did not." As in Kant's tale about the Indian and Chappelle's "Dudes' Night Out," there's no greater foe of laughter than emotion. If the bystander's disturbance causes them to step out of the formation, the triangle collapses, and what's left is a direct, undeniable line between the aggressor and their victim, which, without the emotions signaled by laughter, is much more difficult to pass off as play.

It makes sense that Ford says it is the laughter she remembers most, because it was one of several factors that likely skewed her coordinates of reality. (Being transformed from a subject—a person in control of their own body and desires—to an object at someone else's mercy is another reliable way of doing this, and that disorientation leads to its own form of trauma.) Rearranging another's coordinates of reality, also known as gaslighting, accompanies most forms of abuse, whether physical or emotional, overt or covert. For an adolescent—a foreigner in the land of adulthood—there is also the added pressure of being expected to take things the right way. Several stock phrases are frequently used, like canned laughter is, to control the interpretation of others in hostile circumstances: *Don't take it the wrong way; Lighten up; Can't you take a joke?*

Later in the Senate hearings, when Kavanaugh was being questioned by Senator Amy Klobuchar, he skewed her coordinates of reality as well by flipping their roles and turning one of her questions back onto her:

KLOBUCHAR: So you're saying there's never been a case where you drank so much that you didn't remember what happened the night before or part of what happened.

KAVANAUGH: It's—you're asking about, you know, blackout. I don't know. Have you?

It's clear how much Kavanaugh's inversion of their roles and the power differential between them scrambles Klobuchar's thinking:

KLOBUCHAR: Could you answer the question, Judge? I just—so you—that's not happened. Is that your answer?

This kind of scrambling, evident in the disintegration of Klobuchar's speech ("I just—so you—that's not happened. Is that your answer?"), indicates that her coordinates of reality are momentarily skewed by Kavanaugh, who is trying to determine the axis of reality like history's actors (*We're an empire now, and when we act, we create our own reality*). Perhaps the enaction of this kind of scrambling during the hearings was the strongest evidence presented of why Kavanaugh was not suited to become a Supreme Court justice.

A gaslighter is another version of history's actors, a person who creates their own reality when they act, then insidiously draws another person into that constructed universe. The now-ubiquitous term comes from the 1944 film *Gaslight* and is used to refer to the process by which one person alters another's sense of reality by strategically planting false perceptual cues. The film narrativizes the gaslighting process through a man who seduces and marries a young woman to gain access to her dead aunt's home in hopes of stealing her jewels. To induce her to unsee what she sees, the husband convinces the wife that her perceptions are detached from concrete reality, that what she sees isn't there, including the dimmed lights, which he manipulates from behind the scenes (the source of the film's title). She comes to believe, like Sartre's man at the keyhole, that he knows her better than she knows herself: if he says she is mentally unstable, it must be true.

In a sense, a gaslighter creates a transitional space that bridges a fictional reality and the real one, but with the goal of manipulation. The methodology of a gaslighter is very similar to that of a totalitarian leader, as described by Arendt, in that it takes a premise that is irrational (the fiction the gaslighter wants to create) and deduces from it logically in such a way that the rational deduction, the parade of logical thinking, is foregrounded, while the premise remains hidden behind a burning spectacle of reason. If the deduction is connected to a recognizable idea, the mind will imitate its logic without thinking—fall into the familiar rhythm of its marching song—and without registering the premise upon which it is based. Military marching songs, in fact, use familiar rhythms and rhymes to lull the mind in precisely this way, causing the meaning of the words to disappear. By targeting the body, tendentious messages infiltrate the mind surreptitiously, then influence us from within.

Days after Ford appeared before the Senate, Trump ridiculed her testimony during a political rally in Mississippi ("How did you get home? I don't remember. How did you get there? I don't remember. Where's the place? I don't remember"). The audience behind him roared with laughter. The triangle set up between Trump, Ford, and the audience is a reenactment of the scene of smut between Kavanaugh, Ford, and Judge, with Trump in the role of Kavanaugh attacking Ford, and the audience, acting as one, taking up the position of the third-party bystander, a collective Judge. Trump not only defends Kavanaugh, but reenacts the trauma, much like the phrase *can't you take a joke* redoubles an insult: first by disowning responsibility for aggression by casting it as humor, then by adding the element of shame that emerges from the target's not knowing how to take things—like a foreigner who doesn't grasp the codes (*Foreigners are funny!*).

Not long after the rally, the audience's laughter was publicly criticized, with much of the outrage directed toward a particular laugher standing behind Trump. That figure, Joe Davidson, a Mississippian, had been enlisted to play a part, much as professional laughers and mourners are hired to perform emotions that sweeten the desired message in hopes that it will spread. First, Davidson received a call asking him to be a Trump campaign chair for his Mississippi county during the 2016 election, writes Stephanie McCrummen in a *Washington Post* article, and later he was invited to stand behind the president at the rally described above. Davidson and his friend Kenny, who stood beside him, "were having the time of their life" when Trump began to attack Ford:

> Trump started mocking her spotty memory, repeating "I don't remember!" and "I don't know!" over and over as people in the crowd began laughing and clapping, and Joe had joined in. He clapped and laughed and elbowed Kenny, who laughed too, and soon a video clip of the two of them was flying around the Internet. By the time Joe got back to Cleveland, friends were forwarding him angry online comments from all over the country.

Davidson's laughter, as he described it, had less to do with what Trump was saying than the crowd's "'geehawing,' an old Southernism that meant they were aligned," reported McCrummen. Crowd behavior hinges on this sensation of alignment, when the individual's conscious personality disappears and the unconscious predominates, so that they turn, as Le Bon puts it, "by means of suggestion and contagion of feelings and ideas in an identical direction." This suggestion and contagion have the power to pull the emotions of a crowd in all sorts of directions (think of the Capitol riots on January 6, 2021), which is likely what led to the curation of the figures seen behind Trump's podium during his speeches and rallies.

In 2015, an image went viral of a young Black woman seated behind Trump at a rally, reading Claudia Rankine's groundbreaking book of poetry *Citizen*, which explores everyday racism in America. Twenty-three-year-old Johari Osayi Idusuyi had ended up at the rally by chance. She was not a supporter, but when a friend offered her an extra ticket, she figured, "If you have the chance to see a presidential candidate, why not?" Upon entering the venue, she saw open seats on the stage and moved toward them but was told by an organizer that they were for VIPs. Minutes later, a man approached her and her friends and offered them the seats, which they took. She didn't like what Trump was saying, was disturbed by the way he bullied protesters in the crowd, so she pulled the book out of her bag and began to read.

Later, when the image went viral, it was interpreted as a form of protest—and, in many ways, it was. In turning her attention away from Trump, who was the group's focus, she was publicly withdrawing support from him, because, as literary critic Michael Warner explains, "belonging to a public seems to require at least minimal participation. . . . Merely paying attention can be enough to make you a member." In shifting her focus toward *Citizen*, she not only refused to be a member of Trump's audience but inserted into his public a book that expresses the interiority of a Black person's experience, an image that then functioned as a synecdoche—a part that drew into the scenario the whole of a marginalized perspective that Trump chooses to ignore. As the rally ended and people stood, waved "Trump" signs, and cheered, Idusuyi stood, too, smiled, and waved her copy of *Citizen*.

A person's assertion of a conscious personality in a crowd, like the work of a caricature artist, makes visible deep-seated, previously unacknowledged dynamics, emotions, or fears within the group and magnifies them to unmistakable proportions. The risk of having someone in the camera frame behaving off script, bringing in uncurated issues like race, likely contributed to the strategic casting of laughers at rallies that ensued. It became rare to see a person of color standing behind Trump at televised rallies, whereas hand-picked supporters, like Davidson, could be relied upon to show up, geehaw, and fuel the unconscious of the crowd, compelling everyone to turn in an identical direction, chant familiar rhythms and rhymes, laugh on cue.

When organisms use metacommunication, it is most often to ensure the survival of the species. Certain birds—plovers, for instance—

fake injury, pretend to be easy prey to draw predators toward them and away from the nest. Femme fatale fireflies mimic the flash signals of the females of one of their prey species to attract the males, eat them, and ingest their predator-repelling chemicals. All these modes of metacommunication, like a woman laughing in face of a creepy man, are enlisted as defenses against predation—not to get a vote.

Laughter that has nothing to do with humor or survival but is used to communicate outside of language often crops up in contexts involving aggression, nervousness, or power to manipulate, control, or subvert. Even when its goal is to incite positive emotion—for example, to make someone feel affirmed—non-Duchenne laughter is manipulative. If you genuinely feel positively toward another person, wouldn't they sense it? Why is it necessary to enlist metacommunicative signals to underscore feelings that are already there?

The idea that laughter can be anything but genuine and good-natured is very upsetting to people—there is something sacrosanct about laughter and the message it delivers that most prefer not to complicate. Yet without awareness of the complex cluster of emotions laughter carries, we run the risk of losing touch with what we think and feel, engaging in metacommunicative signaling that triggers implants rather than authentic conversations. Even in therapy sessions, particularly when something emotionally difficult comes to mind, an analysand will often use non-Duchenne laughter to put their social self forward, armor themselves with signals that communicate positive or coded feeling as a way of eclipsing uglier, less-sanctioned parts of themselves they worry will lead to judgment.

Perhaps, then, what makes the laughter that accompanies smut particularly pernicious is the way it hides a malevolent power dynamic behind a surface of good-natured play. Smut conceals a predatory exchange, most often between men, triangulated through an objectified party, most often a woman, fueling a circuit of power and libido at her expense, as Ford put it.

The positions occupied in the triangle can be metonymically displaced by other figures that express equivalent power positioning in the social structure of a particular historical moment. In place of the woman, in other words, one may find a figure subjected to a different kind of oppression (race, class, sexual orientation, physical ability, religion) that maintains the underlying structure even as the surface content changes, the way the original real estate theme in the game Monopoly is continually updated and displaced by pop culture motifs, such as Harry Potter, *Game of Thrones*, or *Stranger Things*, without being altered at the foundational level. The game's formula remains the same, but the shift in theme calls up a new set of associations that will align more closely to what is on people's minds at a particular cultural moment, making it possible to tap into the collective unconscious and draw more players to the table.

The original game that became Monopoly, called the Landlord's Game, was meant to be instructive and had two sets of rules: one anti-monopolist set and another set that became the monopolist game most of us know today. Because crushing opponents with monopolies resonated more with the American collective unconscious in the cultural space-time after the Great Depression than did the idea of an equal distribution of wealth, the monopolist set of rules survived and the anti-monopolist version fell away.

Tapping into the unconscious, provoking pattern recognition, is a critical element in marketing a product, getting a laugh, gaslighting, designing clickbait, or any other process that leads its target to believe someone else holds the missing piece or truth about reality that will reveal who they *really* are. Knowledge about one's own interior can then be accessed only through the other's perspective, by understanding what it is they know.

Years ago, desperate to find a babysitter in a short period of time, I joined two local parents' groups on the web and remained subscribed to them long after my situation had been resolved. I didn't know then that I could receive digests instead of individual messages each time members emailed the group, so my in-box was flooded with messages I never read, messages I would delete ten or twenty at a time.

As I was deleting a group of messages I had received from the Park Slope Parents LISTSERV, a subject heading caught my eye as the delete function took it away: "Arab sex DSC-00465.jpg." I opened my trash folder and found a number of emails in the thread under that subject heading. I clicked on what looked like the original post, but there was no text or attachment. As I searched the folder for the message with the attachment—wondering what it meant, what might be in that JPEG—my curiosity intensified into hunger, a driven disquiet.

"Race is like pornography in the United States," according to journalist Bob Herbert, "the dirty stories and dirty pictures that everyone professes to hate but no one can resist." As I searched my trash folder with the same rush of adrenaline I would have felt flipping through a lover's notebook to discover what they thought of me, to discover who I was from the perspective of another, all I could find was an empty message with an attachment that wouldn't open, one the LISTSERV's filter had undoubtedly kept from going through. The floorboards creaked behind me. Race, pornography, and the odd sense that the missing photograph would somehow have me in it seemed to hush around me, like a joke that couldn't be told in my presence.

I follow the details of war in Iraq and its endless reverberations with a similar intensity: it is the I and the not-I that I am discovering, as though my identity were being revealed through the gazes of others. In college, reading feminist texts, I would read "men" and think "they," "women" and also think "they." I couldn't manage to find myself in the us of them. I was on the outside looking in, stepping into someone else's perspective in order to fit into one of the categories. I find myself in the same state of alienation when I read the newspaper: "Iraqis" are "I" and also "they"—a group I belong to but am separated from by the location of my birth—while "Americans" are similarly "I" and "they"—a "they" that I belong to, thus also a "we," but a "we" that I sometimes feel conflicted about being a part of because of the violence it has done to the rest of us, that other we of me.

There was a radio ad that used to play in the morning as my father drove my brother and me to school. "You're driving," a deep voice began. "Your wife is in the passenger seat. Your children are in the back . . ." Each time I heard the ad I would think, He's not talking to me, and tune out. And why listen? Unless something in the speaker, in the person you imagine the speaker to be, makes you yearn for inclusion, why keep listening, rearrange yourself to fit the shape of the addressee you're picturing?

And why click on the JPEG? Such an impulse is recognizable when it comes to advertising, the illusion that you can transform your very being through a product—just spray Beautiful, Allure, Obsession, Happy, Fame, Romance, Bombshell, Heat, Black Opium, Killer Queen, Poison, Meow!, Exclamation, Euphoria, Passion, Yacht Man, Millionaire, Homme, Eros, Swiss Army, Only the Brave, Dark Rebel Rider, Ultimo, Invictus, or Thallium onto your body and you will transmogrify into the alluring source of others' obsessions behind the wheel of a Humvee or running barefoot along the seashore, hair flowing, disappearing into smoke. These prototypes are clear, heavy-handed. But what would the urge to see Arab sex tap into?

Computer viruses are a form of art and a form of prophecy. They make wagers about the unconscious while simultaneously creating it. The lure at the end of the hook must appear real, juicy enough for us to click, to take the bait. We bring our unconscious to the subject headings of the viruses that float into our in-boxes at the same time as they provide us with a shape, a container into which we can project our unprocessed thoughts.

Walking my children to school one morning, I noticed that each time my daughter took a step with her right foot, it followed a convoluted trajectory in the air, a makeshift *demi rond de jambe*, before touching the ground. I stopped her to ask why she was walking so strangely. She lifted her foot and showed me her shoe: the sole, partially detached from the boot, flapped like a thirsty dog's tongue. Her peculiar gait was an adaptation created to keep her from tripping.

The shoe's structure configured her behavior. Human beings are subject to ontological design: we design our world, and our world, in turn, designs us. The sole, like the soul Michel Foucault describes ("the effect and instrument of a political anatomy"), is something external that inhabits us, brings us "to existence," the way language does: it exists before we come into being, lives inside of us during our lifetimes—shapes our thoughts, relationships, and experiences—then goes back into the world to live on after we die. The soul, according to Foucault, "is the prison of the body."

A person training to become a United States Marine is required to refer to themselves in the third person (*this recruit*). They accept their interior, like a command, from the external world. By no longer identifying as an individual, they become a member of the corps, "the effect and instrument of a political anatomy," a sole or boot on the ground, a synecdoche, or a part that stands in for the whole.

Observing my daughter through the one-way window of her preschool classroom during free play, I noticed that when the teacher asked who was behind a transgression, my daughter looked up from her activity and caught the teacher's eye. By turning around, she accepted the blame, stepped into the role the teacher's question called into being. Philosopher Louis Althusser gives an example of this dynamic, which he calls interpellation, through a scenario in which a police officer on the street calls, "Hey, you there!" and a person standing nearby turns. By turning, answering the call, the person takes the position that is being addressed and, in so doing, becomes a subject of the law and subject to it, an effect of its political anatomy.

As soon as I wondered what Arab sex would look like, the seed of fascination had been planted, was ready to grow. Like the man at the keyhole, I had been interpellated.

When I first saw the subject heading, I couldn't call up anything from my mind that could be used to imaginatively fill in the content of the promised JPEG. I googled "Arab sex" and saw dozens of hits of a pornographic nature, mostly dating sites. A year later, as I was googling "Arab sex" again, it became clear that the virus had proliferated, at least in the collective unconscious. There were YouTube videos, porn sites. One site shows an image of a woman in an abaya that alternates with her naked genitals above frames of her having sex with a faceless man. The text reads, "Layla, liberated MILF from Qatar—Age: 31. Sexy Arab housewife Layla from Qatar takes it for the first [*sic*] from our white stud and loves it! This Arab mom has sexiness dripping from her." Another film plot reads, "Watch this pretty arab village girl get pounded in every hole and her pretty face plastered in cum for the first time on camera." A photo for a different film shows a man grabbing a woman's chin and her head by the hair as he rapes her. "Iraq Babes," created by a Hungarian site called Sex in War, shows photos in which soldiers gang-rape Iraqi women. There was a controversy over whether the women were actors, agents who had chosen to participate in the project, or whether they had been treated like objects and manipulated in its execution.

The fantasy of Arab sex is clearly a fantasy of domination. As the viewer steps into the role of a "white stud," the sexual fantasy becomes a rape fantasy, aggression merges with lust. The sadistic element is portrayed as desired (*and loves it!*), a gift of freedom to be rewarded with flowers and candy—as former vice president Dick Cheney once imagined the invading American soldiers would be greeted—or a home-cooked meal.

The radio was on in the kitchen as I was preparing dinner. We were spending a summer weekend in the country. I could see my daughters through the window on the grassy hill, rolling, rolling. Water was running over vegetables in the sink when snippets of a story caught my ear: "allegations . . . US soldiers raped . . . body burned . . . house burned . . ." I turned off the faucet, walked toward the radio, and increased the volume, but the story had already ended. The voice

recounted a different news story, but my mind spoke over it: *soldiers . . .
raped . . . body burned . . . house burned.*

In an episode of the television comedy series *Ramy*, about a first-
generation Arab American family with two American-born twenty
something children struggling to find their place in the world, Dena,
the daughter, is on date with a fellow graduate student, a White man,
who is fascinated by her ethnic background. He invites her to his
apartment for a home-cooked meal, and after some conversation, they
begin to kiss. As the kissing gets more heated, they move to the bedroom and begin to take off their clothes. He asks Dena to speak Arabic
and, turned on by the sound of the foreign words, says, "Are you sure
you want to have sex with me even though I'm a White infidel?"

> "Um, what?"
> "I can just stick it in your ass and you can still be a virgin. Is
> that what you want?"
> "Wait, what?"
> "What?"
> "What are you saying?"
> "Oh, no, I was just—I was just doing a little roleplay, like."
> "Oh. Oh, okay."
> "Yeah."
> "Uh, yeah. Can we just have normal sex?"
> "Yeah, no, totally. Yeah, yeah, yeah. Yeah sure. . . ."
> "Uh, okay, yeah. Let's get these clothes off you. . . . You can
> just, like, be yourself. I accept you. You don't have to wear a fuck-
> ing headscarf or—"
> "What, dude!"
> "No, right, sorry. I'll stop. Because you want me to stop, right?"
> "Yeah, um, can we just roleplay that I'm a White girl?"

It quickly becomes clear that the two are approaching the encounter
at cross-purposes: while he is turned on by the idea of Arab sex, she is
hoping for the sex to be "normal," which she suggests would require

him to see her as "a White girl" (much like Huck Finn needed to view Jim as "white inside" for him to seem worthy of love).

Ironically, in the 2020 US Census, the section asking respondents to select their race offers as examples of ethnicities that would be considered "White," "Egyptian," and "Lebanese." In *Dow v. United States* (1915), Syrian immigrant George Dow was twice denied citizenship because he was identified as "Asiatic" and not a free White person, as the Naturalization Act of 1790 required. Dow argued that he was Semitic, like European Jews, who were able to become citizens. The judge disagreed, saying, according to historian Sarah Gualtieri, that a European Jew was foremost a European, "racially, physiologically, and psychologically a part of the peoples he lives among." Because the term *White* is imaginary, the criteria for determining race in these cases was subjective. Some judges took into account what they saw as being denoted by skin tone: one dismissed an Arab seeking citizenship as "undisputedly dark brown in color," while in another case involving a Syrian seeking naturalization, the lawyer for the government asked the plaintiff to take his shirt off as proof that he was not White.

At the beginning of the twentieth century, explains Gualtieri, "anxieties over America's 'foreign element,'"—which involved "elaborate theories of the contaminating effect" of immigrants who were "neither white nor black in the southern racial scheme of things" and "linked immigration to contagion and disease"—were fueled by the government, which "quarantin[ed] entire immigrant neighborhoods, ostensibly to control a disease that they believed was spread by immigrant habits." Placing immigrants on one or the other side of the already-problematic binary racial structure of America only reinforces that structure, just as Trump's attempts to seal the border with the Muslim Ban, to create detention camps for people trying to enter the country from Mexico, and to build a wall are really ways of delineating what Ellison calls an "outsider" as a way to create a self.

Dow eventually won the case, but being legally White plays out very differently from being perceived as "white inside"—by oneself or by others. "The Census Bureau counts us as white," explains writer

Laila Lalami, "yet we are often treated as nonwhite in encounters with the state or its agents." Not collecting specific data on Arabs has freed the government to "tes[t] the boundaries of citizenship," keep Muslims and Arab Americans "teeter[ing] on the edge of belonging and unbelonging: They may be citizens, but they are also perpetual suspects, always having to show their allegiance through silence or acquiescence." To count Arab Americans as White is strategic because the census influences how power is distributed by determining congressional redistricting. It is no coincidence that "the [census] bureau's Senior Executive Service is overwhelmingly white," as National Public Radio reports.

The very idea of Whiteness is a carefully curated implant used to control people from within. Though the desire to have basic rights—as well as the more complicated impulse, conscious and unconscious, to align oneself with those in dominant positions in order to amplify one's own sense of power—is understandable, when agency gets conflated with being considered "White," when the metonymic displacement, the movement of the spider crawling out of the ear, is treated as though it were a component of concrete reality, an actual *thing*, we are living in an alternate universe created by history's actors. By not gathering evidence that might adjust ideas about Muslims and Arabs, immigrants—all human beings—they remain subject to perversion, to being twisted to fit fantasies (White/non-White), even by themselves. We are all subject to interpellation.

When I searched my trash folder for the original post under "Arab sex," I noticed a number of other email messages with lures in their subject lines: "fuckin karmasutra pics" and "The Best Video Clip Ever." The text of one of these read, "R U ready 2 be fucked?"

"You know," says film producer Brian Grazer, "in order to make somebody laugh, you have to be interesting, and in order to be interesting, you have to do things that are mean. Comedy comes out of anger, and interesting comes out of angry; otherwise there is no conflict." Conflict, like the tension between contradictory emotions (particularly when one of them is taboo), is a trigger for laughter.

The violation within the ethnic pornography of Arabs that has been in circulation since the attacks of 9/11 also comes out of anger. As does most ethnic pornography and humor, it plays with fetishized tropes and taboos, and frequently expresses a sadistic relation to the ethnic group—here, Arabs—being pornographically displayed. If racism is a form of perversion, then, as with a fetish, there is also likely to be a titillating element within it, an erotics of hatred that drives a person to click on the attachment, object to an Arab woman covering herself up, choosing her narrative. If that person has authority, they may even fine her, as sports federations did Lynch and Osaka, if she doesn't give the public what it wants from her.

On the beach in Cannes with her children in 2016, a thirty-four-year-old Muslim woman, wearing leggings, a tunic, and a hijab, was approached by three police officers, who told her if she didn't remove her headscarf, she would be fined. People on the beach crowded around, called, "Go home!" and "We're Catholics here."

"I felt like I was watching a pack of hounds attack a woman who was sitting down, in tears, with her young daughter," says a French journalist who witnessed the scene.

If you want to hook someone, you need to lure them with bait. For that bait to be enticing, to draw out the hound in you, it has to induce a kind of hunger. For someone to want to see what's in the attachment that a computer virus's heading dangles out, it has to be interesting, and to be interesting, according to Grazer, it has to be mean. If you take the bait, open the attachment, your interest in what the subject heading presents—Arab sex—will have resonated with something already inside you and provoked a response similar to what Clarke terms "*it's so true* humour."

Clarke's theory is based, again, on the notion that completing a pattern, like placing the last piece in a puzzle, elicits a cognitive pleasure that is often marked by laughter. There are different kinds of patterns that provoke this response, and sometimes they can span several psyches, so that the element that completes a pattern in one person's speech is supplied by a different person's mind. It is this sort of recognition that stand-up comedy taps into, in which audience members match a comedian's jokes with mental images, even those that have not previously made their way to consciousness. The laughter that results is expressive in that it reveals that some version of the message within the joke already existed in the mind of the audience member.

Many jokes are constructed through audience participation, as Baron Cohen explains: "When I, as Ali G, asked the astronaut Buzz Aldrin, 'What woz it like to walk on de sun?' the joke worked, because we, the audience, shared the same facts. If you believe the moon landing was a hoax, the joke was not funny." "*It's so true* humour" can be experienced as surprise because it holds a mirror up to beliefs that might not yet be fully formulated in your mind or might not fit with your idea of self. The pattern of recognition then exists "between life and its representation," with "the detail of the individual's memory" acting itself as "a term within the pattern," Clarke says.

That resonance—between an external element and a detail within—is recognized, but, if clocked as inappropriate, will likely cross-circuit laughter, which signifies like-mindedness (*Our laughter is always the laughter of a group*). If a joke is unequivocally offensive to a person, their negative feeling will make laughter impossible—as occurred with me when I read Kant's story about the Indian and likely with audience members watching "Dudes' Night Out" (*Laughter has no greater foe than emotion*). Even as the structure of a performance, the fourth wall, permits the audience to disidentify with the resonant element—the term inside them that completes a joke—it will nevertheless draw them into the pattern. They—all of us—are quantum entangled with everything around them.

The heading "Arab Sex" lures you to participate bodily in the emotion you imagine that the photographer snapping the JPEG possesses, much like Bataille's description of how we experience another's laughter, yawning, excitement, and nakedness from within our own bodies. Seated at a safe distance, the voyeuristic onlooker who clicks on the attachment likely expects something demeaning and titillating, a much softer version of the arousal felt by the US Army soldiers who gang-raped Abeer Qassim Hamza al-Janabi, the fourteen-year-old Iraqi girl they had been watching from their checkpoint. The soldiers shot her parents and six-year-old sister, raped her, put a bullet through her head, crushed her skull, and then set her legs and torso on fire. *Body burned, house burned.* Directionless hate in the form of violence: the desire to fuck, the desire to destroy. The desire to fuck as a way of destroying, a detail of memory finding its element of resonance in the external world.

"Watch tour of the alleged crime scene—2:15," read the hyperlink in a news story on CNN about the soldiers who raped Abeer. I clicked on the link to see the girl's burned-down house, but before I was routed there, an ad for Viagra popped up. The connection was uncanny—that the crime scene of the premeditated gang rape, quadruple murder, and flames set to destroy the evidence (the witnesses, the girl) would conjure erections.

Pop-up ads operate much like derivatives of the unconscious, seemingly random associations that flash before us. When we are browsing the web, we see pop-up ads sprinkled about, along with links, associations, clips from our history—all of which operate like a version of the collective unconscious. As we go about our day, we experience the equivalent of pop-up ads, "you might also like"s—associations, images, memories, fantasy thought streaming from our internal projector—that intrude upon our thinking and reconfigure it.

After gang-raping and murdering Abeer and killing her family, the soldiers—who had planned the crime while drinking whiskey and playing cards—returned to their base and reportedly grilled chicken wings. Did they not draw a connection between burning flesh here and burning flesh there?

Lynndie England, the most famous soldier in the Abu Ghraib photographs, had worked at Pilgrim's Pride, a chicken processing factory in West Virginia, as a mixer in marination. Such plants are notorious for their inhumane treatment of chickens; a PETA activist who worked at the plant undercover found that to reduce the number of chickens on the conveyor belt on their way to being slaughtered, they were thrown into a large bin, where the birds at the bottom suffocated. On one occasion, approximately two hundred live chickens "were slammed against the wall by employees. Several hours later, many of the birds were still alive."

England's sister, Jessie Klinestiver, reported that the workers were told specifically not to have sex with the chickens: "They told me that people there actually fucked chickens," she said. "They'd grab the beaks and rip them apart and make them bigger. Then they shoved their sexual parts into their beaks." So-called standard practices slide easily toward abuse both in the chicken factory and at Abu Ghraib, explain bioethicist Peter Singer and animal advocate Karen Dawn:

> Also common to both situations are issues of status and authority. Slaughterhouse work is unpleasant and poorly paid, and the workers are among society's powerless. At Abu Ghraib, the soldiers abusing Iraqi prisoners were from the lower ranks of the Army. But both the slaughterhouse workers and the soldiers could assert some power, the power they had over their charges.

The chickens and the prisoners had become self-objects, moved around in the external world in order for the perpetrators to move something around—a sense of powerlessness—internally, imply Dawn and Singer.

A rebel army in the Democratic Republic of the Congo, according to journalist Daniel Bergner, cannibalized its rivals because "eating the flesh, especially the organs, of your enemy is a way to augment your own power." Bergner describes UN investigators writing that "cannibalism, particularly concerning the Pygmies' internal body parts such as the heart and liver, can be considered to be pure fetishism aimed at helping the perpetrators to acquire the capacity and ability of the victims to hunt and live in the forest." For there to be fetishism, "pure" or impure, the fetish object would be imbued with psychological meaning, so that rather than working through thoughts and feelings inside themselves, the fetishist would instead modulate their emotions through proxy objects in the external world.

A cannibal incorporates the part they imagine embodies the other's power to make it their own. Projection, conversely, throws the self onto the other, while projective identification—far more complex and insidious—splits off unwanted parts of the self and deposits them into another person, interpolates them, as Cavett attempted to do to Murphy. The person who becomes a container for the other's split-off parts will often feel an unconscious pull to take the position called into being by the unwanted negative parts they then contain, as though they were being controlled from within, or "possessed," as Murphy put it, in highlighting Cavett's attempt to disown his racist part (*Did I say that?*) as a way of reattaching it to Cavett, where it belonged.

Although it is an omnipotent fantasy, projective identification has real psychological effects on both the projector and the person who unwittingly receives the projections, much as the virtual image we have of another person structures the way we deal with them at the phenomenological level—which explains, in part, the violence that is done when someone uses the N-word. Bion terms the projected elements, once deposited into another person, "bizarre bits" because once they have been incorporated, the person containing them transforms into what he calls a bizarre object. Othello, after receiving Iago's projections by way of litotes, becomes a bizarre object, "a figure of projection," according to scholar Alessandro Serpieri, that allows the projector to "affirm in the 'other' all that . . . it refutes or censures in the 'self.'"

A bizarre object, psychoanalyst W. W. Meissner explains, becomes "composed of parts of the self and parts of the object in a relationship of container and contained that strips both of any inherent vitality or meaning." Projecting parts of the self into others not only turns those who then contain those parts into bizarre objects—often violently—but depletes the remaining interior of the person doing the projecting so that, as with Tabensky's emptied-out racist subject or an As-If personality, there is the sense that there is no living person directing the actions or speech of the automaton before you. Like the dog of habit that Beckett describes as chained to its vomit, a projector puts out into the world what was already inside them, then takes it back in as though it were of the world, but with the same repulsion that would accompany drinking their own saliva from a glass.

At the same time, the person whose interior gets filled with what are essentially the implants of others will inevitably lose a sense of inherent vitality or meaning, a connection to their own emotional panelboard. In *Blade Runner*, the aim of the corporation placing implants within the replicants is to fill any opening through which original emotions and meaning might develop. If the replicants merely simulated the feelings, beliefs, and expectations of the implants, they would become programmatic, prototypical As-If characters who were easier to control. Implants, like Foucault's soul, can be the prison of the body.

Genuine feeling and meaning, by contrast, are often tools of resistance and change—of freedom—because they are driven by desires that have been generated from what Bayes called "the source," as opposed to from implanted bizarre bits that signal what it is you *should* want from inside (making it easy to mistake them for your own thoughts and feelings). The most effective way to control people, as colonizers have known for centuries, is to infiltrate their psychology with oppressive ideologies that operate like implants and direct them from within.

One of the goals of psychoanalysis is to know your desire, and part of that quest involves becoming conscious of the implants within you. When writing a love letter, the Marquise de Merteuil, one of the protagonists in Pierre Choderlos de Laclos's *Dangerous Liaisons*, advises her protégée, Cécile, it is important to remember that, because it's "meant for [your recipient] and not for you. . . . You must try not to say what you really think but what you think [your recipient will] most enjoy hearing." This advice helps the young lover achieve success, yet at an ambition that the Marquise de Merteuil—like a colonizer—has implanted inside her. Cécile, strategically manipulated to believe the implanted desires are her own, furthers her adviser's agenda without realizing it, like the replicants in *Blade Runner*, who unknowingly serve the Tyrell Corporation that designed them.

Distinguishing between what you think you want—which is often what you are told or trained to want—and what you truly want is to differentiate between desires emerging from your True Self and False Self, the cake you have the urge to spontaneously swipe as it crosses your pathway and the one you eat to call up pleasure in others.

The sense that achieving your desires can occur only by way of the Other also makes it difficult to discern between what you genuinely want and what you imagine is wanted from you by others, particularly those in a position to dole out rewards. Indicators of desire can sometimes be expressed indirectly—envy, for example, can be such an indicator ("Tell me what you need to spoil," writes psychoanalyst Adam Phillips, "and I will tell you what you want"). To know your desire only through another's perspective, determine its value by reading their emotions or knowledge, is to transform from a subject into an object—to become a great consumer.

⌐▪

As I was about to make coffee one morning, I noticed while reaching for the canister of beans that a creature had chewed through the corner of a plastic bag containing bread. A pile of crumbs lay before the coffee maker, and scattered on and around the mound were tiny bits of shit.

Later that day, while teaching, I suddenly thought, Could it have been a rat? The moment the possibility sprang to mind, I shuddered.

In order to return to my professorial duties and focus on the discussion before me, I pushed the thought into the walls of my mind.

I hoped the creature, too, would slip back into invisibility. I hoped this again later in the day, after thinking about what I would have to do if it did not, what kind of trap I would use (this occurred before the sticky trap revelation in the pantry). Visualizing finding a live rodent twisting in glue or upside down with a trap stuck to its front side, perhaps sounding its pain, was horrific. But the option of a guillotine, or snap trap, was also disturbing because it brought to mind the possibility of blood—of mouse or rat—a stray limb or tail, or a trail of blood leading to a dismembered or partially dismembered body. If I put out poison, though, it could die in the walls and rot there, leaving a telltale stench of my crime. At the same time, I knew I couldn't handle the ethical option, feel a live rodent move against my hands as I carried it in a box to the park, even with a screen between my body and its movements. The sticky trap was the best alternative. But then I would have to—what? Put it in a garbage bag, still alive, and walk it to the corner trash can? That option would best disavow my knowledge, help me to not see or unsee what I would know even if it wasn't seen. Mice, rats, rodents have long been metonyms for knowledge in my personal mythology, knowledge that is known and unknown, the unknown known, the unspoken that slips like a mouse between dreams.

A few hours later, in analysis (all analysts have to go through a training analysis), I talked about the crumbs, the shit, my long-standing musophobia, my anxiety around the idea of a rodent in my home, what I should do. Then I said, But I feel like there's something more—

Yes, my analyst cut in. Somebody intrudes upon your life, shits all over the place, and what are you going to do about it?

That evening, a friend came over for dinner with her child. I told her about the mouse and my anxiety around all the different ways of killing it. She described a more humane solution she had used with the mice in her country house. She had hired someone who gave them something that made them so thirsty that they went outside to find water. I wondered what it was, this magic elixir, but was not prepared to pay an enormous fee to find out. Besides, my engagement with the rodent(s?) had reached psychic proportions. I had to deal with it myself.

Still, I did nothing. I did nothing but hope the rodent would go away of its own accord. Later that night, on the phone with my mother, she suggested poison. But what if they die in the walls and decompose? I asked. The poison, she explained, makes them thirsty, so they go outside to find water. My friend, I realized, had hired someone not only to get rid of the mice but to protect her from the truth and any guilt that might accompany the recognition that she had killed or had ordered the killing of living beings.

When I walked into the kitchen with my daughter the next morning, there was shit everywhere. I thought, That's it! and decided to go to the hardware store to buy traps. My daughter offered to go with me.

I discussed the different options with the man who was helping us. He suggested a snap trap that the rodent crawls into, allowing you to pick up the entire thing, body and all, hidden within the box, and throw it away. I went with what I felt I could handle.

As we were walking home, I told my daughter what my analyst had said: Somebody intrudes upon your life, shits all over the place, and what are you going to do about it? Then, regretting not only that I had used a curse word in front of my daughter but had attributed it to my analyst, I tried to unsay what I had said. But she didn't say "shit," I lied.

Well, you did, my daughter told me.

When?

This morning.

What did I say?

You walked into the kitchen and said, There's shit everywhere. That's it! I'm going to fucking kill those motherfuckers!

That night, after everyone was in bed, I set up the trap exactly as the man in the hardware store had taught me. Afterward, as I was falling asleep, the phrase *Aw, snap!* spontaneously erupted from my mouth.

I wondered briefly if that's where the expression comes from, when you think you're going to get one thing but instead get another, the switcheroo of metonymic displacement happening in the open.

The next morning there was a rodent in the trap. I felt victorious, disposed of it, and set up another trap. Then another. I became a warrior. And, somehow sensing it, those motherfuckers fled.

I realized that my phobia had protected me from the recognition of my own aggression, which is provoked when I feel that other people have intruded upon my life to shit all over the place. Aggression, however, is an unacceptable impulse, according to my superego, so having it attached to me destabilizes my idea of who I am. By splitting off my aggression and projecting it into rodents, I was able to create a phobic object that contained unacceptable feelings that had once been inside me. I could then fear rodents, which had become the containers of my disowned taboo emotions (various forms of aggression), and, by fearing the rodents and staying away from then, I could avoid the destabilizing effects that go along with the emotions I had disowned and that the rodents then contained. (Little Hans, Freud's first child analysand, developed a phobic response to horses that worked in a similar way.)

A phobia operates much like a joke or a dream. The phobic object, like the manifest content of a dream or a joking envelope, is not the source of unsettling emotion but its container, the vehicle through which emotions like aggression, sexual desire, and other id impulses flagged by the superego can be avoided. To decipher the latent meaning encoded within a dream, joke, or phobia, you have to analyze the associations that come to mind in relation to what is manifest, on the surface (rodents), and intentionally propel a metonymic chain of free association into motion.

For example, it would have been helpful for me to explore what I had been thinking while teaching just before the rat skittered into my mind. Was it some form of aggression—annoyance with a student, frustration, impatience—that I needed to veer away from, disavow, so I could go back to performing the identity I needed to think of myself as inhabiting, in order to maintain the psychic equilibrium necessary to play the part of professor and return to the material we were discussing?

Freud often points out in his writing how even the most pathological thought processes exist in so-called normal people in watered-down form. As in a dream, the thoughts and images that are made available to our conscious minds are often rearranged into a low-stakes forms that can evade our mind's censor. The ability to identify these psychological dynamics in ourselves, even in seemingly inconsequential scenarios, helps us better understand how they operate, so we can recognize when someone—including ourselves (the we of me)—is reaching for them and try to step in to prevent anyone from getting hurt.

Before going to work one day, shortly after the remaining rodents had fled my home, I left my dogs in the kitchen with the door closed. Immediately after leaving, I remembered the snap traps, worried they might still be set in a corner. I imagined the possibility of one of my dogs getting a paw stuck in a trap, and I suddenly felt dizzy, nauseated. I rushed home, found and removed the traps, but the queasy feeling persisted, morphed into a kind of self-sickness. How had it been tolerable to kill rodents with traps to which I could not bear subjecting my dogs?

A herpetologist friend of mine finds it ethically twisted that categorizing snakes as vermin makes it legal to kill them in parts of the United States, where most other animal species are protected under the law. It becomes likewise acceptable to kill or commit violence against a human being if you call them a terrorist—as Trump did Soleimani and the protesters in DC—or to treat a person, even a child, inhumanely if they are deemed "illegal," because they are either an immigrant, a member of a gang, or a terrorist (the catch-all term for someone evil). A family friend expressed to her grandson her horror at Navy SEAL Eddie Gallagher stabbing a captive Iraqi teenager for sport ("got him with my hunting knife"). Her grandson, around the same age as the boy who had been killed, said, But, Grandma, he was ISIS!

At a protest in Brooklyn, New York, a few days after the murder of George Floyd, New York Police Department scanners picked up radio chatter, including a voice that replied to a police dispatch about protester movement with "Shoot those motherfuckers." Human beings, like animals, objects, concepts, or words, are susceptible to metonymic displacement. Once you imagine that another person embodies the associations you have with them, it becomes easier to manipulate that person like you would an object and, in so doing, modulate your unwieldy feelings.

The stakes are obviously immeasurably high when dealing with a life. Still, in order to understand how a mind operates, it can be helpful to focus on how a mental process works in high- and low-stakes scenarios. To do so, you must attend to the content and the form, as well as to how different content can be inserted into a particular position within a pattern of thought—as with the theme in Monopoly—and displace what had been there before: rodents, horses, dogs, terrorists, protesters—living beings.

Perhaps the thought of the rat that occurred to me while teaching had something to do with the artwork we had been analyzing. We were unpacking a controversy around *Open Casket*, a painting, by Dana Schutz that had been included in the 2017 Whitney Biennial, which has at its center an abstracted image of Emmett Till. In 1955, Carolyn Bryant, a White woman who owned a grocery store, accused Emmett Till, a fourteen-year-old African American boy, of flirting with her, and four days later her husband and brother-in-law abducted, beat, and killed him, mutilated his body, and threw it into the Tallahatchie River. Decades later, Bryant admitted she had made the story up.

Till's image was said by many to have been exploited by Schutz, a White painter. As artist Hannah Black wrote in an open letter to the

Whitney Museum of American Art about its decision to exhibit the work, "*Open Casket* should not be acceptable to anyone who cares or pretends to care about Black people, because it is not acceptable for a white person to transmute Black suffering into profit and fun, though the practice has been normalized for a long time." This kind of transmutation, which is at the core of perverse thinking and racism—changing evidence as opposed to changing your thinking about that evidence—also structures a phobia, which, like a fetish or the alternate version of reality performed by history's actors, restructures your perceptions so that what you want to see is superimposed onto the real.

Applying to Carolyn Bryant the process by which a phobia operates, one can imagine what might have happened between her and Till: Bryant felt desire toward Till that she deemed taboo, split off that desire, projected it into him, and then experienced it as coming at her from the external world. People, like animals, can become phobic objects, depositories for disowned unwanted feelings and parts of the self—as occurs in what psychiatrist and philosopher Frantz Fanon terms "negrophobia."

Negrophobia describes the psychic process by which people split off hated parts of themselves, project them into Black people, then fear Black people because they believe the split-off parts are coming from them. This mode of racism targets other identities as well, and sometimes has a recognizable name—*homophobia, transphobia, Islamophobia*—and sometimes not. When Robert Aaron Long killed eight people, six of them Asian women, at three Atlanta spas in 2021, officials reported that he claimed he was driven by "a temptation for him that he wanted to eliminate," as National Public Radio reported. As with the structure of a phobia, he projected his despised temptation—which he also referred to as a "sex addiction"—into his victims, then tried to kill what he had split off by murdering the people he had imaginatively transformed into containers for those hated parts.

This psychic process is damaging on many levels. The split-off parts, or bizarre bits, though imaginary, are felt to have actual existence by everyone involved (the projector, the container, others entering their

force field). When a human being becomes a container for someone else's split-off hated parts of themselves, those bizarre bits operate
on them from without (by the projector) and also from within—like
ideology—in psychologically complex ways. Fanon explains "the origin of the Antillean's negrophobia" in his realization that "he has been
living a mistake" because he "knows he is black," and that "one is black
as a result of being wicked, spineless, evil, and instinctual. Everything
that is the opposite of this black behavior is white." This belief in "the
collective unconscious," where "black=ugliness, sin, darkness, and im-
morality," is projected into Antilleans and then experienced by them
as a thought that originated in their own minds:

> If I behave like a man with morals, I am not black. Hence the
> saying in Martinique that a wicked white man has the soul of a
> [N-word]. Color is nothing; I don't even see it. The only thing I
> know is the purity of my conscience and the whiteness of my soul.
> "Me white as snow," as the saying goes.

Whiteness is pure because it has split off its hated parts and projected
them into Black people by way of negrophobia. What is the Antillean
or any other person who has been turned into a human phobic object
infected by toxic parts to do? How do the bizarre bits get expelled?

The call for the destruction of *Open Casket* by Hannah Black and
others points to the painting's having likely become a bizarre object
containing not only the painter's bizarre bits but the split-off hated
parts of White people that have been projected into Black bodies—
including that of Emmett Till, the painting's subject—for so long.

The ideal way of working through this kind of projective identification, from a psychoanalytic perspective, would be for the split-off
parts to be reintegrated into the selves that originally housed them,
for the projectors to take back their disowned parts, as Murphy forces
Cavett to do in reattaching the N-word to him. Otherwise, there's a
risk of propelling a metonymic chain of displaced disowned parts into
motion, passing the unwanted bizarre bits from body to body. Aside
from the violence enacted upon the person the bizarre bits are pro-

jected into, the person doing the projecting gets depleted themselves. Reassimilating the disowned parts into the self they originated in would involve changing that self as opposed to changing the other— changing an idea rather than changing evidence in reality, as perverse thinking does.

This approach is precisely what the therapist in Nina Conti's *In Therapy* recommends to Nina: that she integrate her monkey parts into her concept of self rather than split off and project into the puppet what she perceives to be too risky to express as Nina. At times, however, the stakes involved in reintegrating split-off parts feel too high. Splitting is a psychological defense that can be experienced, in certain contexts, as necessary for survival.

Extremely complex power dynamics come into play when another human being is used as a phobic object. *Muselmann* was a term "given to the irreversibly exhausted, worn out prisoner close to death" in concentration camps, according to Levi in *The Drowned and the Saved*, his essayistic meditation on Auschwitz and survival. The word *Muselmann*—used for these suffering, near-death figures walking around like zombies—oddly, translates as "Muslim," and its usage in this context is something many have struggled to understand. Levi offers two explanations, "neither very convincing: fatalism; and the head bandages that could resemble a turban." Others have suggested alternate rationales; "the most likely explanation of the term," according to philosopher Giorgio Agamben, "can be found in the literal meaning of the Arabic word muslim: the one who submits unconditionally to the will of God." However, "while the muslim's resignation consists in the conviction that the will of Allah is at work every moment and in even the smallest events, the *Muselmann* of Auschwitz is defined by a loss of will and consciousness."

In *Did Someone Say Totalitarianism?* Žižek defines "the Muslims" of concentrations camps as the "'zero-level' of humanity," "a kind of 'living dead' who even cease to react to basic animal stimuli" and who are, in fact, "in a way 'less than animal,' deprived even of animal vitality" or a "'spark of life,' of engaged existence." This, as he understands it, is because the Muslim has "see[n] too much, see[n] what one should not see." Can we see atrocities without unseeing them, perverting the evidence before us so it doesn't overwhelm our psyches, turn us into the living dead?

Unseeing is a defense mechanism that allows us to continue to function when what is before us is too much. Levi depicts the shame many Holocaust survivors later felt in relation to the way the *Muselmann* was treated in the camps. The *Muselmann* was scorned and avoided, explains academic Sharon B. Oster, in "Impossible Holocaust Metaphors," as "a strategy among the living to fend off approaching death, and a renunciation of human solidarity that brought survivors great shame." Disidentifying with the near-deathness of others is a method of survival, of continuing to live, perhaps, by disidentifying with the part in oneself that has the potential to submit to death [*Mr. Musselmann's moan*]. Could the so-called *Muselmann*, in this sense, be thought of as a phobic object, containing what needed to be split off from the self for the most urgent reason: survival?

"We need more understanding of human nature," writes Jung, "because the only real danger that exists is man himself. He is the great danger and we are pitifully unaware of it. We know nothing of man. His psyche should be studied because we are the origin of all coming evil." Psychic maneuvers live behind walls, operate unconsciously. It is critical to gain a fuller understanding of their modes of functioning in variable contexts and degrees of seriousness—achieved by taking in evidence from the universe, what is streamed by the external projector—to gain the awareness necessary to recognize what is happening in the moment and make a crucial choice.

Anna Karenina was a morphine addict. Throughout the second half of Tolstoy's novel, she uses morphine to drug her impulses and spontaneous expressions because she worries that revealing parts of herself that her lover, Vronsky, doesn't like might cost her his love.

The novel's famous suicide scene is preceded by her having taken a double dose of morphine. She is in a delirious state, and "everything that had seemed possible to her before was now so difficult to grasp." With ambivalence and last-minute regret, she throws herself before a train and dies.

Even as she manages her happiness—which is dependent on Vronsky being happy with her—by numbing her emotions, Anna recognizes that those very emotions are connected to what is most valuable in her: "She found it painful for these feelings to be stirred up, but she nevertheless knew that this was the best part of her soul, and that this part of her soul was rapidly being smothered in the life she was leading." Strong emotions, although sometimes painful or confusing, make us feel alive. If we suppress them to avert unpleasant sensations—or to avoid inducing them in others—we become detached from our interiors, and a sense of falsity or deadness ensues. "Can I call this living?" Anna asks herself. "I am not living. . . . I'm restraining myself . . . it's all just a deception, it's all just morphine under another name."

The motivation behind such restraint—corseting any sense of aliveness—is to quiet the anxiety that accompanies it, as Winnicott explained in a letter to an American correspondent:

> If you are "all there" then sooner or later this anxiety beyond what you can tolerate comes over you, and you cannot hold it long enough to look at it and see what is the content of the anxiety. If you could do this you would find that it contains—at root—the deepest source of your own psychic energy, so that when you have to blot it out (or it happens to you that it gets blotted out) you lose the taproot, so to speak.

When we allow ourselves to be "all there"—for all of ourselves to be present, even the difficult, fleshy, unwieldy aspects we fear exposing to the criticism of others—we become anxious, and in our desperation to quell our anxiety, reach for morphine, or whatever quick fix might protect us from a painful emotion, even as it blots out the best part of our soul, "the taproot," our deepest source of psychic energy. ("Deep in their roots," Roethke writes in a notebook, "all flowers keep the light.")

Anna "could only suppress terrible thoughts about what would happen if [Vronsky] stopped loving her with activities during the day and morphine at night." Morphine proper, or by another name, allows us, like Anna, to be there without the risks associated with being "all there," but also without the benefits of feeling on, fully present, alive. Whether with opioids, alcohol, work, exercise, socializing, or other forms of distraction, we all, at some point or another, find a substance or activity to fill our minds so there is little room left for troubling thoughts or emotions to set in.

Though uncomfortable, anxiety is a signal from within that can be useful if you can "hold it long enough to look at it and see" that it contains "the deepest source of your own psychic energy." Rethinking our ideas about disquieting emotions allows us to tap into alternative energy sources. The unsettling changes that stress creates in the brain and body, explains psychologist Kelly McGonigal, make us more "alert . . . raw, vulnerable . . . open to the world around [us]." Tolerating these feelings long enough to harness that "surge of energy that is encouraging [us] to engage" will help us muster the strength to "rise to a moment that matters."

One day, while I was preparing dinner at the kitchen counter, my daughter, then four, who had been playing at the kids' table behind me, approached, glanced at the vegetables on the cutting board, and said, That's going to be horrible. A horrible dinner.

She turned, walked back to the little table, sat on a small wooden rocking chair decorated with yellow ducklings, and added matter-of-factly, Mommy, I hate you.

Without responding, I continued preparing the horrible meal. Ten minutes later, after rocking back and forth in her chair, singing, kneading clay, she called out tenderly, Mommy, I love you.

First you hate me, I said, then you love me—

Mommy, she cut in, rapturously, I everything you!

One of Winnicott's most important contributions to psychoanalysis was the idea of a "holding environment," an atmosphere that communicates to another person—a child, an analysand, a lover—that whatever they express will be accepted: the good, the savage, and the ugly. Having the space and opportunity to be fully oneself gives a person the chance to become a self, as opposed to an assemblage of feelings and behaviors they have been conditioned to adopt in exchange for affirmation or love.

A former analysand of Winnicott's, Margaret Little, described a moment in her analysis in which, feeling utter despair, she "attacked and smashed a large vase filled with white lilac, and trampled on it." The next day, when she showed up for her session, she found that "an exact replica had replaced the vase and the lilac." Although "a few days later he explained that [she] had destroyed something that he valued, . . . [n]either of [them] ever referred to it again," letting her know that nothing had changed. A holding environment creates the security necessary for a person to express their impulses and intuition, rather than to act on the strategic desire to manage how they are received.

There is comfort in letting go, being able to be yourself without the risk of rejection or of losing love. The desire to feel held and contained—emotionally swaddled—is a primal instinct. When feeling Margaret Little–level despair, my daughter used to crawl under the kitchen table and sob, saying, I want to go back into my mommy's belly! Animal behaviorist Temple Grandin—inspired by the observation on her aunt's cattle farm that the animals, when placed in a V-shaped squeeze box meant to hold them still during vaccinations, appeared consoled—invented a hug machine, a concrete holding environment to soothe autistic children by simulating the comfort of being contained. Winnicott recognized not only how crucial the sensation of being held is in the development of a child, but how necessary it becomes for the feeling to be re-created in an analytic setting, particularly for someone who did not experience it often enough during childhood to have the chance to recognize who they were before having to adjust that self to social demands.

Is it merely coincidence, then, that Winnicott's father, the father of the father of the holding environment, was a merchant specializing in women's corsets? A corset holds with an inverse objective—to tuck away rather than spill over; it is used to hide flesh, an excess of body—being *too much*—with the aim of avoiding critical judgment. Fathers in Winnicott's theories, those trafficking in the corsets of laws, codes, and regulations, are largely absent.

At best, *mothers*, the term Winnicott uses for primary caregivers, encourage their small children to express themselves freely by remaining receptive to all communications, however vicious or wild. A baby who cries or bites and is then punished for being bad will learn to restrain themselves to access the rewards that accompany good—which is to say, desired—behavior.

Giving the mother what she wants in exchange for affirmation and care is the only way a baby can control its environment. In fact, "there is no such thing as an infant," according to Winnicott, without a relationship: "Whenever one finds an infant one finds maternal care, and without maternal care there would be no infant." Because all babies need a caregiver to survive, they quickly learn to adapt to maternal demands—a tactic that gets carried over into adulthood, although it is rarely literal survival that is at stake.

Someone who perceives early on that moving things around on the outside (making the mother feel good) is a way of moving them around on the inside (feeling loved themselves) is likely, later in life, to use people, objects, and substances as vehicles to modulate their feelings and thoughts. This basic principle is encapsulated in the precept "it's not what you know but who you know"—an inevitable dynamic in infancy, when one's agency is at the mercy of the parents. But what is for some a phase to grow out of can, for others, become calcified into a belief system, particularly if receiving care was connected to gratifying the demands of others in childhood.

Of course, every parent has to set boundaries that will feel, when they curtail freedom, like demands. One of the most difficult parts about being a mother is snuffing out my children's impulses, teaching them to disconnect from their interiors in order to display proper behavior (*Inside voice; Don't stare; Pretend that you like it even if you don't*). It is my maternal duty to watch over their survival—literal and social—but also to guard over their connection to their spontaneous, instinctive selves, so that they remain emotionally alive as well.

Politeness, civility, means, in part, not acknowledging your perceptions or emotions, but acting into a mold, following protocol to maintain the status quo, an anesthetized state of belonging. The cost of getting caught up in a role is that it becomes easy to lose connection to your inner thoughts and desires. The reward, on the other hand, is that you are more likely to be given the job, affirmation, a sense of belonging.

Anna Karenina is a book of orphans. Anna herself is an orphan. Tolstoy makes no mention of her parents, only of two aunts: one who brought Anna up and another who freeloads off her while she is living with her lover, Vronsky. We know nothing of Anna's childhood or early adulthood, or of what her life was like with the aunt who raised her, beyond the fact that the aunt pressured the tedious but dutiful Karenin—Anna's husband (also an orphan), whom she leaves for Vronsky—into marrying her niece by making him believe his honor was at stake. He complied with what was asked of him in exchange for a respected position in society.

Their forced match locked Anna into a loveless marriage and a life that placed appearances over desires and needs, the external above the internal. The impression Anna's sister-in-law, Dolly, had "of visiting the Karenins"—Anna and her husband—was that "there was something false in the whole cast of their family life."

The False Self put forward in accordance with the codes and expectations of others brings social rewards at the expense of the True Self, the deepest core of our being, the part of us that feels "alive" and "real." We all have False Selves—it is necessary to have a protective skin to go out into the social world. One of the purposes of the False Self, in fact, is to shelter the True Self. But a False Self that is so fortified by layers of compliant behavior that it loses contact with the raw impulses and expressions that characterize the True Self often results in a person feeling as though they don't really know who they are beyond what is signaled about their interior through the ideas, interests, friends, and achievements they have accumulated from the outside world (imposter syndrome). When contact is made with the True Self, however, wires touch, switching on an inner light.

When I first read *Anna Karenina*, in high school, I was captivated by Anna, who is all of light. Tolstoy introduces her to us through Vronsky's eyes as "so brimming over with something that . . . showed itself now in the flash of her eyes, and now in her smile." I aspired to be Anna, wondrously lit yet "deliberately extinguishing the light" even as "it shone against her will." As she comes into contact with Vronsky's force field, "the joyful light kindled in her eyes," and he, too, felt the pull.

Isn't it amazing when you see someone who has the light? artistic director Oskar Eustis asked during a toast he gave at Bayes's book launch. The clowns in the room—all having been transformed in some way by Bayes's light—nodded emphatically. Once a certain way of being has been cognized, you recognize it everywhere. The light was the wax lining the paper cup of my childhood.

Transmissions that cannot be explained logically pass between people all the time, though only some give them attention. When Vronsky first glimpses Anna, he "felt the need to glance at her again—not because she was very beautiful" but because of "an abundance of something," a "radiance" that "overflowed her being." That something—radiance, light—has less to do with looks than a living energy emitted by "anyone," as Gaulier purportedly has it, "in the grips of freedom or pleasure."

Because this beauty flows outside circuits of social currency, it is unlikely to be apprehended by those unattuned to its frequency. Tolstoy seems ambivalent about whether value can be given to passion that is not aboveground, connected to social mores or religion. "Eruptions of sexual desire cause confusion," he writes in a notebook, "or rather an absence of ideas: the link with the world is lost. Chance, darkness, powerlessness." Can we trust desire if it cannot be transposed onto an idea, linked to the logical world? And can a character—a woman at that—who chooses to leave her (dreary) husband and beloved child to pursue passion be permitted pleasure and light?

Even as Tolstoy allows Anna to be all there, he punishes her for it by making her unable to control her light when it's not refracted through a socially sanctioned structure: what had previously brimmed over against her will begins to blaze, and, though "her face shone with a vivid glow . . . it was not a joyous glow—it resembled the terrible glow of a conflagration on a dark night." Chance, darkness, powerlessness. In Tolstoy's hands, the light leads to Anna's suicide—a death that served as a warning of what might become of me as well if I didn't shroud my light.

"Only the True Self can be creative," writes Winnicott, ". . . feel real." The hallmark of a False Self, by contrast, is a lack of "creative originality." The capacity to be creative develops out of a sense of being held in a reliable context that makes it safe to *everything* one another, to be all there, flesh out, able to access the taproot, that deepest source of psychic energy, in ourselves and others.

Anna is a thinker, reader, and writer of great intelligence. She has "remarkable knowledge" of architecture, machinery—topics she discusses confidently with the men at her and Vronsky's table. She speaks "in a natural, clever way" and "read[s] a great deal—both novels and the serious books . . . foreign papers and journals." Anna's brother describes her to his friend Levin, the character based on Tolstoy, as having "inner resources." She even writes a children's book, he relays. Then, looking at Levin's reaction, he adds, "I can see you are smiling ironically, but you're wrong."

Levin isn't the only character who doubts the intellectual capacity of Anna and women in general (*I hate intellectual women*). One of Anna's major fights with Vronsky occurs when he makes fun of girls' high schools and women's education more widely. Anna is offended because she sees it as an allusion to her own reading and intellectual pursuits, even as she is the one who does the research for his projects. Anna downplays her knowledge, her artistic capabilities—for example, likening her writing to basket-weaving—in order to minimize anything that might threaten, elicit ironic smiles, or cause men to find her less appealing. ("A woman who has a head full of Greek," writes Kant, ". . . might as well have a beard.") Anna's behavior is choreographed to manage the impression others have of her—a False Self concern that will inevitably dampen any creativity that hinges on a person's connection to their internal world.

Bobbie Louise Hawkins, a poet and prose writer of the Beat generation, was married to the poet Robert Creeley for eighteen years. "When Bob and I were first together, he had three things he would say," Hawkins recalls:

> One of them was "I'll never live in a house with a woman who writes." One of them was "Everybody's wife wants to be a writer." And one of them was "If you had been going to be a writer, you would have been one by now." That pretty much put the cap on it. I was too married, too old and too late, but he was wrong.

Complying with these precepts would have prioritized external demands over internal drives. At a 2019 tribute to Hawkins at St. Mark's Church-in-the-Bowery in New York, poet Eileen Myles relayed an anecdote Hawkins liked to tell about a time when writer Lucia Berlin babysat for her and Creeley's children:

She would tell this story and then she would smile and that was really the last line, where it was just like, there was an element of triumph . . . Bob and Bobbie had gone out and Lucia babysat for them . . . and I think Lucia was in her aspiring writer mode and writing, and she had given Bob some work. So he was driving her home after she babysat and on the way home he pulled over under this tree and she thought, "Oh, he's going to talk to me about my work." And they sat there for a moment in the moonlight looking at this tree, and he said, "Lucia, see that cottonwood tree?" And she was like, "Yeah, Bob." And he said, "Be like that tree for your man."

Hawkins and Creeley eventually divorced, and Hawkins pursued her artistic ambitions while teaching for many years at the Naropa Institute. At St. Mark's Church-in-the-Bowery, poet Reed Bye recalled sitting in on a class Hawkins taught, in which she advocated for "the virtue of surprising turns that short-circuit discursiveness." A surprising turn takes you off the moving walkway, and, like an infant's spontaneous gesture, brings you back to impulse and intuition:

She ended the class with her paraphrase from a poem by Lew Welch called "Small Sentence to Drive Yourself Sane." And the poem:

The next time you are doing something absolutely ordinary, or even better

the next time you are doing something absolutely *necessary*, such as pissing, or making love, or shaving, or washing the dishes or the baby or yourself or the room, say to yourself:

"So it's all come to this!"

"Like, whatever you're doing," Bobbie said, "just stop in the middle of it, look around and say, 'So it's all come to this.'"

Anna tries to be that cottonwood tree, but the more she suppresses her emotions, the more they build up and press for release. Because Anna's husband, Karenin, will not grant her a divorce, she and Vronsky live together in a relationship that society won't sanction, and they are not accepted as a couple into the social world. Vronsky, however, is granted admittance on his own, while Anna, completely cast out, can see people only when they visit her. Vronsky genuinely loves Anna, is willing to give up being firmly installed in society to be with her, but he isn't willing to lose his "male independence." He has been trained from an early age to prioritize external demands over his emotions, and therefore remains ambivalent about completely giving up the rewards society offers to those who follow its codes.

When we first meet Vronsky, we learn that "in his soul, he did not respect his mother, and, without being conscious of it, did not love her, although in keeping with . . . his upbringing, he could not imagine his attitude to his mother being anything other than extremely obedient and deferential." When his mother tries to undermine his relationship with Anna, his obedience is pitted against his love. Anna, perceiving this, panics, tries to turn Vronsky against his mother by speaking disparagingly of her and dissuading him from going to see her. Vronsky asks that she "not speak disrespectfully about [his] mother," aligns himself with the demands of his upbringing. Unable to corset herself, Anna ramps up her attack.

When Anna is *all there*, Vronsky, rather than being able to offer a holding environment in which he tolerates her full range of emotions, says, "No, this is becoming unbearable," gets up, tells her his "patience . . . has its limits," and, choosing obedience over love, walks out to see his mother. Anna takes a double dose of morphine.

In a drug-induced delirium, with ambivalence and last-minute regret, Anna throws herself onto the train tracks. Like Margaret Little, Anna smashed a vase, but unlike Winnicott, Vronsky wasn't able to withstand her despair, restore the vase—communicate to her that she was more important than the vase, the prohibition against breaking it—and remain present.

The "'destructive' . . . aliveness of the individual," writes Winnicott, ". . . has vital positive function." Winnicott explains the "positive value of destructiveness" in his radical, groundbreaking paper "The Use of an Object." It is essential, he says, for the infant to destroy the mother to move from a primitive narcissistic relationship (in which the mother is recognized solely as a means of getting its needs met) to a more mature relationship (in which she's understood as a separate person, possessing her own mind). It is when the infant is ruthless toward the mother and sees that the mother is hurt—rather than angry or frustrated, which is how the infant feels—that it can recognize that the mother has her own emotions existing outside the infant's omnipotent control. Because the mother has her own feelings, she is separate; and because she is separate, she is real. It is only then, in the mother's realness—not as a projection, but as a separate subject— that she can become available for what Winnicott terms "use."

If the mother retaliates, she is feeling the infant's feelings. In other contexts, this is a useful mode of communication, but when the feelings are destructive (despair, rage), it can mean the infant has gotten inside the mother's head and is controlling her from within. That degree of power is terrifying to a child because a mother who is an extension of the infant and not a separate person is not only incapable of being used but is a mere projection and thus unreal, not really there at all. The mother needs to demonstrate that she is separate and real, all there, which she does by tolerating the infant's being all there as well.

For a mature relationship to exist, individuals must encounter each other in their separateness, which is established once they become available to each other for use by surviving a destructive attack. It is when each person is able to recognize the other's independent existence that the other becomes real and seen—and, in feeling seen, real to themselves as well. Only then, when individuals come together as separate, can they love and be loved.

"We never fight," psychoanalyst Danielle Knafo records a new analysand telling her, describing his two-year relationship. ". . . She's not the kind of girl who could ever give me a reason to fight with her." He went on to explain how this relationship was different from his two marriages or that of his parents, in which his father had "nothing left of his manhood"—or, in Vronsky's terms, "male independence."

People often mistake a lack of conflict for a working relationship, the way a baby who doesn't fuss, is seen and not heard, will often be deemed "good." Not infrequently, when I'm working as a psychoanalyst, an analysand will say that their partner has asked them to talk to me about going on antidepressants. When we explore the request, we find that it is rooted in a hope that the antidepressant will make the couple's problems go away by subduing difficult feelings, much as Anna hopes morphine will do for her relationship with Vronsky.

The perfect girlfriend described by Knafo's analysand—the woman who met his needs without compromising him in any way—was a high-end sex doll. These dolls have become increasingly popular across the globe. At realdoll.com you can build your ideal partner with all the physical attributes you desire. The life-sized human figure, covered with flesh-like silicone, is equipped with both vaginal and anal orifices fabricated to feel real without the mess of interiority.

Feeling real, however, is not that simple. In order to feel real, in Winnicott's terms, a person has to have had the opportunity to express themselves spontaneously without worrying about losing love. An infant, according to Winnicott, feels real upon seeing recognition register in its mother's face, which is different from looking into a mirror and seeing its own reflection. The infant must feel real before being able to recognize the reality of another person, which is grasped when it is seen to exist outside the infant's omnipotent control. If the infant perceives that the mother has the capacity to experience an attack (*She has her own emotions*) and survive that attack without retaliating (*It's okay to express oneself*), the mother will have been, in Winnicott's formulation, *found*. Through finding the other, one finds the self.

My younger daughter's first word was *mama*. Mama was a name, but also a word attached to me that meant *I want it*; *Get it*; *Give it to me*; *I hate it*;

I'm about to attack. A couple of months after she first said it, rather than calling me *mama*, she began to use the name *Mimi.* It seemed like an odd regression, until one day I heard in her enunciation our combined selves: *Me* (her self) and *Me* (my self, which was also hers): *Me-Me.*

Oedipal representations—when a child is four or five—are different. At four, my other daughter called me over to look at a drawing she had made of our family. There were four figures: a little girl, a littler girl, a father, and a cat. Where am I? I asked. Here, she answered, handing me her pencil. You can draw yourself.

When working as a psychoanalyst with analysands whose issues are preoedipal—originate in a developmental phase that is primarily pre-linguistic and merged—it is necessary to tune in to communications that are transmitted outside of words. An experience that occurs before words are available will register in nonrational, imagistic terms within the body, as opposed to linguistic, rational ones—making it more difficult later, after language has been acquired, to recollect and communicate the memory in words than through images and sensations.

When an adult relationship involves merging, it replicates that early relationship between mother and infant, in which the other person does not fully exist but functions as a vehicle toward getting needs met. The stakes are likely to feel connected to survival, as they do in infancy, prompting desperation and compliance to kick in, along with the restraint of any part of the self that seems too dangerous to express. Genuine spontaneous expression will always involve a degree of risk.

I use a wooden match as a bookmark.

"Who can say," Winnicott quotes Pliny asking, "whether in essence fire is constructive or destructive?"

Indigenous communities across the world believe in setting controlled, intentional fires that protect against wild ones. "At the core of those tribal or indigenous philosophies," explains research ecologist Frank Lake, is the view that "fire is medicine and when you prescribe it in the correct way, it can enhance and maintain ecosystem service production." Prescribed fires can be used, according to Chook-Chook Hillman, land steward for the Karuk Tribe, "to set the landscape on a trajectory to accept fire in a good way," to become "ready to take it." When fires are avoided, even criminalized, an "unnatural situation" results. Human beings "have to reconcile," Hillman advises, their "relationship with fire":

> The way that it's talked about here in the US and in other places, when a human has some relationship to fire they're called a pyromaniac. We talk about it like it's a mental health issue when really it's not. It's our responsibility to the world to use fire to keep the world healthy.

Aggression, likewise, when released in the "correct" way—in the form of a joke, for example—can function like a fire and help maintain the social ecosystem, harness the destructive aliveness of individuals, and channel the burning energy in a positive direction by creating cracks in the walls that divide us. Humor, like a prescribed fire or a boundary, can express healthy forms of aggression that protect against the wilder kinds.

Winnicott, who was based in London, presented "The Use of an Object" for the first time in New York at the New York Psychoanalytic Society and Institute, the oldest psychoanalytic institute in America, where the predominant approach to psychoanalysis did not then involve much consideration of the preoedipal period of development, during which nonverbal communication predominates. (This is also the institute with which Green of Malcolm's *Psychoanalysis: The Impossible Profession* was affiliated, and where I began my own psychoanalytic studies.) The paper took many surprising turns—in a way Hawkins would appreciate—veering sharply away from the thinking of the discussants and using terms that were common to them in defamiliarized ways. Winnicott broke ground and they retaliated.

After he finished giving his paper, the discussants subjected it to a wildfire of ruthless attacks. In response, Winnicott told the group that "his overall concept had been torn to pieces and he would be happy to give it up." The vase had been shattered and no one was there to help him pick up the pieces. He went back to his hotel room that night and had a heart attack.

Bringing one's creative projects to light is a way of exposing the True Self, which most people—out of a desire to protect what is most precious—keep hidden. Though Winnicott's health improved, he never fully recovered and died two years later.

Still, as I imagine it, Winnicott would not have felt regret. ("Oh God!" he writes in "Prayer." "May I be alive when I die!")

I overhear my daughters in the next room:

DAUGHTER 1: I can't believe you flushed my barrettes down the toilet! Those were my best ones.
DAUGHTER 2: I know! They were so cute!
DAUGHTER 1: How could you?
DAUGHTER 2: (*cheerfully*) I was so angry.

"It is perhaps the greatest compliment we may receive," Winnicott suggests, "if we are both found and used."

"Look at your aggressiveness," Winnicott writes in a letter; ". . . it provides one of the roots of living energy." By numbing aggression, as by suppressing anxiety, you may avoid conflict with those around you, but you will also lose access to the taproot, the ability to feel creative, alive, connected to others, real. By harnessing your living energy—aggressiveness, anxiety, primitive destructive impulses, savage complexity—you can, as McGonigal suggests, "use some of this energy, use some of this biochemistry to make choices or take actions that are consistent with what matters most."

Anna Karenina laughs in front of Levin, and, unlike with the laughing Frenchwoman whom he "swiftly moved away from . . . as from some dirty place," he enjoys it. Perhaps his response has something to do with the gratification he feels in recognizing that Anna's laughter is sparked by a comment he has just made. Levin says of French art that after taking stylization to its extreme, the French returned to realism and "saw poetry in the fact that they were no longer lying."

Anna, who at this point in the novel is living openly with her lover, is, like the French, no longer lying. When Levin puts words to an unarticulated thought or feeling that was already inside her—there's poetry in honesty—she laughs in "the way that one laughs when one sees a very true likeness in a portrait." The resonance between his words and something within creates pattern recognition: her "face suddenly completely lit up" and "she burst out laughing."

Laughter has the capacity to mark all kinds of recognition, including a transfer of power, which Spence describes as a "gift" (*The power others possess is the power I give them*). Anna amplifies Levin's power through her laughter in the same way that laughing at another person's joke does, which is why in dating profiles a person might say they like to laugh or like to make people laugh as a way of signaling a preferred power position (submissive, dominant).

The ability of laughter to redistribute power, Weber cautions, is "violent" and "dangerous" because it occurs at the bodily level, without a person's conscious consent. The sensation of being overpowered by laughter or infected by another person's emotion occurs against a person's conscious will, and may make them feel, as Bartleby's employer describes it, "impotent" and "unmanned." For Homer's gods in the *Iliad*, writes Weber, "laughter is as 'unquenchable' as a conflagration [wildfire], as uncontrollable as a highly contagious illness." This contagion exists not only with laughter but when you come into contact with someone who has the light, which, when it happens, like witnessing a yawn or sexual activity, "rules out the possibility of dispassionate observation," writes Bataille. When we are infiltrated, infected by another's aliveness, we "participate" with the other person's emotion "from inside [our]sel[ves]," like it or not.

Levin's wife, Kitty, learns of his encounter with Anna and becomes threatened and enraged, accuses him of having "fallen in love with that nasty woman" who "bewitched" him. Anna's light, like a witch's magic or a spontaneous outburst of laughter, has the force to redistribute the balance of the world, making her—like Trump said of Clinton—a "nasty woman."

A nasty woman, like the reporter's "nasty question" or Bion's "nasty hole," creates an opening for, as Bion puts it, "mental curiosity . . . wanting to know something about the universe in which we live." Like a vacuum that the hoarder needs to fill with space stoppers, this hole where "one hasn't any knowledge at all" is often blocked by premature and precocious answers, shut up in prose.

Although an opening, like an appoggiatura in music, can create longing, let in light, spontaneity, freedom, and beauty, it can also threaten the unknown and cause, as Tolstoy experienced with sexual desire, "an absence of ideas: the link with the world is lost." Rather than risk being left with "chance, darkness, powerlessness," Kitty and Levin stop up the space with knowledge, rules, and conventions, flipping Anna from a beautiful woman to a hag.

I recall the optical illusion as I do most literary devices, through the specific terms that were used when I first encountered it in elementary school: *beautiful woman, hag.* The illusion, originally a 1988 German postcard, was published by cartoonist W. E. Hill as "My Wife and My Mother-in-Law" (1915). The title itself reinforces the idea of a woman as double: we see her as she is, which is inseparable from where she is headed, a destiny inscribed in her from the start. According to Urban Dictionary, the contemporary acronym PFH (propensity for hagdom) refers to "a girl usually in her early to mid-twenties who looks good now because of her age, but you can tell that she will look like [actor] Sean Penn of Geddy Lee when she gets older." Female sexuality is treated like a seductive trap, a biased coin rather than an effect of the viewer's splitting, even though a weighted coin is known to be impossible in reality, the unicorn of probability.

Anna, we later learn through Tolstoy's narrative, transfers power to Levin as a way of eliciting a transfer of power to her, like a con man who gives his target his confidence in order to elicit a mirrored response that places reciprocal confidence in him. She manipulates Levin, like acoustically extreme laughter does its audience, to feel positively toward her: "She had unconsciously spent the whole evening doing all she could to arouse in Levin a feeling of love for her (as she did with all young men lately)." This, too, is morphine by another name: the hope that moving things around on the outside—making the token land beauty-side up—will move them around internally.

To many, a pleasing False Self is easier to interact with than a person committed to the expression of genuine thoughts and feelings: "A wanton inclination (*coquetterie*)," writes Kant, "in a refined sense, namely an effort to fascinate and to charm, is perhaps blameworthy in an otherwise decorous person, yet it is still beautiful and is commonly preferred to the honorable, serious demeanor." Giving others what they want—like the actor playing to the majority—and reaping the rewards associated with doing so may push a person's social position or career along, but will the individual genuinely feel the pleasure most assume accompanies success if it is achieved in a False Self way?

If one does not have one's True Self, spontaneous gestures, accepted in early life by a parent, one is likely, like Anna, to develop a strong False Self, which will seek that affirmation in metonymically displaced others: Vronsky, Levin, all young men. (One can only begin to imagine the extent to which the vacuum created by parental absence would intensify this dynamic in an orphan's psyche.) By filling an opening, a nasty hole, with morphine—the drugging of genuine feeling—one becomes agreeable, easier for others to be around, which will, in turn, affect their sense of self as seen from the imagined view-point of those others.

After my daughter's first year in elementary school, we received in the mail a detailed four-page written report of her performance. What are you reading? she asked, noticing the intensity of my interest. Your report from school, I said. Do you want to see it? Sure, she replied, accepting the bundle from me and sitting at the kitchen table. After a minute or two of reading bits and flipping impatiently through pages, she put it down and headed to her room. Aren't you curious what your teacher thinks of you? I asked. She has her idea of me, she said matter-of-factly. And I have my own idea of me.

What if Anna had not been, like Tolstoy, an orphan, and had experienced a holding environment in early life that gave her the sense that her uglier emotions would not flip her to hagdom? Or what if she had been in analysis with Winnicott rather than a character in Tolstoy's narrative? What if, alternatively, she had remained a character, but had been placed in the hands of an author who granted her permission to feel and express her emotions fully?

On the first page of novelist Elena Ferrante's *Days of Abandonment*, we learn that the main character, Olga, has just been abandoned by her husband. Every subsequent page offers the reader an unmediated sense of the emotional and physical struggle that ensues. Olga tries to make herself appear beautiful to rekindle her husband's desire and conceal the fact that "the life had been drained out of [her] like blood and saliva and mucus from a patient during an operation." But falsity doesn't sit well with her. In contrast to Anna, who dresses up and takes morphine to align herself with Vronsky's desire, Olga can't swing it. She becomes forlorn, and fluids—from tears to menses to bile—begin to seep out from her interior:

> Immediately I felt depressed. My eyelids were heavy, my back ached. I wanted to cry. I looked at my underpants, they were

stained with blood. I pronounced an ugly obscenity in my dialect, and with such an angry snap in my voice that I was afraid the children had heard me.

Unlike Giuliani, who secretes synthetic compounds like an android controlled from within by the corporate machinery of Trump Inc., what seeps out of Olga are her living animal substances. Storytelling, writes Ferrante, "gives us the power to bring order to the chaos of the real under our own sign." But when the sign controlling the narrative comes so frequently from outside of us, we "internaliz[e] the male method of confronting and resolving problems . . . [and] end up demonstrating that we are acquiescent, obedient and equal to male expectations." We stop up all our holes so nothing can leak out but the motor oil used to grease our implanted beliefs.

Feminine narratives have the potential to express a different kind of order. By removing the corset of laws, codes, and regulations, each individual body, narrative and idea is free to spill over, take its own direction. A Danish television show for children, *Ultra Strips Down*, has people stand naked on a stage, revealing that the figures we are trained to seek out and desire are unrealistic. Similarly, each narrative, like a body, has its own shape, and a writer who gains awareness of their methods of confronting and resolving chaos is free to make conscious choices, including the choice to take off the corset of social dictates and let be.

It is important to note that feminine narratives are not limited to women, just as male methods are not utilized solely by men ("I'm not a boy, not a girl," says one volunteer who stripped down on the Danish show, "I'm a bit of everything"). Internalized masculine methods, in fact, often cube men with even greater intensity. "In order to live a fully human life," writes poet Adrienne Rich, "we require not only *control* of our bodies (though control is a prerequisite); we must touch the unity and resonance of our physicality, our bond with the natural order, the corporeal grounds of our intelligence." The natural order, like corporeal intelligence, the True Self, embodied knowledge, is neither gendered nor socially coded.

When Olga's husband judges her outburst of emotion through standards of social behavior—one should not get angry in front of children—and asks her, as Vronsky asks Anna, to change the way she is speaking, she responds uninhibitedly:

> I don't give a shit about prissiness. You wounded me, you are destroying me, and I'm supposed to speak like a good, well-brought-up wife? Fuck you! What words am I supposed to use for what you've done to me, what you're doing to me? What words should I use for what you're doing with that woman? Do you lick her cunt? Do you stick it in her ass? Do you do all the things you never did with me? Tell me! Because I see you! With these eyes I see everything you do together, I see it a hundred thousand times, I see it night and day, eyes open and eyes closed! However, in order not to disturb the gentleman, not to disturb his children, I'm supposed to use clean language, I'm supposed to be refined, I'm supposed to be elegant! Get out of here! Get out, you shit!

Olga's rage, like Anna's, is followed by an exit.

Near the elevator of my office building is a sign:

> YOU ARE HER
> EXIT

The sign makes me think of Anna Karenina's predicament. I wonder what it would have taken for Vronsky to have been "here" rather than "her exit"—to have been all there, fully present, and, in the present, not *there* but *here*. What does it take—not only for Vronsky, but for anyone—to be *all here*?

The simple answer is an "e."

In mathematics, *e* is known as Euler's number, an irrational figure, about 2.71828. It exists in mathematics, physics, nature—and I would like also to imagine a metaphorical equivalent in interpersonal relationships. This imagined application of *e* would offer a way of addressing the irrational, incalculable component that is necessary in experiencing a connection as alive and real.

What Winnicott terms the True Self, Lorde would call "the erotic"—our "physical, emotional, and psychic expressions of what is deepest and strongest and richest within each of us." Yet we are raised, she says, to fear this energy, marked by "nonrational knowledge"—"the *yes* within ourselves, our deepest cravings"—because it threatens the social system, which is based not on primal impulses, or the body, but on logic and power. A sense of nonrational bodily aliveness marks one's having accessed the wellspring of living energy characteristic of the True Self.

Love is irrational—if you can explain it, it's likely an illusion. And it is precisely this irrational component that creates radical possibility. Even as it was progressive of Anna to leave her husband and live with her lover, she realigned herself with dominant structures in using morphine to numb the best parts of her soul as a way to avoid the loss of Vronsky's love.

The corset brings rewards, the positive gaze of others, but it also buries the taproot and stifles one's ability to feel creative and alive. Lorde champions the power of erotic nonrational knowledge because it taps into an energy that all radicalism must harness. Every move that feeds the False Self—places external demands over internal desires—may protect the True Self but will invariably strengthen the system that pushed it into hiding in the first place. "The master's tools," as Lorde puts it, "will never dismantle the master's house."

Freud had a tendency to be very un-Freudian. Analysts in the United States in the second half of the twentieth century determined what should be considered Freudian analysis with rules that Freud himself did not always follow.

In the notes to his Rat Man case, Freud describes a moment in which he burst out laughing. The laughter provided him with a way of disassociating from the Rat Man's "most frightful transferences"—a fantasy involving Freud and his siblings being hanged, combined with the accusation that Freud's family had a criminal past:

> My mother was standing in despair while all her children were being hanged. . . . I was not able to guess the explanation he produced for having the phantasy. He knew, he said, that a great misfortune had once befallen my family: a brother of mine, who was a waiter, had committed a murder in Budapest and been executed for it. I asked him with a laugh how he knew that, whereupon his whole affect collapsed.

The Rat Man, Freud continues in his notes, "explained that his brother-in-law, who knows my brother, had told him this, as evidence that education went for nothing and that heredity was all." Regardless of how Freud lived his life, the Rat Man seemed to be saying, he was fated to be crooked because his heredity was stained.

Anxiety around one's origins—another angle on the question of who you are according to another—is characteristic of obsessionals and is addressed directly by Freud in the Rat Man case: "The predilection felt by obsessional neurotics for uncertainty and doubt leads them to turn their thoughts by preference to those subjects upon which all mankind are uncertain . . . chief [among them] . . . paternity." Easier than attempting to resolve any doubt surrounding your origin—whether you are upstanding, orphaned, or a criminal—is to negate its trigger, and there's no better way to do so than through a burst of Duchenne laughter, which gets rid of a threat metaphorically by expelling it from the body.

Freud's laughter in response to the Rat Man's accusation, psychoanalyst Richard Gottlieb explains, had an "impulsive, action-like quality" characteristic of countertransference, a psychoanalytic term for an emotional reaction an analyst experiences when associations to people and events from the analyst's past are transferred onto the material presented by an analysand, in the same way that an analysand's associations and expectations from the past get transferred onto the analyst in transference. Viewed through Arlow's model of consciousness, countertransference indicates resonance between what is projected onto the mind's screen from the external world—which in a session is made up largely of the analysand's material—and what streams from the internal projector, the analyst's mind.

Countertransference can undermine a psychoanalyst's ability to orient around the analysand's psyche and keep their personal emotions out of court. Ideally, during a session, an analyst will set the knob of their internal projector to standby and wait until the analysand has exited the consulting room to turn it back on and analyze the stream of data. Unfortunately, that is not always possible—an analyst is, after all, a human being and "when two personalities meet," as Bion has it, "an emotional storm is created." Such storms are inevitable, Bion continues; "the problem is how to make the best of it." A stormy unconscious entanglement between an analyst and an analysand can be fruitful if it is unpacked, analyzed, and eventually understood. Countertransference, like a fire, can be useful if handled in the right way—but may lead to a wildfire if it is not.

The Rat Man's fantasy would not have elicited countertransference in Freud unless it resonated with some element from his interior that was called up and, in line with the pattern recognition theory of humor, was inserted into the structure of logic before him. The history behind what was stirred up by the accusation—the data being projected by Freud's internal projector—likely related to the Freud family's actual criminal past. Freud's paternal uncle was arrested, according to Gottlieb, for "possession of one hundred counterfeit 50-ruble notes (Russian) as he attempted to sell these to an undercover agent." When he was nine and ten, Freud undoubtedly "knew a great deal about the events relating to his Uncle Joseph's criminal activities, arrest, trial, and sentencing," and, given public accusations, "*must have wondered* if his older half brothers" and father "were involved in these crimes as well." The fact that there were indeed criminals in his family "may have conditioned his countertransferential responses to the Rat Man's Train Murder fantasy," prompting the expulsion of the old feelings, likely threatening to him as a child, that had resurfaced.

Rather than analyze the Rat Man's fantasy, Freud disputes it and assures him that no one from his family had anything to do with the murder. The analytic position would be to resist any reassurance and, instead, explore the fantasy, accept the role projected onto you—wear the criminal suit—long enough for the analysand to describe their feelings and thoughts while in the midst of experiencing them. Instead, Freud rejected the role that had been transferred onto him by assuring the Rat Man that it was not true. He even supplied facts from his life in substantiation—he "never had any relatives in Budapest"—disavowing both the fantasy and the feelings it aroused.

This "non-interpretive denial" or "negation," in Gottlieb's terms, of the Rat Man's accusation that Freud's family was criminal would be described by self-proclaimed Freudians as very un-Freudian. In practice, however, the classical (Freudian) approach of interpreting the fantasy without addressing its objective veracity—foregrounding psychic reality, placing the internal life ahead of the external—can be emotionally challenging if the fantasy resonates in some way with a fantasy in the analyst's own mind, which is why it is critical that every analyst undergo their own analysis. Freud, however, as the first psychoanalyst, had to be his own analyst. Moments of countertransference were inevitable.

The brevity of Freud's outburst—the fact that it occurred "temporarily and impulsively"—points, as with parapraxis, to an eruption from the unconscious. During stressful situations, laughter can create distance, scientists Dacher Keltner and George Bonanno's research suggests, "dissociation from the subjective experience of distress," by creating "a shift from negative to positive emotion" and strengthening interpersonal bonds.

But wait! Bonanno is the researcher who suggested that female victims of sexual abuse who smiled or laughed when he interviewed them would do "better" because they were able to keep "negative emotions in check." He seems to value making oneself agreeable over working through "the subjective experience of distress," lining up the external chips and letting the internal chips fall where they may. Strengthening interpersonal bonds can sometimes cause alienation from oneself, making a meaningful connection unlikely.

Even as Freud's laughter appeared to keep negative emotions in check, it did so in a way that was not helpful to the Rat Man. Freud notes that after he laughed, the Rat Man's "whole affect collapsed," but what was going on with him internally was not explored. By functioning as an analytic sneeze, Freud's burst of laughter enabled him to expel his feelings around his analysand's accusation and reestablish the therapeutic alliance, or interpersonal bond, that had been shaken on both ends, but in a way that was more social than analytic. An analyst who bursts out laughing, as Freud did, has the space to deny the nuances within their response, because we are primed for such disavowal daily through a ready stock of phrases that pass off more complicated emotions as humor (*Just joking; Can't you take a joke; Lighten up*). Laughter lets the truth slip out while simultaneously evading detection.

Freud's case studies are sprinkled throughout with evidence of such un-Freudian behavior. In his notes on the Rat Man case, Freud writes simply, "He was hungry and was fed." Freud's biographer Peter Gay calls this "a heretical gesture for a psychoanalyst: to gratify a patient by permitting him access to his analyst's private life, and to mother him by providing food in a friendly and unprofessional setting." Any analyst would agree that his action was technically inappropriate. At the same time, many would also admit in a safe setting—the kind in which Duchenne laughter commonly erupts—that such rules are broken all the time. (During the pandemic, with sessions conducted by phone or video calls, this inevitably became even more true.)

My own analyst offered me food on occasions when I hadn't had time to eat, and extended to my children pretzels and warmth, permission to wait on the couch outside the consulting room on days I didn't have childcare. On one such occasion, when my daughters were six and eight, I asked them to be well behaved and kind to each other as I set them up with activities on the waiting room couch. My main worry was that the shy one would get nervous and need me, because, in the past, she had knocked on the door of the consulting room to either ask a question (*Would it be okay for me to eat my sandwich?*) or to just let me know she loved me.

Everything went smoothly. The two rooms shared a wall, so I figured I would hear anything out of line. But when I entered the waiting room and saw their faces, I could tell they had been fighting. One daughter sprang to her feet, bursting to tell me something, while the other, still seated, avoided eye contact by staring straight ahead. My zipper was down: I signaled to them to remain silent and follow me through the door. As soon as we were in the hallway, the animated one pulled out the old iPhone I had given them to play with, excited to show me what she had captured. Her sister had been so naughty! she told me. Without evidence, I would never believe it. The guilty child, so dreading the exposure of what had been videotaped, began to weep the moment her sister pressed play. In the video, my shy criminal held over her head one of the fancy decorative pillows from the waiting room couch, looked directly at the camera (her sister), and pummeled.

What disturbed me was not so much the act itself—though I demonstrated appropriate shock to discourage the impulse from being indulged in the future. I was unsettled instead by what crawled out of my daughter's expression as she looked at her sister just before attacking (*horror at pleasure of her own of which she herself was unaware?*). Again, regardless of how well you believe you know another person, you can never fully know what's inside them. Perhaps more disconcerting, you never fully know what's inside yourself.

When I was pregnant with my first child, I thought of my unborn fetus as a New York City neighbor—someone who, despite my awareness of her rhythms and movements, was essentially anonymous to me. Knowledge of this neighbor's name and sex might have organized my fantasies about her, but pregnancy placed me in an odd relation to this being, in that she existed to the same degree in fantasy as in concrete reality.

To make the fantasy feel more real, I consulted a pregnancy book that included sketches of what a fetus looks like week by week. At around eight weeks, it has webbed fingers and toes. On the ultrasound, she appeared otherworldly, an alien creature suspended in a hammock of light. It was far more pleasing, I discovered, to turn to images in my head than to envision what was happening inside me through technical diagrams and representations.

For a month, I woke every night at 1:00 a.m. with excruciating abdominal cramps. My organs were moving around, I learned, to make room for the machinery. My body, too, began to seem alien. We are, of course, always alien to ourselves without direct access to the unconscious, but the more aware I became of the wall separating me from the neighbor within, the more inaccessible my interior seemed to become to the external world, of which I was suddenly more a part. I came to access that universe, as with the unconscious, indirectly— through my baby's kicks, for instance, which I approached as an unrecognizable variant of Morse code.

I lived for years next door to a man I never encountered. I knew when he couldn't sleep, when he was ill, when agitation prompted him to pace the floor at 3:00 a.m. One night, he banged on my door with a hammer during a party. The friend who opened it described him looming above her like a serial killer from a horror movie, hammer cocked, ready to hit. Days later, the neighbor slipped a note under my door. He wasn't crazy, he wrote. The music was too loud. No one could hear his knocking.

I empathized. When he was sick, I heard his cough through the wall. I heard it from the stairs. It hurt my entire body. I knew him only through indescribable aspects, the kind Elizabeth Bishop tried to get at in her poetry. I loved this unknown neighbor as a poem, but did I love him as myself? Is that even generous if one is self-critical? Perhaps the precept should be inverted: love yourself as you love your neighbor, your poems—or, preferably, your unborn child. "Higher than love to your neighbor," Nietzsche writes, "is love to the furthest and future ones; higher still than love to men is love to things and phantoms."

The morning before my due date, I woke to use the bathroom at dawn. It was then that I grasped what was meant by a mucus plug. Understanding often occurs retroactively. Even in writing this, I feel myself far from understanding. I don't know what idea it will deliver or what meaning might be unplugged, but I'm afraid I am turning around too soon and there will be a cost.

In a recent dream, I get into my car and start driving. After a few feet, I realize someone has altered my rearview and side mirrors. Unable to see anything behind or to the sides of me, only what is directly before my eyes, I fear I will crash. I am able, in my dream, to see the past, which is ahead of me, but the present—which is to the sides and the future in the rearview mirror—has been tampered with, adjusted to fit someone else's desire or need. Perhaps we are always rearranging around another figure, either internalized from the past or still to come, as with Nietzsche's distant figures, whether stranger, unborn baby, or future self waiting to be known.

Within minutes of my daughter's birth, someone handed her to me. My first words upon seeing the strange creature that looked like she had stepped out of a *Saturday Night Live* Coneheads sketch was, What's up with her head? Then, realizing those were not the first words I would have chosen to utter to my newborn child, I added, Hi, sweetie. I'm your mother. Her name had already been chosen, but immediately after her birth, seeing her in the flesh, there seemed to be a disconnect. When you name what you do not know, you are naming your fantasy of what that unknown will become.

One summer, home from college, where I was studying neuroscience, I worked in a sleep lab. The research conducted at the time aimed to determine how sleep deprivation affects psychomotor activity in rats. First, electrodes were placed on the brain of each rat so its activity could be recorded, then the rats were placed in cages that had a circular disk at the base that was suspended above shallow water on one side. When the rats entered REM sleep, the disk would rotate, tossing them into the water to be awoken. The idea was to deprive them of sleep and study the repercussions.

Even though my newborn daughter was outside of my body, she remained attached to me by invisible electrodes that controlled me from within, tracked my brain activity so that each time I entered REM sleep—or had the rare thought about anything other than her—the disk rotated and I fell, ratlike, into a splash of maternal wakefulness. She materialized to dispel my dreams and fantasies, keeping me connected to the real by pummeling the cushions of my slumber and insisting that I know her as she was rather than as I imagined or hoped her to be.

A year and a half later, I became pregnant with my second daughter. As soon as I began to show, I explained the situation to my almost-two-year-old. I'm going to have a baby, I told her. Your baby sister is in my belly. She stared at me for a few seconds, stuffed the yellow baby blanket she carried everywhere under her shirt, and said, And *your* baby sister is in *my* belly. His name is Jako.

Before giving birth the second time, I worried about what would happen to my toddler if I suddenly went into labor and had to rush to the hospital, so I decided to be induced. It was infinitely easier the second time around to envision the baby, to know what to expect and how to handle it. Immediately after she was born, I breastfed her while the umbilical cord was still intact. I asked my husband to run out and buy a large Coke on ice, as I used to have in my teens after long Saturdays at the ballet studio. There were no hospital rooms available, so they let us stay in the delivery room with the baby and order food. Holding my newborn baby with one hand, I ate a grilled cheese with the other.

I knew exactly what to do, what was needed, but sometimes following a script can muffle the signals emitted from within. I hadn't anticipated the effect it would have on my daughter not to have been able to decide when to enter the world. Even now, she is averse to change, has trouble transitioning from one activity to another, needs me to put her to bed in the same way each night in order to fall asleep. If I nudge, she holds fast, says, It's because you didn't let me choose my birthday! Now whenever I think of an induced birth, the phrase *rude awakening* comes to mind.

But all changes aren't so sudden. The man I lived with and loved for over a decade, the father of my children, gradually became a neighbor to me. I explained our divorce to our daughters this way: We were two overlapping circles. The overlapping space was where we connected, but as we each came to know ourselves better and pursued what was important to us—things we believed in, felt passionately about— each of us gravitated toward opposite ends of our circles and the over-lapping space diminished. We were faced with a dilemma: Should we continue to move toward the parts of ourselves that felt alive, even if it meant no longer hearing the other's knocking?

▶

When my daughter was a toddler, she had a book about colors. There was a two-page spread for each color with images of objects in that color (a frog, waves). Each time we flipped to the pages for red, I was struck by how pink the red looked and wondered whether learning the word and category *red* would stop her from seeing the nuances of the actual color before her, as marriage can sometimes do to the per-ception of a relationship.

Learning the words for colors is perhaps a process of unseeing. Once we become able to connect whatever is before us to a category or set of familiar expectations, we apply what we've gathered from previous experiences to the present situation and use that to frame our interpretation. When those experiences we refer back to are not our own but are implanted within us to cushion our responses, we lose the capacity to distinguish between the simulated and real, like the replicants in *Blade Runner*. By the time we are adults, this process becomes second nature. With little perceptive input and little emotional output, we know how to take things.

The danger is that the facility we develop in moving from what is before us to attached words or meanings keeps us from using our perceptive abilities. Rather than cognizing, we re-cognize, refer the thing to a category and, in effect, no longer see the thing but its generic image.

Expectations surrounding an encounter take us out of our bodies into the meta level, and we assess the extent to which the present moment matches what we had anticipated. It's like reading a review of a film before seeing it, hearing about a city before visiting it, being told what sex is like before losing your virginity. We become psychologically habituated, and the ability to have a genuine reaction is short-circuited.

The more access we have to cultural information, the more difficult it becomes to resist mediating our experience of the world through knowledge and expectations. This is an enormous issue at the moment in relation to sex, and to the prevalence of porn in particular, the way it strengthens expectations around how sex should go, what turns people on, what the goal is—not merely orgasm, for some, but a money shot.

There sometimes seems to be a money shot quality to writing, and to the endings of poems in particular. A money shot ending, schematic in a similar way to a set joke, calls up third-person pleasure (*This is what one likes*), stirs the sole to the corps. When art becomes programmatic, it follows set structures that fulfill our expectations in serviceable ways. There's no dissonant note.

Rather than focus on consummation, on "getting" the meaning or message through interpretation, Sontag calls for an erotics of art, a poetics that centers around effect. "Paint, not the thing," advises poet and critic Stéphane Mallarmé, "but the effect it produces.... The line of poetry ... should be composed not of words, but of intentions, and all the words should fade away before the sensation." How, then, can poetry, and by extrapolation, experience, be red—not the word, the adjective, but the effect it produces erotically in the body?

"In a poem," poet Joseph Brodsky said in an interview, "you should try to reduce the number of adjectives to a minimum. So if somebody covered your poem with a magic cloth that removes adjectives, the page would still be black enough because of nouns, adverbs and verbs. When that cloth is little, your best friends are nouns."

When I picture enacting that advice, I imagine unfolding a napkin and placing it over a slice of pizza to absorb the grease. Adjectives, to me, are greasy. Colors are adjectives. And, like words for colors that categorize and limit perception, I think of them as other-directed. In fact, most language that strives to be understood in a particular way by its recipient feels greasy. (Freud writes in a letter to Jung about the "oily excuses" of a man saying what he thought would appease Freud after the latter confronted him about something he had written rather than engage with what he had expressed.) I use fewer adjectives when perceiving the world or talking to myself than when describing my perceptions to others. If my dogs were able to communicate in words, they wouldn't use adjectives either.

Barthes calls the adjective "that poorest of linguistic categories." "The man who provides himself or is provided with an adjective is now hurt, now pleased," writes Barthes, "but always *constituted*." Adjectives constitute us because they are linked to coded expressions: "rude, austere, proud, virile, solemn, majestic, warlike, educative, noble, sumptuous, doleful, modest, dissolute, voluptuous." We recognize how we are supposed to understand them, shift from potentially cognizing whatever is before us—the real thing—to recognizing a set interpretation. They call up meaning that has been implanted within us to shape how we take things. Adjectives are the canned laughter of language.

To provide oneself with an adjective is to be what Barthes terms a "user" as opposed to a "creator." In discussing the influence of toys on children, he describes certain toys as "essentially a microcosm of the adult world" in that they teach children to adopt adult roles—the doll that pees, the stethoscope that makes a beating sound when you press it against a surface, the play kitchen with its plastic chicken leg and glass of orange juice, eternally half-full. Such function-oriented toys train the children who play with them to become users, and, in performing the functions to which the toys correspond, to adopt roles. In a sense, they are users of roles rather than creators of their own identities and interactions with others and the world—great consumers. Abstract toys, like wooden blocks, require imagination, and, by not calling a role into being, train children to become creators. It is the difference, essentially, between adopting a prototypical life and creating your own structure out of basic building blocks.

Subjecting understanding to logic, the sentence—being shut up in prose—is to accept a scripted role, take your position on a stage and in a performance that, like bodily processes, is controlled by codes. As with Sontag's programmatic art, when what we perceive is linked to coded meaning—a certain chord progression eliciting happiness—we get it, know how we are supposed to respond, understand logically without necessarily feeling much of anything at all.

Adjectives, like non-Duchenne laughter, operate metacommunicatively and are therefore useful for the same reason that they're problematic. In fact, not everyone sees them in a negative light. "Adjectives," writes Anne Carson, "... these small imported mechanisms ... are the latches of being." Even as she seems to adopt a positive angle, Carson also describes adjectives as connectors, which is what Barthes objects to, the way they link up to coded expression, constitute us, latch our being.

Finding a way around the problem of the adjective wouldn't mean stopping using adjectives altogether but understanding what made you reach for them in the first place, just as a psychoanalyst wouldn't advise you to simply get rid of your defenses but to understand why you use them when you do, how they might have worked in the past but will inevitably turn on you once they become automatic, come to constitute you, program (and calcify) your responses.

Barthes's suggestion is to tune in to what he calls the "grain" of the voice: "The 'grain' is the body in the voice as it sings, the hand as it writes, the limb as it performs." The grain, like beta elements do, puts your body in direct erotic relation to the body of the singer, writer, musician:

> I know at once which part of the body is playing—if it is the arm, too often, alas, muscled like a dancer's calves, the clutch of the finger-tips (despite the sweeping flourishes of the wrists), or if on the contrary it is the only erotic part of a pianist's body, the pad of the fingers whose "grain" is so rarely heard.

A "contingent work," which Barthes opposes to a coded one, would necessarily be embedded with elements from the specific physical context it was born out of: the environment, the singer's emotional and physical state when singing, the situation—emotional and physiological—of the specific body the voice passes through, and, of course, the voice itself.

"Can I get some of that tea? Some of that tea," singer-songwriter Lauryn Hill asks between songs on her *MTV Unplugged* album:

> I know I sound raspy, but that's, hey, I used to go on tour, you know, and . . . I'd be this prisoner in a hotel, you know, drinking tea and, you know, telling the children, you know, "Mommy has to sleep" cause I wanted to maintain this, you know, immaculate sounding voice, but that's not realistic. You know, reality is, sometimes I stay up late, and this is what I sound like when I wake up the next day, and you know, it's a voice. You know, and to me, the more I, uh, I focus less on myself the more I realize I can be used to spread a message. 'Cause when I'm, I used to be so, you know, oh my God, if I sound harsh and raspy I can't go out there. And that's a lie, you know, I just sound like a singer with a lot of stuff in her throat.

A lot of grain. And what's transmitted through the grain—the blood, saliva, and mucus Ferrante equates with life—is different from what the immaculate voice carries. "Today," Barthes writes, ". . . there seems to be a flattening out of technique, which is paradoxical in that the various manners of playing are all flattened out *into perfection.*" Auto-tuned. There is no "space of pleasure, of thrill, a site where language works for *nothing.*" He mocks singing teachers' emphasis on proper breathing: "The lung, a stupid organ (lights for cats!), swells but gets no erection; it is in the throat, place where the phonic metal hardens and is segmented, in the mask that *significance* explodes, bringing not the soul but *jouissance.*"

Years ago, I spent the day with a man I met at a party. We went to lunch, looked at art. I knew I was interested in him but couldn't read his feelings toward me. Later that evening, I received an email from him. The content was mundane, offered no inkling of interest, but in it was a typo that contained a world.

Somewhere near the beginning of the email, where the man had meant to write, *It was great to see you, although . . .* , he wrote, It was great to see you, althought. With that *t*, he created a condensation that was loaded with meaning—it was great to see you, *although all thought,* which is to say, *It was great to see you although it was all thought, no body.* The lowercase *t*, which is also the symbol for addition, stitched his body into the message, making palpable the finger that made the slip, slipped in—erect, as Barthes would say—to transform an uncommunicative email into a titillating one, "language carpeted with skin."

The more perfect—coded—a work, the more likely it is to inoculate pleasure, just as an analysand who guards against letting the messier parts of themselves slip out is less likely to access transformative insight. Poking fun at himself and his own tendency toward such inoculation in a letter to a friend, Proust imaginatively projects himself into a third-person perspective that criticizes his performative gestures, placing them on par with adjectives: "I must own that I rather dislike him with his everlasting grand impulses, his busy manner, his grand passions, and his adjectives." (Proust and Bergson were cousins by marriage.)

Artists who perform unplugged, directly, without the amplification of adjectival gestures, make way for new life, the unknown. Work that preserves the grain—the fluids and funk that flow through a living body—brings you back to a moment of cognition because, as Barthes puts it, "the symbolic . . . is thrown immediately (without mediation) before us." You feel the stuff in the singer's voice, the finger that sticks through what was meant to be two-dimensional space. This "directness," Sontag writes, ". . . entirely frees us from the itch to interpret." We can feel (*rapid motion of wings*).

What is thrown directly, unmediated before us is a sense of the unconscious, which we cannot willfully access but can get an inkling of by following the grain with techniques similar to those used in psychoanalysis.

Write not the idea but the effect it produces.

"When one goes at ideas directly," poet John Ashbery says in an interview, "with hammer and tongs as it were, ideas tend to elude one in a poem. I think they only come back in when one pretends not to be paying any attention to them, like a cat that will rub against your leg." Ashbery goes on in this interview to explain the associative process he used in writing the poem "What Is Poetry." By leaning on "one's automatic temptation to connect something with something else," he leaped from the town of Chester, England, to foreign boy scouts, to the Empire State Building (because it was a beautiful day), to school, to the teachers, to how they "tried to make everything simple and understandable, by combing out the snarls in one's thinking." (*The lines I love now have all their knots left in.*)

Free association, whether in writing or in psychoanalysis, helps you gain access to the unconscious. It is during the session in which an analysand says, "I have no idea where I'm going with this" that revelation pokes through. By pursuing whatever arises in the mind without strategy or investment—the random thought, slip of the tongue, sensation of a cat—you become able to discover meaning rather than make it. Even a snippet of overheard speech can enter into the space-time of your writing and redirect its trajectory, as is the case with Ashbery's poem's last line: "It might give us—what?—some flowers soon?" Ashbery explains that he often uses overheard speech in poems and that he "overheard a boy saying that particular line to a girl in Brentano's bookshop where [he] was browsing."

Incorporating the speech of others into writing makes the consciousness of the work simultaneously singular and collective. In her poetry collection *Sleeping with the Dictionary*, Harryette Mullen lifts familiar phrases and recasts them ("We are not responsible for your lost or stolen relatives. / . . . Your insurance was cancelled because we can no longer handle / your frightful claims"), provoking the reader to feel the vibration between different levels of meaning, eliciting an emotional response in the body similar to the one triggered by a singer's vibrato. Poet Wanda Coleman, in her poem "Wanda Why Aren't You Dead," choreographs the heard speech of others—whether real or imagined—so that the body of "wanda" is positioned in direct relation to the reader's body, although she makes only an implied appearance as the figure being addressed:

> wanda when are you gonna wear your hair down
> wanda. that's a whore's name
> wanda why ain't you rich
> wanda you know no man in his right mind want a
> ready-made family
> why don't you lose weight
> wanda why are you so angry
> how come your feet are so goddamn big
> can't you afford to move out of this hell hole
> if i were you were you were you
> wanda what is it like being black
> i hear you don't like black men

tell me you're ac/dc. tell me you're a nympho. tell me you're
into chains
wanda i don't think you really mean that
you're joking. girl, you crazy
wanda *what* makes you so angry
wanda i think you need this
wanda you have no humor in you you too serious
wanda i didn't know i was hurting you
that was an accident
wanda i know what you're thinking
wanda i don't think they'll take that off of you

wanda why are you so angry

i'm sorry i didn't remember that that that
that that that was so important to you

wanda you're ALWAYS on the attack

wanda wanda wanda i wonder

why ain't you dead

Despite having been written in multiple voices with no interior representation of "wanda" in its language, the poem causes the reader to
feel into what they imagine to be her shape, to hear these lines from
within a conjured body. The figure of "wanda" becomes a "symbol of
limits," in Ellison's terms, a "reliable gauge"—like negative space—
for others to determine, through disidentification, who they are. Even
the adjectives enlisted (rich, ready-made, angry, big, black, crazy, serious, dead) highlight the forces that latch "wanda"'s being to associations that were already in the mind of the reader—as with "*it's so true
humour*"—chaining her individual circumstances to broader dynamics, both social and political.

"Power links," Blanchot writes, "un-power detaches." Adjectives and other forms of coded linguistic expressions, Arendt explains in "Thinking and Moral Considerations," lead us to transfer our attention and power to conventional assumptions rather than to what the facts and events of concrete reality reveal:

> Clichés, stock phrases, adherence to conventional, standardized codes of expression and conduct have the socially recognized function of protecting us against reality, that is, against the claim on our thinking attention which all events and facts arouse by virtue of their existence.

Attention arouses, whereas standardized codes of expression and conduct ease us into collective sleep, habitualization—allowing us to close our eyes to what we would prefer not to see. When we choose not to act, not to express ourselves freely, and instead turn and face the direction that is indicated, take our position in a social script, we reinforce the power dynamics within the culture to which we are bound. We are our choices, including whatever it is we become by default when we decide to transfer our power to others and let them choose for us.

If the unconscious, as Lacan proposes, is structured like a language, then it would make sense to apply poetic principles to our approach to the self, others, and the world we collectively inhabit. By incorporating contingent elements into your thought process—what passes before you visually, aurally, parapraxes, snippets of speech—you situate yourself in space and time, which situates your addressee in space and time, lets you have a body, lets them have a body, and within it the capacity to experience erotically. "No interpretation is any good," Bion writes, "unless it is reminiscent of real life." You have to be able to receive unconscious transmissions, hear the music, the other's knocking.

Rather than reiterating what you already know, delivered from your intellect to another's in language, however skilled and beautiful, speaking and writing then become processes of discovery—not merely of yourself, but of interpersonal relationships, the irrational parts, the world, of which you are only a small (hopefully moving) part. The idea that we are separate and enclosed is an illusion: other people's speech, like it or not, lives inside us, buoys us, metastasizes. We are quantum entangled with our universe and everything in it.

That is not to say that you can't also reach for inward contingencies—your own internal knocking. Overheard internal speech can also be useful—what your inner voice says without your participation when it's unmiked. I hear my mind most clearly when walking my dogs—moving through space without destination—and in dreams. Freud uses the term "involuntary thoughts" in *The Interpretation of Dreams* to describe "ideas that seem to emerge 'of their own free will'" when one manages to get around "the critical function that is normally in operation against them." Uncritical self-observation is necessary for free association and "poetic creation," as he explains through quoting the following letter by Schiller:

> It seems a bad thing and detrimental to the creative work of the mind if Reason makes too close an examination of the ideas as they come pouring in—at the very gateway, as it were. . . . Where there is a creative mind, Reason—so it seems to me—relaxes its watch upon the gates, and the ideas rush in pell-mell, and only then does it look them through and examine them in a mass.—You critics, or whatever else you may call yourselves, are ashamed or frightened of the momentary and transient extravagances which are to be found in all truly creative minds and whose longer or shorter duration distinguishes the thinking artist from the dreamer. You complain of your unfruitfulness because you reject too soon and discriminate too severely.

For Schiller, those moored to Reason become watchers at the gateway of the mind, critics, rejecting ideas too quickly: "Looked at in isolation, a thought may seem very trivial or very fantastic; but it may be made important by another thought that comes after it, and, in conjunction with other thoughts that may seem equally absurd, it may turn out to form a most effective link." As in dream analysis or poetry writing, following a trail of associations will lead to unexpected, previously unknown revelations. But inhibitions need to be lifted for that to be possible.

When you free yourself from the goal of making meaning, pleasing the watchers at the gateway of the mind with Reason, whatever will be interpretable to others—prototypes, adjectives, the money shot, unerotic pornography—you leave open the possibility of connections created with the participation of more than just the logical faculty, which hankers after meaning and themes because that is what feels, like processed foods, easiest to digest.

"Thematicism," writes Derrida, "necessarily leaves out of account the formal, phonic, or graphic 'affinities' that do not have the shape of a word, the calm unity of the verbal sign." Because I write by hand, I often cannot read a word or phrase I've jotted down, and the graphic affinity my eyes find in my illegible writing is invariably more profound or surprising than what I had intended. The same goes for autocorrect, which seems to tap into my unconscious (*I'm writing to let you know how dirty I am*). Phonic affinities play into the music of writing but can also be taken as the basis of meaning itself, as with homophonic translation, which translates work from another language not by the meanings of words but by their sounds—as poet Louis Zukofsky does in his translation of Catullus. He listened through the words in Latin to hear English words he discovered within their sounds and translated that heard meaning. By listening not only to words, fleshless skeletons, "but also to the music," as Bion puts it, you tune in to the grain.

During my childhood, when my brother and I would wake our mother—an obstetrician who had to get up at all hours to deliver babies—while she was napping, she would yell, *Zucknaboot!* We would look at each other and say, Suck my boot? We understood the Arabic phrase through homophonic translation to mean, *You'll get a boot in your mouth if you don't quiet down.*

A child listening to the *muzz muzz* of adult conversation, regardless of the language, will hear in the sounds words they know—or will understand what they see, hear, or otherwise perceive based on what they can relate to it through the process of recognition. Yet without having first cognized a broad set of reference points, the child will turn to what is available—the internal projector's stream of fantasy thought—and rediscover its contents in the world around them. Finding meaning in the sounds of words or world, and other perceptions, taps into the unconscious in the same way that a Rorschach inkblot does: what you perceive reflects your unconscious beliefs and desires, how they structure your emotional world.

When my daughters made drawings in preschool, the teacher would ask what they had drawn and write the word for it in the lower right-hand corner (*flower, cat, house*). At age three, nearly a year after her sister was born, my older daughter came home with a sheet of paper that had on it, instead of a sketch, the word *baby* in an emphatic scribble. In the lower right-hand corner, in the teacher's hand, was her infant sister's name. As I looked at the drawing, the symbolic was thrown, without mediation, before me, the word in her hand all grain, made flesh.

Often while working as a psychoanalyst, I feel the grain, the flesh, the billowing of the veil as it is briefly lifted, the clumsy touch of something that has slipped through an opening. As with a screen memory, I catch among the mulching leaves the ranke scent of ciphered meaning.

The creation of a screen is an encoding process: the overwhelming thought or emotion that has been turned away from is retained within the screen in encrypted form. If free association can help get at the screened-out meaning in a memory or dream, perhaps using a poem, sensation, or experience, in Ashbery's terms, as a "launching pad for free associations" can be a way of transmitting at the sensory level what lies beneath the associations—what has been screened out—without approaching it directly, taking it as a subject and combing through its snarls to make it appear presentable, available for interpretation.

A poem—whether on the page or in the world (*Everyone is a poem*)—can be apprehended as a screen memory, which, like Barthes's contingent work, becomes encoded with meaning and emotion that is not limited to what is carried in dictionary definitions or recognizable logic, but loaded with unconscious, encrypted meaning and emotion, beta elements. In contrast to adjectives, ideas, coded meaning, and money shot endings that defend against unlatched being, a poem has the potential to track "being . . . stepped out into the unconcealedness of its being," as Heidegger has it—*jouissance*—the effect that conjures a body, a poem continuously being written, what teeters over the brink of being known. Discoveries about the unknown, the unconscious, restore our sense of aliveness. But, like a shark, you have to keep moving.

"Movement is the principle element in dance, it's plot," according to dancer Bronislava Nijinska, dancer Vaslav Nijinsky's sister. To me, movement is also the principle element in poetry, relationships, experience—anything that contains the throbbing pulse of being. The plot rests neither in narrative nor in idea, but in a tracking of the grain, the feeling in your hands as they rest on the dancer's jumping body (*how like thought!*), whatever might have been screened out but can nonetheless be perceived, like music, by nonrational faculties.

The experimental composer John Cage describes music as "purposeless play," which is "an affirmation of life—not an attempt to bring order out of chaos nor to suggest improvements in creation, but simply a way of waking up to the very life we're living." His process involved using what he termed "chance operations"—rolling dice, consulting the *I Ching*—that invite random, irrational elements into a controlled situation, much as psychoanalysis encourages free association within a fixed frame (the set elements of a session: from environment and time to expectations surrounding the analyst's demeanor).

The "very life we're living" encompasses everything in the space-time we occupy without weighted value or purpose.

Merce Cunningham, Cage's life partner, also incorporated chance operations into his method of composition.

> When I choreograph a piece by tossing pennies—by chance, that is—I am finding my resources in that play, which is not the product of my will, but which is an energy and a law which I too obey. Some people seem to think that it is inhuman and mechanistic to toss pennies in creating a dance instead of chewing the nails or beating the head against a wall or thumbing through old notebooks for ideas. But the feeling I have when I compose in this way is that I am in touch with a natural resource far greater than my own personal inventiveness could ever be, much more universally human than the particular habits of my own practice, and organically rising out of common pools of motor impulses.

Cunningham creates a transitional space by way of play that allows him to travel freely between personal inventiveness and the universally human. In reaching beyond what is known and tapping into natural resources belonging to the universe—its energy and impulses—an artist has the potential to create works that jolt us awake.

One summer afternoon, as I lay on my back on the carpeted floor reading Stendhal's *The Red and the Black*, the enormous novel extended above me, my then seven-year-old daughter entered the room, lay beside me, and, knowing I had also been bingeing on *Mad Men* at the time, asked, Mommy, which do you like better—*Mad Men* or Stendhal? The moment she put the two sagas side by side, I realized that their main characters—Don Draper and Julien Sorel—are, in fact, quite similar, both slipping through openings created by desire to upset the social order.

I don't think my own personal inventiveness could have come up with that connection: for me to see it, the components needed to be brought together by a force outside my will, the way I sometimes recognize a resonance between ideas merely because the books housing them have landed haphazardly beside one another on a table or a shelf. Books can become metonyms for the ideas they contain, which is why sometimes, to engage with a thought I am not ready to think, I find myself placing books charged with unthought elements beside one another in a space where they can commune without my active participation.

The chance procedures used by Cunningham as a choreographic tool were the subject of a master class taught by Jean Freebury, a former Merce Cunningham company dancer, that I took at Mark Morris Dance Center in Brooklyn. We were first introduced to Cunningham's use of dice, and to how he would ask questions about where to take his choreography that a throw of dice would answer. Next we were asked to put this idea into action. Freebury presented us with basic dance moves from one of Cunningham's solos and then placed us in groups of three to compose a piece using the moves and a handful of dice.

I learned pretty quickly that matching up yes-or-no questions to even or odd answers was the easiest way to work: Should the dance begin with the dancers on- or offstage? Would the dancers all perform the same moves? Would they perform at the same time? In her book *Motherhood*, Sheila Heti uses a coin toss in a similar way, seeking answers to yes-or-no questions that seemingly direct her thinking and writing ("Is it wrong to have an audience in mind when setting out on a work of art? yes"). The limitation I found in my own use of this method was that, even as it involves play, it is not quite purposeless: the framing of closed-ended questions latches being in a similar way to adjectives, in that both bring coded, answer-slapping order to openings to stop up chaos.

The universe is rarely ordered in binary ways. Even "the terms *alive* and *dead* are ones whose meanings are wholly psychological," according to psychoanalyst Charles Brenner, because "physiochemically, they merge into one another." There is "no definable point at which a living organism dies," so, although "the terms *living* and *dead* have obvious meanings psychologically, . . . there is no such clear difference between the two for a chemist." As with binocular rivalry, the binary splits we perceive are often illusions. If the "no" of a coin toss were a thing with physical existence, then I imagine at the physiochemical level it would similarly merge with its psychological opposite and possess a tinge of "yes." "The wrong answer," as designer Bruce Mau has it, "is the right answer looking for a different question." Within each crack is light.

I roll a single die—a four—and meditate on it.

My parents recently moved out of my childhood home. As I rifled through boxes of letters and notebooks, deciding what to keep, I was stopped by a ripped sheet of paper that had on it a list of four items and a map: "1st kiss Fraine's basement (in the fucking closet) / #2 Blues Fest / 3&4 Jimmy's." I knew immediately who had written it—heard the words in his low mumble—and what the map represented—the street in front of Jimmy's, the local bar, where kiss 4 took place. The piece of paper (a placemat from Jimmy's) had embedded within it a cross section of time: the uncertainty of the moment, the touch of our bodies, the strip of Fifty-Fifth Street a block away from the house I grew up in, the foot-shaped stones in the front garden (*Would my feet ever get that big?*), the smell of the garbage truck that provided kiss 4's cover, the worry that I would be seen, wouldn't be seen, would miss curfew, would follow the map's road leading uphill into possibility, risk, the unknown. I placed the sheet of paper in the "save" pile, where many of the more prototypical love letters, which used the phrase "I love you" [*sound of latch fastening*], didn't land.

Though it wouldn't necessarily be detected through a formal or physiochemical analysis, the map of four kisses—the inverse of Baudrillard's simulation—transmits the grain, as do Niedecker's poems written on calendar pages ("Wade all life / backward to its / source which / runs too far / ahead"), or Dickinson's fragments on envelopes ("We talked with / each other about each other / though neither of / us spoke"). The wall between me and these writings, as with the "baby" in my daughter's drawing, is full of openings: I feel the touch of a hand loop toward me, much as Keats, in his "O for a life of Sensations rather than of Thoughts!" letter, describes how hearing a "delicious voice" provokes the listener to form "the Singer's face"— and, perhaps, as with appoggiatura, yearn for it as well.

I am continually running away from the subject, along with the "I" of Keats's letter—

Yet the subject, like an idea, eludes me when I go after it with a hammer and tongs. Perhaps the aim is to talk without speaking, wade backward to the source—a life of sensations rather than of thoughts. But where to begin?

"Begin anywhere," says Cage.

The night before dropping off my older daughter at overnight camp, we had dinner with one of her friends who was to attend the same camp. It was my daughter's first time at sleepaway camp. Everyone was excited—or so it seemed, until she pulled me aside, rubbing her temples, and asked, What if I miss you too much? She inherited my tendency to get what I termed in childhood "birthday headaches": incapacitating mental pain that sets in whenever there is pressure to be happy (birthday parties, school trips, holidays). Joy, for me, has always been script-resistant.

Before my daughters went to sleep that night, they played cards on the hotel bed next to mine. At one point, my older daughter reprimanded her sister, You're bleeding! You're bleeding! The phrase, they taught me, means you are holding your hand such that your cards show.

Maybe we are all afraid of bleeding. I picture the pages of this book streaked with red and cringe—

"Only some of you will guess," Fanon writes in the introduction to *Black Skin, White Masks*, "how difficult it was to write this book." Perhaps his difficulty was inevitable: "A great book," according to Deleuze, "is always the inverse of another book that could only be written in the soul, with silence and blood." Unplugged. But "great," to me, has always meant being able to create change, not some joke revolution.

One of the exercises in clown school was to take the stage with others and spontaneously create a game. The first initiated action functions as a proposal that is then collaboratively developed through improvisation. When I performed this exercise, one of the actors onstage with me lifted his shirt and another spontaneously slapped his belly. We then created a game of shirt-lifting and belly-slapping.

However, as anyone who has participated in a group project knows, there is invariably an alpha participant, who, believing they have an idea superior to the one at hand, directs their energy toward changing course, switching from shirt-lifting and belly-slapping to some other game that has been proposed by them that is more in line with how they would like to be perceived.

One of the most meaningful lessons I learned in clown school was offered by Bayes in the moment when one of the actors onstage with me tried to do just that. "There's no better game," he admonished, "than the one you're playing."

Or, as in driving, always turn your wheel in the direction of the skid—

The gap between who one is and who they would like to be—castration anxiety—often compels them to want to switch from what they have mastered or what comes naturally to a different profession, game, or life they think of as better.

However, being a master of one's craft, regardless of what it produces, affords one the freedom to create without having to take direction from others, explains Tsvetaeva, discussing the poet through the example of the shoemaker. Were a banker or politician to give a shoemaker advice, the shoemaker would "laugh" at him (*I'm sorry for you*), "either up his sleeve or to [his] face." The value of what is produced, the shoes, is inseparable from the freedom and emotion experienced in the process of creation, the accompanying consciousness, which is then transmitted through beta elements to the one who wears the shoes or reads the poem.

Shelley, in "A Defence of Poetry," argues that poetry exercises the imagination and, because imagining yourself in another's shoes is the first step in ethical thought, it can indirectly develop your ethical faculty regardless of its subject matter. When you exercise the imagination, in other words, you are simultaneously exercising your ethical faculty. Reading or writing poetry, then, is an imaginative act—no matter what its content—that helps you strengthen your ethical musculature so you are prepared to fight the necessary fights, make critical changes, and affect the world.

Shelley's argument, when I first read it as a graduate student, offered enormous relief. At the time, I had been feeling conflicted about the work I was writing, the game I was playing, because it didn't directly involve the ethical and political concerns that were on my mind. Despite being bothered by the gap between what I was writing and what I wanted my writing to be, I was able to accept my work on its own terms because I told myself—or heard Shelley telling me— that I was exercising my ethical faculty by proxy.

After delving deeper into Shelley's personal writings, however, I discovered he actually valued political writing above poetry, the shoe you walk around in as opposed to the one you imbue with encoded meaning. Nevertheless, because he suffered what his biographer Richard Holmes describes as "hysterical and nervous attacks" of both somatic and psychosomatic origin, Shelley felt too weak to write in the form he held in highest esteem (only some of you will guess how difficult it would have been for him). His defense—that ethics could be approached indirectly through poetry, that one form can metony-mically deliver another—was, in short, projective autobiography.

Still, this failing led to some of the most important poetry of the nineteenth century as well as to a rallying call for the Labour Party in the twenty-first. Lines from "The Mask of Anarchy" were recited in 2017 by British politician Jeremy Corbyn ("Rise like Lions after slum-ber / In unvanquishable number— / Shake your chains to earth like dew / Which in sleep have fallen on you—"). The poem was so well known that some in the crowd were reported to have joined in at the last line, which, in modified form, became a campaign slogan ("For the many, not the few"). His poetry, in the end, managed to transmit political meaning.

Recently, I noticed the *moth* in the word *mother*, a tendency toward light. They are my little lights, my daughters. But my unhappiness as a mother has always been about the sense that I should be hankering after something brighter.

As they grow, my hankering does too. Every night, my daughter asks me to put her to bed. An evening shortly after she has turned thirteen, I pull myself impatiently from my work, stay five minutes or so, then lean forward to give her a kiss. Don't go yet, she says. I know you think I'm a stinking teenager now and want to get away, but I'm still me.

On the radio, I hear a scientist, Jeff Lockwood, describe the breed of crickets he studies, *gryllacrididae*, as so aggressive they are like "crickets on steroids." These bulky crickets have not only strong jaws and sharp mandibles but also a tendency to fly into vicious rages. To keep them from attacking one another, which is their tendency, he housed each in its own cage, where it would build a "nest" it considered a home. He came to realize that each recognized its nest through a particular scent that it identified as its own.

Because these crickets were aggressive with everyone, not just with one another, Lockwood used a special tool when opening their cages to maintain a safe distance. After one bit off the end of his tool, however, he began anesthetizing them before opening their cages by placing them in the refrigerator. One time, as he opened the door to a cage, the cricket inside started to slip out. Lockwood used his tool to quickly shove the cricket back in and mistakenly injured it, creating a slit along its abdomen.

Out of this slit seeped the cricket's viscera (*You're bleeding! You're bleeding!*). After a pause, the wounded insect turned its head downward and began to eat what it must have recognized olfactorily as part of itself. This behavior, the scientist explained, is evolutionarily sound: the viscera likely smelled like fat, and fat is hard to come by in nature. A survival instinct, in other words, compelled the cricket to eat its own body.

Regardless, one of the hosts of the *Radiolab* episode found the unplugged viscera repulsive. "Wow. That is disgusting," he said. It is indeed repellent to most of us for our interior to be presented to us in the external world and then to be reassimilated into our bodies, to drink our own saliva from a cup, take our voice back in through our auditory cavity, reencounter our viscera in published form (*Only some of you will guess*). Who among us can harness such animal vigor, celebrate the whole dimension of our organism unveiled, spill our viscera, only to eat it up again and sing, along with Whitman, "laugh[ing] at what you call dissolution," "I find no sweeter fat than sticks to my own bones"?

Dancer and choreographer Agnes de Mille, after the "flamboyant success" of work she thought "only fairly good," confided in Martha Graham that she "had a burning desire to be excellent, but no faith that [she] could be." De Mille recorded Graham's response in her biography, *Martha*:

> Martha said to me, very quietly: "There is a vitality, a life force, an energy, a quickening that is translated through you into action,

and because there is only one of you in all of time, this expression is unique. And if you block it, it will never exist through any other medium and it will be lost. The world will not have it. It is not your business to determine how good it is nor how valuable nor how it compares with other expressions. It is your business to keep it yours clearly and directly, to keep the channel open. You do not even have to believe in yourself or your work. You have to keep yourself open and aware to the urges that motivate you. Keep the channel open. As for you, Agnes, you have so far used about one-third of your talent."

"But," I said, "when I see my work I take for granted what other people value in it. I see only its ineptitude, inorganic flaws, and crudities. I am not pleased or satisfied."

"No artist is pleased."

"But then there is no satisfaction?"

"No satisfaction whatever at any time," she cried out passionately. "There is only a queer divine dissatisfaction, a blessed unrest that keeps us marching and makes us more alive than the others."

Schiller wanted to hug the world. That was what stood out to me when I first encountered his work in graduate school, although the only evidence I've ever found of his having said that is in my mental library beside Freud's daughter's strawberry cake. Across Schiller's poems and philosophical essays are a multitude of embraces, including within the poem that was the inspiration for Beethoven's ninth symphony, *Ode to Joy*. In December 1989, after the fall of the Berlin Wall, Leonard Bernstein conducted *Ode to Joy*, replacing the word for "joy" (*Freude*) with the word for "freedom" (*Freiheit*): *Ode to Freedom*. After hearing this fact repeatedly, as it was reported quite a bit at the end of 2019 for the thirtieth anniversary of the fall of the Berlin Wall, I came to hear in the *Freude* of the symphony a phonic affinity with the Freud of psychoanalysis—which, for me, has been a similar ode, both to freedom and to joy. To come to know your desire—what you really want as opposed to what you think you want or what will fulfill the desires of others, those watchers at the gateway of the mind—is essential to psychological freedom. ("Emancipate yourselves from mental slavery," sings Bob Marley. "None but ourselves can free our minds.") It is fitting that a contingent trail of free associations—Schiller, Beethoven, Bernstein, the Berlin Wall, *Freude*, his Schiller, the watchers who inoculate against extravagances—led me to this sense of world joy, a state of mind that is difficult, if not impossible, to conjure by will.

World joy, like Lecoq's universal poetic sense or Graham's queer divine dissatisfaction, can flip into savage complexity, along with the unwanted truths, the viscera, leaking from it. "To dare to be aware of the facts of the universe in which we are existing," Bion writes in his final paper, "calls for courage":

> That universe may not be pleasing and we may be disposed to get out of it; if we cannot get out of it, if for some reason our musculature is not working, or if it is not appropriate to run away or retire, then we can be reduced to other forms of escape—like going to sleep, or becoming unconscious of the universe of which we do not wish to be conscious, or being ignorant. . . . (I use "ignores" as the process requisite to reaching "ignorance".)

To remain present to the aliveness of the universe, for an authentic conversation to take place and for the quickening to be translated through us into action, we must be willing to take in rather than ignore the facts of that universe, along with the full range of emotions that come up—remain accurate and honest, awake. Doing so, however, requires that we become aware of the destructive and disgusting—visceral—tendencies within ourselves and others, keeping in mind "the fact that something *could* go wrong does not mean that we are in danger," as writer Sarah Schulman says in *Conflict Is Not Abuse*. "It means that we are alive."

The act of "going to sleep," becoming unconscious when we don't want to be conscious, is raised at the end of William Stafford's poem

"A Ritual to Read to Each Other." The speaker "appeal[s] to a voice, to something shadowy / a remote important region in all who talk":

> though we could fool each other, we should consider—
> lest the parade of our mutual life get lost in the dark.
>
> For it is important that awake people be awake,
> or a breaking line may discourage them back to sleep;
> the signals we give—yes or no, or maybe—
> should be clear: the darkness around us is deep.

We stay connected by creating cracks in the wall of darkness around us. Through these openings, we transmit conscious and unconscious communications in the form of words, beta elements, provocations, embodied knowledge, and laughter in hopes of keeping one another awake.

But binary splits—like a yes-or-no coin toss—are often illusions that limit our modes of apprehension. It is when binocular rivalry is suspended through laughter, or when some other spontaneous gesture from the True Self is released, that we unveil the wholeness of our being, feel alert and alive. "I would make a distinction," writes Bion, "between existence—the capacity to exist—and the ambition or aspiration to have an existence which is worth having—the quality of the existence, not the quantity; not the length of one's life, but the quality of that life."

I recently discovered, while searching for the Schiller passage, that he was not, in fact, the philosopher who wanted to hug the world. I now possess that knowledge, but what is known is dead. Knowledge in and of itself does not carry vital meaning. A psyche must take in and process knowledge for it to be enlivened. "When you're writing," James Baldwin explains, "you're trying to find out something which you don't know. The whole language of writing for me is finding out what you don't want to know, what you don't want to find out. But something forces you to anyway." The same can be said of living—or, rather, of remaining alive.

When I did not know, I wondered, and when I wandered, I impro-vised, kept moving, played. "Exuberance is Beauty," as William Blake writes, most self, that sweeter fat. Knowledge, similar to an answer, has the potential to be a space stopper, a *straling*-snuffer. It corsets the free flow of viscera, like the person Roethke encapsulates in a note-book with "he'd turn the light off on a moth."

The lure in failure is that it creates an opening, and through that opening can emerge a flash of spontaneity, freedom, momentary chaos, something akin to a bird's pain (and fear) before flight. The artist's blessed unrest. "I love only that which is written with blood," writes Nietzsche. "Write with blood: and you will discover that blood is spirit." Alive and present, you tune in to the grain, the knocking, the flow of pure becoming, that unconscious life-energy that is neither created nor destroyed but transferred and transmitted, continuously moving, changing shape. "It is not your business," as Graham advises, "to determine how good it is nor how valuable nor how it compares with other expressions. It is your business to keep it yours clearly and directly, to keep the channel [nasty hole?] open."

"My propositions," writes Wittgenstein, "serve as elucidations in the following way: anyone who understands me eventually recognizes them as nonsensical." Or, in Barthes's terms, "What I can name can-not really prick me." The goal is less to line up the external chips, to get things right, than it is to be alive while living, alive when you die.

Can you just tell me I'm a good mother? I say to my younger daughter. We are alone in the kitchen. I've just had an argument with her teen-age sister and am feeling guilty. Even though part of me recognizes I do this each year the night before my older daughter leaves for sum-mer camp—create conflict, distance between us that will somehow make the separation feel a little bit easier—another part of me can't handle the enormity of my emotion, wants to look away, unknow what I know, and insist upon my parade of logic. On the drive to camp the next morning, my older daughter and I will work through the impending loss metacommunicatively: I will mistakenly take a wrong turn to gain time with her; she will lose her phone in the trunk of the car while pulling a sweatshirt out of her duffel bag at a rest stop to gain time with me. It all comes to this.

Yeah, I will, my younger daughter responds, taking her phone out of her pocket to look at the screen. Someone's calling me. [*Walking out of the room.*] Okay, you're a good mother. Hello?

A Shrewdness of Thinkers & Feelers

Books

Mikhail Bakhtin, *Rabelais and His World*, trans. Hélène Iswolsky (Bloomington: Indiana University Press, 1984).

——. *Speech Genres and Other Late Essays*, trans. Vern W. McGee, ed. Caryl Emerson and Michael Holquist (Austin: University of Texas Press, 1986).

James Baldwin, *No Name in the Street* (New York: Dial Press, 1972).

Charles Baudelaire, *The Essence of Laughter and Other Essays, Journals, and Letters*, ed. Peter Quennell (New York: Meridian Books, 1956).

Roland Barthes, *Image, Music, Text*, trans. and ed. Stephen Heath (New York: Hill and Wang, 1977).

——. *The Pleasure of the Text*, trans. Richard Miller (New York: Hill and Wang, 1975).

——. *Roland Barthes*, trans. Richard Howard (Berkeley: University of California Press, 1994).

Georges Bataille, *Erotism: Death and Sensuality*, trans. Mary Dalwood (San Francisco: City Lights Books, 1986).

Jean Baudrillard, *Simulations*, trans. Paul Foss, Paul Patton, and Philip Beitchman (New York: Semiotext(e), 1983).

W. R. Bion, *Attention and Interpretation: A Scientific Approach to Insight in Psycho-Analysis and Groups* (London: Tavistock Publications, 1970).

——. *Clinical Seminars and Other Works* (New York: Routledge, 2018).

Maurice Blanchot, *The Writing of the Disaster*, trans. Ann Smock (Lincoln: University of Nebraska Press, 1995).

Jorge Luis Borges, *Twenty-Four Conversations with Borges: Including a Selection of Poems: Interviews, 1981–1983*, ed. Roberto Alifano (New York: Grove Press, 1984).

Charles Brenner, *Psychoanalysis or Mind and Meaning* (New York: Psychoanalytic Quarterly, 2006).

Craig Brown, *Hello Goodbye Hello: A Circle of 101 Remarkable Meetings* (New York: Simon & Schuster, 2012).

Jacqueline A. Bussie, *The Laughter of the Oppressed: Ethical and Theological Resistance in Wiesel, Morrison, and Endo* (New York: T. & T. Clark International, 2007).

Anton Chekhov, *Notebook of Anton Chekhov*, trans. S. S. Koteliansky and Leonard Woolf (New York: Ecco Press, 1987).

Alastair Clarke, *The Pattern Recognition Theory of Humour* (Cumbria, UK: Pyrrhic House, 2008).

Charles Darwin, *The Expression of the Emotions in Man and Animals* (CreateSpace Independent Publishing Platform, March 16, 2012).

Gavin de Becker, *The Gift of Fear: And Other Survival Signals That Protect Us from Violence* (New York: Dell, 1998).

Gilles Deleuze, *Essays Critical and Clinical*, trans. Daniel W. Smith and Michael A. Greco (Minneapolis: University of Minnesota Press, 1997).

Agnes de Mille, *Martha: The Life and Work of Martha Graham* (New York: Random House, 1991).

Emily Dickinson, *The Complete Poems of Emily Dickinson*, ed. Thomas H. Johnson (Boston: Little, Brown & Company, 1960).

———. *The Gorgeous Nothings: Emily Dickinson's Envelope Poems*, ed. Marta L. Werner and Jen Bervin (New York: New Directions, 2013).

Guillaume-Benjamin Duchenne, *The Mechanism of Human Facial Expression*, ed. and trans. R. Andrew Cuthbertson (New York: Cambridge University Press, 1990).

Paul Ekman, *Emotions Revealed: Recognizing Faces and Feelings to Improve Communication and Emotional Life* (New York: Times Books, 2003).

Frantz Fanon, *Black Skin, White Masks*, trans. Richard Philcox (New York: Grove Press, 2008).

Elena Ferrante, *The Days of Abandonment*, trans. Ann Goldstein (New York: Europa Editions, 2005).

Anna Freud and Dorothy T. Burlingham, *War and Children* (New York: Medical War Books, 1943).

Sigmund Freud, *The Complete Standard Edition of the Psychological Works of Sigmund Freud*, ed. and trans. James Strachey (London: The Hogarth Press, 1971).

Malcolm Gladwell, *Blink: The Power of Thinking without Thinking* (New York: Little, Brown and Company, 2005).

Immanuel Kant, *Critique of Pure Reason*, ed. and trans. Marcus Weigelt (New York: Penguin Books, 2007).

John Keats, *The Selected Letters of John Keats*, ed. Lionel Trilling (New York: Farrar, Straus and Young, 1951).

Danielle Knafo and Rocco Lo Bosco, *The Age of Perversion: Desire and Technology in Psychoanalysis and Culture* (New York: Routledge, 2017).

Rem Koolhaas, *Delirious New York: A Retroactive Manifesto for Manhattan* (New York: Monacelli Press, 1994).

Jacques Lacan, *Ecrits*, trans. Alan Sheridan (New York: W. W. Norton, 1977).

———. *The Seminar of Jacques Lacan: The Ethics of Psychoanalysis, 1959–1960, Book VII*, ed. Jacques-Alain Miller, trans. Dennis Porter (New York: W. W. Norton, 1992).

Jacques Lecoq, *The Moving Body: Teaching Creative Theatre*, trans. David Bradby (New York: Routledge, 2001).

Primo Levi, *The Drowned and the Saved*, trans. Raymond Rosenthal (New York: Summit Books, 1988).

Audre Lorde, *Your Silence Will Not Protect You* (London: Silver Press, 2017).

Janet Malcolm, *In the Freud Archives* (London: Granta Books, 2018).

———. *The Journalist and the Murderer* (London: Granta Books, 2018).

———. *Psychoanalysis: The Impossible Profession* (London: Granta Books, 2018).

Tara McKelvey, *Monstering: Inside America's Policy of Secret Interrogations and Torture in the Terror War* (New York: Basic Books, 2009).

Friedrich Nietzsche, *Thus Spoke Zarathustra: A Book for Everyone and No One*, trans. R. J. Hollingdale (New York: Penguin Books, 1969).

———. *Writings from the Late Notebooks*, ed. Rüdiger Bittner, trans. Kate Sturge (New York: Cambridge University Press, 2003).

Martha C. Nussbaum, *Upheavals of Thought: The Intelligence of Emotions* (New York: Cambridge University Press, 2001).

George Orwell, *The Collected Essays, Journalism, and Letters of George Orwell* (New York: Harcourt, Brace and World, 1968).

Adam Phillips, *Winnicott* (New York: Penguin Books, 2007).

Sylvia Plath, *The Unabridged Journals of Sylvia Plath 1950–1962*, ed. Karen V. Kukil (New York: Anchor Books, 2000).

Plato, *Republic*, trans. G. M. A. Grube (Indianapolis: Hackett Publishing Company, 1992).

Valerie Preston-Dunlop and Susanne Lahusen, *Schrifttanz: A View of German Dance in the Weimar Republic* (London: Dance Books, 1990).

Robert Provine, *Curious Behavior: Yawning, Laughing, Hiccupping, and Beyond* (Cambridge: Harvard University Press, 2012).

———. *Laughter: A Scientific Investigation* (New York: Viking, 2000).

Theodore Roethke, *Straw for the Fire: From the Notebooks of Theodore Roethke: 1943–63*, ed. David Wagoner (New York: Doubleday, 1972).

Oliver Sacks, *The Man Who Mistook His Wife for a Hat: And Other Clinical Tales* (New York: HarperCollins, 1999).

———. *On the Move: A Life* (New York: Knopf, 2015).

Jean-Paul Sartre, *Being and Nothingness*, trans. Hazel E. Barnes (New York: Washington Square Press, 1993).

———. *Existentialism and Human Emotions*, trans. Bernard Frechtman (New York: Philosophical Library, 1957).

Friedrich Schiller, *Aesthetical and Philosophical Essays*, trans. Nathan Haskell Dole (Boston: Francis A. Niccolis & Company, 1902).

Arthur Schopenhauer, *The World as Will and Idea*, ed. David Berman, trans. Jill Berman (New York: Everyman Paperbacks, 1995).

Sarah Schulman, *Conflict Is Not Abuse: Overstating Harm, Community Responsibility, and the Duty of Repair* (Vancouver: Arsenal Pulp Press, 2016).

George Sheldon, *Trauma and Race: A Lacanian Study of African American Racial Identity* (Waco: Baylor University Press, 2016).

Susan Sontag, *Against Interpretation* (New York: Farrar, Straus and Giroux, 1966).

William Stafford, *The Darkness around Us Is Deep*, ed. Robert Bly (New York: Harper Perennial, 1993).

Richard F. Sterba, *Introduction to the Psychoanalytic Theory of the Libido* (New York: R. Brunner, 1968).

Leo Tolstoy, *Anna Karenina*, trans. Rosamund Bartlett (Oxford: Oxford University Press, 2014).

Marina Tsvetaeva, *Art in the Light of Conscience: Eight Essays on Poetry*, trans. Angela Livingstone (Tarset, UK: Bloodaxe Books, 2010).

Bessel van der Kolk, *The Body Keeps the Score: Brain, Mind, and Body in the Healing of Trauma* (New York: Penguin Books, 2014).

Michael Warner, *Publics and Counterpublics* (New York: Zone Books, 2002).

Ludwig Wittgenstein, *Notebooks 1914–1916*, ed. G. H. von Wright, ed. and trans. G. E. M. Anscombe (Chicago: University of Chicago Press, 1979).

Walt Whitman, *Leaves of Grass*, ed. John Hollander (New York: Library of America, 2011).

D. W. Winnicott, *The Collected Works of D. W. Winnicott*, ed. Lesley Caldwell and Helen Taylor Robinson (Oxford: Oxford University Press, 2017).

———. *The Maturational Processes and the Facilitating Environment: Studies in the Theory of Emotional Development* (London: Hogarth Press, 1965).

———. *Playing and Reality* (New York: Routledge, 1992).

Slavoj Žižek, *Did Somebody Say Totalitarianism?* (New York: Verso Books, 2001).

———. *How to Read Lacan* (New York: W. W. Norton, 2007).

Articles, Essays, and Letters

Jacob A. Arlow, "Fantasy, Memory and Reality Testing," *Psychoanalytic Quarterly* (38:1, 28–51, 1969).

Francis Baudry, "Winnicott's 1968 Visit to the New York Psychoanalytic Society and Institute: A Contextual View," *Psychoanalytic Quarterly* (78:4, 2009).

Isabel Behncke, "Evolution's Gift of Play: From Bonobo Apes to Humans," TED Talk (March 29, 2011).

Daniel Bergner, "The Most Unconventional Weapon," *New York Times* (October 26, 2003).

Richard J. Bernstein, "The Illuminations of Hannah Arendt," *New York Times* (June 20, 2019).

W. R. Bion, "The Psycho-Analytic Study of Thinking," *International Journal of Psycho-Analysis* (vol. 43, 306–310, 1962).

Keren Blankfeld, "Lovers in Auschwitz, Reunited 72 Years Later. He Had One Question," *New York Times* (December 8, 2019).

"Chappelle's Story," Oprah.com (February 3, 2006).

Kate Conger, "Twitter Places Warning on Congressman's Tweet for Glorifying Violence," *New York Times* (June 1, 2020).

M. Fakhry Davids, "The Impact of Islamophobia," *Psychoanalysis and History* (11:2, 175–91, 2009).

Karen Dawn and Peter Singer, "Echoes of Abu Ghraib in Chicken Slaughterhouse," *Los Angeles Times* (July 25, 2004).

Jacques Derrida, "The Animal That Therefore I Am (More to Follow)," *Critical Inquiry* (28:2, 368–418, winter 2002).

Helen Deutsch, "Some Forms of Emotional Disturbance and their Relationship to Schizophrenia," *Psychoanalytic Quarterly* (11:3, 301–21, 1942).

Jeff Dolven and Joshua Kotin, "J. H. Prynne: The Art of Poetry No. 101," *Paris Review* (issue 218, fall 2016).

Ralph Ellison, "What America Would Be Like without Blacks," in *Going to the Territory* (New York: Random House, 1987).

Thomas Erdbrink and Martin Selsoe Sorensen, "A Danish Children's TV Show Has This Message: 'Normal Bodies Look Like This,'" *New York Times* (September 18, 2020).

Elena Ferrante, "A Power of Our Own," *New York Times* (May 17, 2019).

Mike Fleming Jr., "Sacha Baron Cohen on Unseen Shocking Scenes in Trump-Inspired Golden Globe–Nominated Series 'Who Is America?,'" *Deadline* (December 19, 2018).

Vittorio Gallese, "Mirror Neurons and Intentional Attunement: Commentary on Olds," *Journal of the American Psychoanalytic Association* (54:1, March 1, 2006).

René Girard, "Perilous Balance: A Comic Hypothesis," *Comparative Literature* (87:7, 811–26, 1972).

Richard M. Gottlieb, "Technique and Countertransference in Freud's Analysis of the Rat Man," *Psychoanalytic Quarterly* (58:1, 29–62, January 1989).

Philip Gourevitch and Errol Morris, "Exposure: The Woman Behind the Camera at Abu Ghraib," *New Yorker* (March 17, 2008).

Martin Heidegger, "The Origin of the Work of Art," trans. Roger Berkowitz and Philippe Nonet, Academia.edu (2006).

Bob Herbert, "Overkill and Short Shrift," *New York Times* (May 3, 2008).

"How 'Horror Smells' Are Helping People with Dementia," BBC (October 30, 2019), www.bbc.com/news/av/uk-england-dorset-50166820.

Colby Itkowitz, "A Yazidi woman from Iraq told Trump that ISIS killed her family. 'Where are they now?' he asked," *Washington Post* (July 19, 2019).

Harmeet Kaur, "A right-wing group got pranked at a rally and they believe Sacha Baron Cohen is behind it," CNN (June 29, 2020).

Daniel Kane, interview with John Ashbery, www.writing.upenn.edu /~afilreis/88v/ashbery-interview.html.

Dacher Keltner and George A. Bonanno, "A Study of Laughter and Dissociation: Distinct Correlates of Laughter and Smiling during Bereavement," *Journal of Personality and Social Psychology* (73:4, 687–702, October 1997).

Lady Gaga, "Lady Gaga on Sex, Fame, Drugs, and Her Fans," interview by Lisa Robinson, *Vanity Fair* (August 2, 2010).

Laila Lalami, "I'm a Muslim and Arab American: Will I Ever Be an Equal Citizen?," *New York Times Magazine* (September 17, 2020).

Tara McKelvey, "Lynndie England in Love," *American Prospect* (July 23, 2007).

Janet Malcolm, "The Real Thing," *New York Review of Books* (January 9, 1997).

Andrew Marantz, "Good Evening. Hello. I Have Cancer," *New Yorker* (October 5, 2012).

David Marriott, "Corpsing; or, The Matter of Black Life," *Cultural Critique* (vol. 94, 32–64, fall 2016).

Collier Meyerson, "Why Claudia Rankine Writes for the Resistance," *Nation* (January 12, 2018).

Sharon B. Oster, "Impossible Holocaust Metaphors: The *Muselmann*," *Prooftexts* (34:3, 302–48, fall 2014).

Frank Richards, "Frank Richards Replies to George Orwell," www.friar dale.co.uk/Ephemera/Newspapers/George%20Orwell_Horizon _Reply.pdf.

Heather Cox Richardson, "Letters from an American" (September 12, 2020), https://heathercoxrichardson.substack.com/p/september-12 -2020.

Richard Schiffman, "Laughter May Be Effective Medicine for These Trying Times," *New York Times* (October 1, 2020).

Marc Segar, *Coping: A Survival Guide for People with Asperger Syndrome*, (1997), https://www-users.cs.york.ac.uk/~alistair/survival/.

Alessandro Serpieri, "Reading the Signs: Towards a Semiotics of Shakespearean Drama," trans. Keir Elam, in *Alternative Shakespeares*, ed. John Drakakis (New York: Methuen, 1985).

Viktor Shklovsky, "Art as Technique" (1917), warwick.ac.uk/fac/arts /english/currentstudents/undergraduate/modules/fulllist/first /en122/lecturelist-2015-16-2/shklovsky.pdf.

Alexis Soloski, "The Joy of Corpsing: Why Giggling Fits the Theatre," *Guardian* (October 21, 2010).

Alice Speri, Ryan Devereaux, and Sam Biddle, "New York Police Are Attacking Protesters—They Know They Won't Face Consequences," *Intercept* (June 2, 2020).

Ron Suskind, "Faith, Certainty and the Presidency of George W. Bush," *New York Times* (October 17, 2004).

Evan V. Symon, "I'm Paid to Mourn at Funerals (and It's a Growing Industry)," *Cracked* (March 21, 2016), www.cracked.com/personal -experiences-1994-i-am-professional-mourner-6-realities-my-job .html.

Pedro Alexis Tabensky, "The Oppressor's Pathology," *Theoria: A Journal of Social and Political Theory* (57:125, 77–98, December 2010).

Samuel Weber, "Laughing in the Meanwhile," *MLN* (102:4, 691–706, September 1987).

Patti A. Wood, "Shooting the Breeze about Sneezing," www.pattiwood .net/article.asp?PageID=11594.

The Yes Men, "Don't Forget the Funny," Occupy.com (April 11, 2012).

Correspondence

Elizabeth Bishop, letter to Donald E. Stanford (March 1934).
Sigmund Freud, letter to Martha (September 25, 1882).

Films

Tim Burton, *Pee-wee's Big Adventure* (1985).
Larry Charles, *Borat: Cultural Learnings of America for Make Benefit Glorious Nation of Kazakhstan* (2006).
Morgan Neville, *Won't You Be My Neighbor?* (2018).
Ridley Scott, *Blade Runner* (1982).
George Tillman Jr., *The Hate U Give* (2018).
Moshe Zimerman, *Pizza in Auschwitz* (2008).

TV and Video

"Bobbie Louise Hawkins Tribute," YouTube (April 29, 2019).

"'Keep your voice down': Trump berates female reporter when questioned over Covid-19 response," YouTube (April 20, 2020).

"Still Face Experiment," Dr. Edward Tronick, YouTube (November 30, 2009).

Radio Broadcasts

"The Ballad of the Tearful: Why Some Songs Make You Cry," *All Things Considered*, National Public Radio (February 13, 2012).

"Can We Reframe the Way We Think about Stress?" Kelly McGonigal, *TED Radio Hour*, National Public Radio (August 2, 2019).

"Laughter" *Radiolab*, National Public Radio (February 25, 2008).

"How Tribal Members Are Shaping the Federal Government's Wildfire Strategy," *The Takeaway*, National Public Radio (January 6, 2020).

"Killer Empathy," *Radiolab*, National Public Radio (February 6, 2012).

Thank you to those who have hosted or housed parts of this book in alternate forms: *BOMB*, Book Works in London, the Centre for New and International Writing at the University of Liverpool, *The Cut*, Faber & Faber, Glasgow Women's Library, *Granta, Labor Day, Literary Hub, New York* magazine, the *New York Times Magazine*, New York University's Low-Residency MFA Writers Workshop in Paris, the Non-Human Encounters: Animals, Objects, Affects, and the Place of Practice forum at New York University, the *Poetry Review, Studies in Gender and Sexuality*, Tate Liverpool, and the *White Review*.

Thank you to my agent, Harriet Moore, and to the teams at Graywolf Press and Fitzcarraldo Editions, all of whom lent their brilliance to the book. I am particularly grateful to Ethan Nosowsky, Anni Liu, and Katie Dublinski at Graywolf Press and to Jacques Testard at Fitzcarraldo Editions. This book would not have been possible without Jacques, whose belief in the project offered me the freedom and space to play.

Thank you also to the following people who read and engaged with the book, in part or in its entirety: Rachael Allen, Youmna Chlala, Heather Christle, Josh Cohen, Sophie Collins, Jameson Fitzpatrick, Nick Flynn, Jonathan Lethem, Sandeep Parmar, and Claudia Rankine.

Most of all, for everything, thank you, Isadora and Sabine. This book is for you.

NUAR ALSADIR, a poet and psychoanalyst, is the author of *Fourth Person Singular*, a finalist for the National Book Critics Circle Award in Poetry and the Forward Prize for Best Collection, and *More Shadow Than Bird*. She lives in New York City.

The text of *Animal Joy* is set in Arno Pro.
Book design by Rachel Holscher.
Composition by Bookmobile Design & Digital
Publisher Services, Minneapolis, Minnesota.
Manufactured by McNaughton & Gunn on acid-free,
100 percent postconsumer wastepaper.